BLESSED ARE THE CONSUMERS

BLESSED ARE THE CONSUMERS

Climate Change and the Practice of Restraint

Sallie McFague

Fortress Press

Minneapolis

BLESSED ARE THE CONSUMERS
Climate Change and the Practice of Restraint

Cover image: Seedling growing in cracked mud © Ocean / Orbis

Cover design: Laurie Ingram

Library of Congress Cataloging-in-Publication Data

McFague, Sallie.

Blessed are the consumers : climate change and the practice of restraint / Sallie McFague.

p. cm.

Includes bibliographical references.
ISBN 978-0-8006-9960-4 (alk. paper) — 978-1-4514-3867-3 (ebook)
1.   Human ecology—Religious aspects—Christianity. 2.   Consumerism (Economics)—Religious aspects—Christianity. 3.   Christian saints—Biography. I. Title.
BT695.5.M4428 2013
261.8'8—dc23   2012034991

Print ISBN: 978-0-8006-9960-4
Digital ISBN: 978-1-4514-3867-3

The paper used in this publication meets the minimum requirements of American National Standard for Information Sciences — Permanence of Paper for Printed Library Materials, ANSI Z329.48-1984.

Manufactured in the U.S.A.

To Michael West, editor par excellence and my longtime friend and fellow theologian.

Contents

Preface: Religion, Ecology, and Economics

Over the years, when people have asked me what I do, and when I have answered that I am a theologian who investigates the connections of religion with economics and ecology, they often give me a funny look. What does "religion" have to do with financial and environmental matters? Isn't religion about God and human sin and salvation, or maybe human peace and comfort? At any rate, money and the earth have not figured largely in many Westerners' understanding of the role of religion in life and culture.

But times have changed. The 2010 edition of the annual environmental publication *The State of the World*, subtitled "Transforming Cultures from Consumerism to Sustainability," contains a lead article by Gary Gardner suggesting that the religions must be major players in the most important two-sided crisis of our time—that of economics and ecology. Gardner applauds the religions for their recent attention to environmental concerns—from "greening" church buildings to reevaluating their Scriptures for ecological friendly doctrines—but bemoans the fact that the religions have not given comparable attention to economics. Somehow they fail to see the intrinsic connection between environmentalism and consumerism. Increasingly, however, we are becoming aware that these apparently disparate fields—economics and ecology—are tightly interlocked, for it is the rampant use of energy that both creates our consumer paradise as well as depletes the planet's resources and contributes to global warming. To put it as simply as possible: it is not sufficient to consume in a "green" fashion; rather, we must consume *less*, a lot less. Buying a Prius does not permit one to drive *more*, although that is often the underlying rationale of many people. Quantity still matters; in fact, we are at such a level of consumption in relation to the carrying capacity of our planet that reduction must take a major role in sustainability. No one wants to face this fact; changing from an SUV to a Prius is not enough—we may have to reconsider the use of automobiles.

"Thus it becomes clear that while shifting technology and stabilizing population will be essential in creating sustainable societies, neither will succeed without considerable change in consumption patterns, including reducing and even eliminating the use of certain goods, such as cars and airplanes, that have become important parts of life today for many."[1] This casual statement from the 2010 *State of the World* causes a global gasp—

"reducing and even eliminating" the use of cars and airplanes! Surely not. The shock, however, causes us to realize how far we have to go in both our attitudes and our practices. As the essay points out, we human beings are so embedded in the culture of consumerism that asking us to curb it (let alone eliminate precious forms of it) is like asking us to stop breathing—"they can do it for a moment but then, gasping, they will inhale again."[2] It is important to take this seriously: the "culture of consumerism" is not just a form of life that we can accept or reject; it has now become the air we breathe. This is the "nature" of "culture"—culture becomes nature, it becomes "natural."[3] Consumerism is a cultural pattern that leads people to find meaning and fulfillment through the consumption of goods and services. Thus the well-known comment that consumerism is the newest and most successful "religion" on the globe is not an overstatement. Consequently, the task of changing culture—from consumerism to sustainability, for instance—is immense. If one accepts the analysis that our planetary society is in serious condition, then one also must accept that "preventing the collapse of civilization requires nothing less than a wholesale transformation of dominant cultural patterns."[4]

The religions are being handed a challenge here—a significant but difficult one. They are being asked to take on what no other field has been willing to assume, something at the heart of all religions: "a wholesale transformation of dominant cultural patterns," particularly at the level of consumerism. As the 2010 State of the World asserts, "Of the three drivers of environmental impact—population, affluence, and technology—affluence, a proxy for consumption, is the arena in which secular institutions have been the least successful in promoting restraint."[5] There it is: the most significant challenge the religions could undertake for the well-being of our planet and its inhabitants—but a challenge for which no other field is so well prepared—is "restraint." Restraint at all levels, summed up in the Golden Rule (a variation of which most religions take as their central practice), is the one thing needed now, and is, I believe, both a gift from the religions and a challenge to them. It could be considered a "coming home" for the religions as well as their greatest contribution to the economic/ecological crisis facing us. As Gardner sums up so well:

> Often pointed to as conservative and unchanging institutions, many religions are in fact rapidly embracing the modern cause of environmental protection. Yet consumerism—the opposite side of the environmental coin and traditionally an area of religious strength—has received relatively little attention so far. Ironically, the greatest contribution the world's religions could make to the sustainability challenge may be to take seriously their own ancient wisdom on materialism. Their special gift—the millennia-old paradoxical insight that happiness is found in self-emptying,

> that satisfaction is found more in relationships than in things, and that simplicity can lead to a fuller life—is urgently needed today. Combined with the new found passion of many religions for healing the environment, this ancient wisdom could help create new and sustainable civilizations.[6]

I consider this paragraph, from one of the standard-setting texts of our time—the carefully researched and thoughtful series of annual volumes on the state of the world—to be marching orders for the religions, and to be the central theme of my modest effort in this book. As Gardner points out, "Advocating a mindful approach to consumption could well alienate some of the faithful in many traditions" (probably an understatement!). But such a position would not only serve the planet but would also signal a return of the religions to their own spiritual roots and cause them to recognize how far they have deviated from them.[7] The insidious message that the purpose of human life is to consume is a heresy, and should be condemned as such. The religious traditions may well find that such a return revitalizes their basic message—restraint, not for the sake of ascetic denial of the world, but in order that the "abundant life" might be possible for all.[8] My small contribution to condemning the heresy of consumerism is to take up this challenge with an in-depth study of one form of restraint in one religion—"kenosis," or self-emptying, in Christianity. It is interesting to note that in the 2010 *State of the World*, which contains over twenty-five articles on a huge range of topics—from business and education to health and media—only seven pages are given to the topic of religion's absolutely critical role in transforming dominant cultural patterns. How can such a critical task be accomplished in a few pages? There is an obvious disconnect here. While study after study points to the "spiritual" nature of our problem—that it is one of changing both minds and behaviors—it is still often neglected or marginalized. It is also marginalized in the 2010 *State of the World*, but what it does is critically important: it calls on the religions to do what they have traditionally and essentially done and should do—present a radical alternative to the good life for both people and planet. If the religions do their own centuries-old job, which no other field can or wants to do, of presenting wholescale alternatives to conventional worldviews of the "abundant life," they will be neither comforting nor popular. But they might be right.

This particular essay is but one modest attempt to suggest a contribution from the religions, and especially from Christianity. Increasingly, the issue of how to live well has become one of *how to change from how we are living now to a different way*. As our crises worsen, more and more people are questioning the reigning anthropology of insatiable greed, and they are coming to the conclusion that the prospects of the consumer culture have been greatly overrated and that serious change at a fundamental level—of who we think we are and what we must do—is necessary. Change at this level is incredibly difficult, and many people find it impossible. Yet it is precisely change at this fundamental level that most religions prescribe. Christians call it "conversion," and it demands thinking and living differently than conventional society recommends.

Hence, my modest contribution to this task as a Christian theologian will be as follows: Some reflections on why I have undertaken to look at conversion (chapter 1); a study of our present context that demonstrates why such radical change is necessary (chapter 2); the stories of some saints—John Woolman, Simone Weil, and Dorothy Day—whose lives express deep change (chapter 3); an analysis of the process of conversion to the kenotic way of life emerging from these stories (chapters 4 and 5); a depiction of kenosis in areas ranging from the arts to parenting, and in most religions (chapter 6); a summary of kenotic theology and how it affects the Christian understanding of God, Christ, and human life (chapter 7); and a consideration of the special role of middle-class, well-off people for deep, kenotic change (chapter 8).

Throughout the entire book, we will follow a central theme: a fourfold process of conversion our saints' lives and writings express. Succinctly, the argument of the book is as follows.

Given our twin planetary crises of climate change and unjust financial distribution, what is needed is not more information but the will to move from belief to action, from denial to profound change at both personal and public levels. The religions of the world, countercultural in their assumption that "to find one's life, one must lose it," are key players in understanding and promoting a movement from a model of God, the world, and the self focused on individualistic, market-oriented accumulation by a few, to a model that sees self and planetary flourishing as interdependent. We live *within* our models and make decisions on the basis of them. "Be careful how you interpret the world. It *is* like that."⁹ The interdependent model demands self-emptying (Christian kenosis) or "great compassion" (Buddhism) on the part of the well-to-do, so that all human beings and other life-forms may live just, sustainable lives. One small but necessary task is to present an in-depth analysis of the process by which such a change can occur. This essay, then, is addressed to the so-called first world, its values and followers, wherever they might live: The fourfold process from belief to action contains the following steps.

1. *Experiences of "voluntary poverty"* to shock middle-class people out of the conventional model of self-fulfillment through possessions and prestige, and into a model of self-emptying, as a pathway for personal and planetary well-being. It can become a form of "wild space," a space where one is available for deep change from the conventional model of living to another one.

2. *The focus of one's attention to the needs of others*, especially their most physical, basic needs, such as food. This attention changes one's vision from seeing all others as objects for supporting one's own ego to seeing them as subjects in their own right who deserve the basic necessities for flourishing. We see everything in the world as interdependent.

3. *The gradual development of a "universal self,"* as the line constituting one's concern (compassion or empathy) moves from its narrow focus on the ego (and one's nearest and dearest) to reach out further and further until there is no line left: even a caterpillar counts. This journey, rather than diminishing the self, increases its delight, but at the cost of one's old, egoistic model.

4. *The new model of the universal self operates at both the personal and public levels*, for instance in the planetary house rules: (1) take only your share; (2) clean up after yourself; (3) keep the house in good repair for those who will use it after you.

Thus, while other fields contributing to solving our planetary crises often end their studies with the despairing remark, "Of course, it is a spiritual, an ethical problem," the religions of the world should offer their distinctive answer: "Yes, it is, and let us look at the process of change from belief to action."

This is what we are attempting in the following pages. As we enter this project, I need to set its parameters: what it *does not* plan to cover and what it *does*. First, as the choice of the three saints discussed in chapter 3 shows, I make no attempt to be comprehensive or even representative. One could choose many others, but I have spent a lifetime on these figures. Hence, I have come to know and love them. I have learned much of what I say about them through long reflection. With this limitation in mind, I will focus not on all aspects of their contributions, but specifically on their insights into the process of conversion from belief to action. A second qualification is the limitation of the chosen saints to Western, middle-class people like myself and like the audience addressed in this project. Third, while I make reference to other religions, especially to Buddhism, I have limited this study to Christianity, the tradition from which I come and that I know best. Nevertheless, as will become clear as the argument progresses, the process described here is not "Christian" or even "religious" in the narrow sense. What emerges is an understanding of humanity's place in the scheme of things; therefore, I focus not on "belief in Jesus" or "belief in God" per se so much as the theme, common in most religions, that loving one's neighbor is tantamount to loving God. If the "neighbor" is understood to include all living creatures, and indeed the planet itself, then what matters is not a discrete belief in a God (or "gods") so much as an understanding of the self—its duty and its delight—as radically inclusive love. The implication is that one should focus on what one sees (the visible neighbor) rather than on what one does not see (the invisible God). Thus, if one understands God to be not a "substance" but the active, creative love at work in the entire universe, then "loving God" is not something in addition to loving the world, but is rather the acknowledgment that in loving the world, one is participating in the planetary process (which some identify as "God") of self-emptying love at all levels. By understanding both "God" and the world in this way—that is, as radically kenotic—this essay can be read as both Christian *and* interfaith. Thus all can participate in the kenotic paradigm as a way of loving the neighbor, a process in which God's own self may also be seen at work.

One must not be overly optimistic about such attempts—nothing any one of us does will solve the immense problems we face. But to do nothing is not permitted.

Acknowledgments

I wish to thank the good folks at Fortress Press who have, as with my other books, offered expert advice for its publication. I am deeply grateful to people who have helped me with this book, especially Michael West, Janet Cawley, Janet Gear, Sharon Betcher, Sister Mary Aquin O'Neill, and the many students over the years who have taken my courses covering material in the book. I also wish to thank the Vancouver School of Theology where I wrote this book in my fine office overlooking the ocean and mountains.

Notes

[1] Gary Gardner, "Engaging Religions to Shape Worldviews," *State of the World 2010: Transforming Cultures from Consumerism to Sustainability*, ed. Linda Starke and Lisa Mastny (London: Earthscan, 2010), 7.

[2] Ibid., 3.

[3] "Cultures arise out of the complex interactions of many different elements of social behaviors and guide humans at an almost invisible level. They are . . . the sum total of all 'social processes that make the artificial (or human constructed) seem natural" (Ibid., 8).

[4] Ibid., 3.

[5] Ibid., 26.

[6] Ibid., 28–29.

[7] Ibid., 26–27.

[8] In a recent book, Gary Gardner speaks of "Progress as Bounded Creativity," which commends the energy of the twentieth century that has created genuine progress for many. However, he notes that our human creativity during the last century was "like a river without banks, the flow of innovation impressive but unchanneled. One missing riverbank was ecological wisdom . . . which might have helped rich and poor alike build more dignified and fulfilling lives" (*Inspiring Progress: Religions' Contributions to Sustainable Development* [New York: W. W. Norton, 2006], 3). In other words, restraint is not the opposite of energy and creativity, but its necessary partner in sustainable progress.

9 Erich Heller, *The Disinherited Mind: Essays in Modern German Literature and Thought* (Cleveland: World, 1961), 211.

1

"But Enough about Me"

What Does Augustine's Confessions Have to Do with Facebook?

How to Live Well

In a *New Yorker* essay titled "But Enough About Me: What Does the Popularity of Memoirs Tell Us about Ourselves?" Daniel Mendelsohn notes that our culture is inundated with "unseemly self-exposures," in a rich variety of forms: reality TV, addiction and recovery memoirs, Facebook, tales of sexual and physical abuse by parents, and so on. "The greatest outpouring of personal narratives in the history of the planet has occurred on the Internet," which has provided a cheap and convenient means to broadcast one's fascination with the self endlessly and without censorship.[1] This outlet for our narcissism is a new phenomenon, at least in its current breadth and depth: never have so many been able to share so shamelessly with so many others the secrets of their personal lives. There are several contributing factors to this situation, such as the blurring of the real and the artificial (does "reality" TV show "real" people?) as well as the confusion between private and public life (why are we forced to overhear private cell phone conversations in public places?).

Things used to be quite different—in fact, very different. Memoirs, auto-biographies, diaries, and journals were considered not only private but also questionable. They occupied an odd and ill-defined place among the various genres (history, fiction, philosophy). Were they "true" and if so, in what fashion? How do we know that people don't "lie" (or are in denial) about their stories? Are these forms history or fiction? Are they closer to photographs or paintings? They are highly suspect these days too, because they assume a stable author with a privileged point of view, when in our postmodern context even the existence of a "subject" is questionable. So, why has the personal narrative gained such widespread popularity?

I suggest the reason is both simple and deep: personal narrative addresses the most central issue of human life—how to live well. Regardless of the corrupt forms it has assumed in contemporary culture, it is concerned with the same question that motivated Augustine to write the *Confessions*: who am I and what should I be doing with my life? Whether this question takes the form of one of the greatest pieces of Western literature, as in the case of the *Confessions*, or a desperate report by a recovering alcoholic at an AA meeting, the intent is similar. How to live well?

This question has been at the heart of my own life and theology. Two essays, written almost forty years apart, one in 1970 and the other in 2008, illustrate my journey with this question. The first essay is a proposal for submission to a publisher, in which I outline one avenue for investigating the question of who we are and what we should do from a Christian perspective. While I never sent the outline to a publisher, I have taught a course (with many variations) on this topic since 1970 and have learned a great deal by doing so. I have come to the conclusion that that outline contained a germ for one way of addressing the question, a way that has parallels in most religious traditions, although I have conducted my investigation from within Christianity.

Before sharing this document, I would like to suggest why I think it might have contemporary relevance. We are facing an economic and environmental meltdown of more serious proportions than any generation of human beings before us. It is no exaggeration to speak in apocalyptic language, at the most elemental levels of basic physical needs, of the prospects for people and the planet. The years since the 2007 report by the UN Intergovernmental Panel on Climate Change and the 2008 crash of the stock market have opened our eyes to the seriousness of our planetary health at all levels and for all creatures. Every field of endeavor, including the religions, is being called on to offer its deepest and best thinking and action to address this crisis. In studies of the contributions by the sciences and technology, the closing sentence is often something like the following: "But of course it is really a spiritual problem—a problem of changing hearts and minds so that people will live differently." And there is probably nothing more difficult or discouraging than such a conclusion, for people do not change easily. In fact, can they, will they, change at all—at least in ways sufficient to make a difference in the use and misuse of the planet's resources? The answer may be no, in which case we may well be damned to a future we do not want to contemplate. However, many of us are not willing to accept this answer.

In the proposal I wrote almost forty years ago, I see a germ of an idea for us to consider, a germ I will call "kenosis," or self-emptying, so that others may live. This "radical" stand can be found in different ways in many religious traditions, as well as in other fields of study, and it focuses on a portrait of human existence fundamentally at odds with the conventional assumption that human beings can be fulfilled by self-aggrandizement. It makes the outrageous claim that "to find one's life one must lose it," and it makes the further claim that this process contains an ethic not only for personal life but also for public well-being. It makes this connection between the personal and the public on the basis of interrelationship in both religion and science: the transcendence of self-centeredness at the heart of the religions and the evolutionary reciprocity of all life forms at the biological level. Religion and economics also both underscore interdependence as the heart of well-being at personal and public levels.

It is important at the outset to distinguish ego from self. It is not easy to do so, given the myriad meanings used by different schools of psychology as well as common confusion between the terms. Thus the words *egocentric* and *self-centered* both refer to excessive focus on the self in a narcissistic fashion; however, *ego* is a narrower term and often a negative one (egotism, egomania, ego trip, etc.), while *self* has a broader range, all the way from self-abasement and self-satisfaction to self-discipline and self-fulfillment. (In fact, my dictionary contains over 150 hyphenated words beginning with *self*.) *Self* is a neutral term, veering toward the positive, whereas *ego* is a term veering toward the negative. It is important to distinguish the terms, since religious traditions have often been accused of negative forms of self-sacrifice, including ascetic and particularly female subordinationism. In the following chapters, *self-fulfillment* will play a major role, and it will be intimately related to *self-sacrifice* (kenosis). In other words, self-fulfillment is achieved through a form of self-sacrifice (or, perhaps more accurately, ego-sacrifice).

Here is the 1970 document, unedited and complete with masculine pronouns and a prefeminist consciousness!

Case Studies of Some Radical Christians

The question here might run something like this: What is the difference between a lukewarm and a radical Christian? The assumption is that most of us *are* lukewarm and stand in awe of Christians whose total lives are committed to Christ. This study is to be an inquiry into *how* and *why* certain Christians have taken radical stands. It is to investigate, by means of journals, letters, and papers written by the individuals, the actual process that eventuated in their radicalism. By "radicalism" I mean deep and abiding commitment and this refers to religious stands as well as social and political ones. "Radical" does not necessarily mean extreme, "left," or odd, except according to "lukewarm" estimates, but as its derivation from root implies, radical has to do with depth, rather than any direction to the right or left of some imagined center.

It is the depth of commitment as it affects a mode of life, then, which we would investigate, and especially the *way* such commitment occurs. This will be approached through a study of a select number of writings of radical individuals in the hope of discovering some of the "insides" of such commitment. Perhaps the finest text for such a study is the journal of the eighteenth-century Quaker John Woolman. Others that might be included are Bunyan, Sir Thomas More, the French novelist and essayist Leon Bloy, William Lloyd Garrison, Bonhoeffer—and I am on the lookout for others (especially contemporary men, though the right sort of texts are hard to come by). The study would by no means be historical in nature; it would, perhaps, be closer to psychology of religion. The method I have chosen has the advantage of being concrete, situational, and individual—it points a direct finger at the reader. It is difficult, for instance, to read Woolman's journal which gives the portrait of a man of absolute integrity, wholly committed to the will of God, however unpopular that might cause him to be with his contemporaries (as it did cause him to be on the slave trade issue), without feeling a finger pointed at oneself. All the radical Christians with whom I would deal are worldly rather than ascetic; that is, they are involved in the public issues of their day and not merely in private sanctification.

The theological problem which lies behind this study and which prompted me to undertake it is the issue of God's power and man's will; that is, the age-old problem of how a man can say "all is of God" and "yet I will it too" or as Paul says in Gal.2:20, "I have been crucified with Christ; it is no longer I who live, but Christ who lives in me; and the life I now live in the flesh I live by faith in the Son of God, who loved me and gave himself for me." There are, of course, many ways to tackle this problem, but one way is to see how it works out in actual lives which are totally committed to God and at the same time totally immersed in the historical ambiguities and complexities of real life. The supposition here is that reality is richer and more thought-provoking than theory. Both as an assumption of the study and an undercurrent within it, will be the suggestion that radical Christians, both religiously and socially, ought really to be called normative Christians, for what one sees immediately upon reading the texts mentioned is that religiously, such Christians are "fanatics" only in the sense of deep commitment to God and such total commitment to God gives them rare and clear insight into the just stance for the issues of their day, the issues of slavery, war, poverty, etc.

The point, then, of such a study is to help the Christian to get some perspective on his *own* "destiny," that is, what God wills for him, what his world has made of him, and what he makes of himself—the total context in which and by which he has become *this* man and no other. The issue will be dealt with through case studies; it will not be necessary to draw "conclusions," but I will point up in detail how the destinies of certain totally committed Christians have unfolded. This method has some of the advantages of the sort of wisdom about human life and destiny one gains from reading novels, for it illumines through a story of a life, not through concepts. But it also has disadvantages, for just as the "point" of a novel is not in the conclusion or in any paraphrase of the theme, so the point of a study of the lives of the saints (for that is what it is) is in the study itself and not the conclusions. A life, like a work of art, cannot be summarized; it can be pointed to and highlighted, but the reader himself must get into the experience of another's life or a work of art through empathy and imagination.

What are some of the features of this proposal that might address our economic and ecological crises? What might one religious perspective—a Christian one, with parallels in other religions—offer to the planetary conversation? I will mention a few: first, a redefinition of "normal" religious/Christian from its usual "lukewarm" character to "radical" as the new norm; second, a refocusing of religious/Christian concern from the "personal" to the "personal/public"; third, the redirection of the goal of human life from self-fulfillment to self-emptying, with the paradoxical assertion that divine empowerment and human fulfillment are the same; and, fourth, a reinterpretation of the form of ethical instruction from the essay to the life story, with the assumption that change or "conversion" is more likely to happen through the power of lived experience than the logic of argument.

These features have informed my theology over the last forty years, and in various books I have investigated different aspects of them. The present essay is intended to deal more directly with them, especially as they suggest an alternative to the reigning "anthropology of individualism," which has reached its culmination in market capitalism and its mantra of more, more, more—an anthropology that is undercutting the health of our planet and the happiness of its human beings. The religions suggest a very different view of the abundant life, one capable of critiquing the model that market capitalism and its endless advertising campaigns promote as the "truth." Probably the most serious conversation of our day is expressed in these questions: How should we live? How can we live well? Why are we here, and what should we be doing? Behind Augustine's *Confessions* and at the base of numerous Facebook entries and agonizing addiction memoirs are the same questions. In times of great planetary crisis, they arise even more urgently, and ours is certainly such a time.

How might these features of my humble, embryonic, perhaps "naive" proposal from forty years ago help us answer these questions in such a way as to benefit not only our personal fulfillment but also the planet's well-being?

A second essay, a sermon delivered nearly four decades later, picks up on these four themes, but with more depth and from a twenty-first-century perspective.

A Sermon on Kenosis

I am teaching a course this semester on spiritual autobiography. I have taught it many times; in fact, it may be the first course I taught over forty years ago. It is about folks like Teresa of Avila, John Woolman, Dietrich Bonhoeffer, Simone Weil, Mohandas Gandhi, Jean Vanier, Martin Luther King Jr., Nelson Mandela, and Dorothy Day, people who live lives of extraordinary love for others, especially the weak and vulnerable. I always find new insights teaching the course, and this year is no exception. I have been struck by a characteristic shared by many of them, the rather shocking practice of self-emptying, of what the Christian tradition has called "kenosis." The text from Philippians sums it up well: "Let the same mind be in you that was in Christ Jesus, who, though he was in the form of God, did not regard equality with God as something to exploited, but emptied himself, taking the form of a slave, being born in human likeness. And being found in human form, he humbled himself and became obedient to the point of death—even death on a cross." What an inversion this is of triumphal, imperialistic views of Christianity!

The reason I am struck by self-emptying is because I believe it suggests an ethic for our time, a time that is characterized by climate change and financial chaos. These two related crises are the result of excess, our insatiable appetites that are literally consuming the world. We are debtors twice over—financially and ecologically. The very habits that are causing the financial crisis are also destroying the planet. We are living way beyond our means at all levels: our personal credit cards, the practices of the financial lending institutions, and the planet's resources that support all of us.

Could the crazy notion of self-emptying, a notion found in different forms in many religious traditions, be a clue to what is wrong with our way of being in the world as well as a suggestion of how we might live differently? Whether in Buddhism's release from desire by nonattachment or Christianity's admonition that to find one's life one must lose it, religions are often countercultural in their various ethics of self-denial for the sake of genuine fulfillment. While in some religious traditions, such self-denial moves into asceticism and life-denial, this is not usually the underlying assumption.

I am thinking of John Woolman, an eighteenth-century American Quaker who had a successful retail business and gave it up because he felt it kept him from clearly seeing something that disturbed him: slavery. He came to see how money stood in the way of clear perception of injustice: people who had a lot of property and land needed slaves to maintain them (or so these folks reasoned). He saw the same problem with his own reasoning—he said his "eye" was not single because whenever he looked at an injustice in the world he always saw it through his own eye, his own situation and benefit. It was as if he had double vision. If he was able to move himself out of the center, then his eye became "single." Once he reduced his own level of prosperity, he could see the clear links between riches and oppression. He wrote: "Every degree of luxury has some connection with evil."[2] Reduction of his lifestyle gave him insight into the difference between "needs" and "wants," something our insatiable consumer culture has made it almost impossible to recognize. As an ethic for a time of climate change, Woolman suggests the clarity of perception into others' "needs" that can come about through the reduction of one's own "wants."

However, Woolman did not find such self-emptying negative or depressing; rather, he found it fulfilling. He has a dream in which he hears the words "John Woolman is dead" and realizes, now that his own will is dead he can say with Paul that he is crucified with Christ, that Christ might live in him. We find ourselves by losing ourselves. That deeper desire is the desire for God, for nothing less will fill the hunger in us. Augustine says that we are drawn to God as a sheep is drawn to a leafy branch or a child to a handful of nuts. To empty the self is not an act of denial, but of fulfillment, for it creates space for God to fill one's being. We are satisfied by nothing less than God; our deepest desire is to be one with God, even as Jesus was. Made in the image of God, our destiny is to become one with God, so that we too can say, not my will but God's be done. This is not a loss, but again, the greatest gain.

What we see here is not an ascetic call for self-denial to purify ourselves or even a moral injunction to give others space to live; rather, it is more basic. It is an invitation to imitate the way God loves the world. In the Christian tradition, kenosis, or self-emptying, is a way of understanding God's actions in creation, the incarnation, and the cross. In creation, God limits the divine self, pulling in, so to speak, to allow space for others to exist. God, who is the one in whom we live and move and have our being, does not take all the space but gives space and life to others. This is an inversion of the usual understanding of power as control; instead, power is given to others to live as diverse and valuable creatures. In the incarnation, as Paul writes in Philippians 2:7, God "emptied himself, taking the form of a slave," substituting humility and vulnerability for our insatiable appetites. In the cross, God gives of the divine self without limit to side with the poor and the oppressed. God does not take the way of the victor, but like Jesus and the temptations, rejects absolute power and imperialism for a different way. Therefore, Christian discipleship becomes a "cruciform" life, imitating the self-giving of Christ for others.

Another example of kenotic living is the case of the French philosopher and unbaptized Catholic Simone Weil. She lived a radical and brief life of solidarity with her poorest and often starving fellow citizens during World War II. She practiced what she called "decreation," a form of self-emptying in which she sees herself diminish as God grows in her. Decreation, or the death of the will, is giving up control over one's life, so that God can subvert the self's exorbitant and constantly growing desires. The point is not mortification but a discipline of emptying herself so that God can be all in all. To eat when and what one wants when others are starving is a symbol of control over finitude, of exceptionalism, which she refused to embrace. Food is a symbol of basic physical limits, and unless we can limit our own voracious appetites, we will not be able to attend to the hunger in others— their abject suffering, both physical and emotional. Our tendency is to love others because of our needs, not theirs, our hunger, not their hunger. Our fat, relentless egos want more, more, more: this is the insatiability of the consumer culture, which has resulted in climate change and more recently in financial collapse.

Simone Weil says that human beings are naturally "cannibal-istic": we eat instead of looking, we devour rather than paying attention, we consume other people and the planet in our search for self-fulfillment. Augustine claimed something similar in his understanding of sin: voracious, lustful desire to have it all for oneself. From the twenty-first-century ecological perspective, sin is refusing to share, refusing to live in such a way that others—other people and other life-forms—can also live. For us in our time, sin is refusing to live justly and sustainably with all others on our planet. It is refusing to share the banquet of life.

This is not a new understanding of sin; rather, it is built upon the traditional view that, as Augustine puts it, sin is "being curved in upon oneself" rather than being open to God. In our ecological age, we now see that "being open to God" means being open to the other creatures, upon whom we depend and who depend upon us. We cannot love God unless we love God's world. Christians have always known this, because an incarnate God is a world-loving God; but now it takes on new meaning and depth as we realize the radical interrelationship and interdependence of all forms of life.

As with Woolman, the problem as Weil understands it is the inability to really see others. She writes: "The only people who have any hope of salvation are those who occasionally stop and look for a time, instead of eating."[3] The United Nations Earth Charter, a document that lays out principles for a just, sustainable planet, agrees. Its first principle reads: "Recognize that all beings are interdependent and every form of life has value regardless of its worth to human beings." An ethic of self-emptying begins with the recognition that something besides oneself really exists and needs the basics of existence.

Paying attention to others, looking not eating, is a somber, thoughtful ethic for our time of climate change. Put simply, climate change is the result of too many human beings using too much energy and taking up too much space on the planet. "Environmentalism" is not simply about maintaining green spaces in cities or national parks; rather, it is the more basic issue of energy use on a finite planet. Thus space and energy, the basic physical needs of all creatures—a place to live and the energy to sustain life day by day—is the issue. In other words, the crisis facing us is one of geography, one of space and place and habitability. It is not about time and history and human meaning; rather, it is physical, earthly, worldly, fleshly—the basics of existence. Christianity has often focused on time, history, and human meaning; for example, salvation has been understood to be eternal existence in another world for individual human beings. But an "incarnational" Christianity, a Christianity that believes in an incarnate God who loves the world and inhabits the world, is radically mundane. In Irenaeus's wonderful words: "The glory of God is every creature fully alive."

This is a strange "crisis" to face: it does not have the immediacy of a war or plague or tsunami. Rather, it has to do with "how we live" on a daily basis—the food we eat, the transportation we use, the size of the house we live in, the consumer goods we buy, the luxuries we allow ourselves, the amount of long-distance air travel we permit ourselves, and so forth. We are not being called to take up arms and fight an enemy; rather, the enemy is the very ordinary life we ourselves are leading as well-off North Americans. And yet, for all its presumed innocence, this way of life, multiplied by billions of people, is both unjust to those who cannot attain this lifestyle and destructive of the very planet that supports us all.

A very different form of life is suggested by another extraordinary Christian. Dorothy Day, who identified totally with the abject poverty of people in the ghettoes of New York City during the Great Depression, lived a life of joyful sharing, a form of the abundant life totally contrary to our consumer understanding. If Woolman and Weil belong to the prophetic strain in Christianity, the strain that underscores the way to God through self-emptying, Day belongs to the sacramental path that, while acknowledging self-emptying, revels in the fulfillment that follows. She found the abundant life in voluntary poverty: she did indeed find her life by losing it, and it was a rich, full, joyful life. In the postscript to her autobiography, she writes of her community:

We were just sitting there talking when lines of people began to form, saying, "We need bread." We could not say, "Go, be thou filled." If there were six small loaves and a few fishes, we had to divide them. There was always bread. . . . There is always room for one more; each of us will have a little less. . . . We cannot love God unless we love each other, and to love we must know each other. We know Him in the breaking of bread, and we know each other in the breaking of bread, and we are not alone any more. Heaven is a banquet and life is a banquet, too, even with a crust, where there is companionship.[4]

GOD'S CALL, OUR RESPONSE

The kenotic paradigm in Woolman, Weil, and Day is not for the sake of asceticism or self-flagellation. It is not a negative statement about the earth and life; rather, it is the recognition that life's flourishing on earth demands certain limitations and sacrifices at physical and emotional levels. The ego that demands everything for itself—honor, power, money—is the same cannibalistic self that devours all the food and land. As St. Francis well knew, "possessionlessness" is a matter of the spirit and the body: it demands giving up not only some of one's possessions but also one's claim of exceptionalism. While the self-emptying pattern might have been seen in other times as a peculiarly religious way of being in the world, I think we can now see how it might be the germ of a personal, professional, and public ethic for the twenty-first century.

Two things characterize our time: first, an awareness of our radical interdependence on all other life-forms—as evident in the vital climatic system of our planet—and second, an increasing appreciation of the planet's finitude and vulnerability. These two realities of our time mean that the vocabulary of self-limitation, egolessness, sharing, giving space to others, and limiting our energy use no longer sounds like a special language for the saints, but rather, as an ethic for all of us. The religions may be the greatest "realists," with their intuitive appreciation for self-emptying and self-limitation as a way not only to personal fulfillment but also to sane planetary practice. Could it be that the religions might take the lead in exploring and illustrating how an ethic of self-limitation might function in light of the twenty-first-century crisis of climate change? The banquet of which Dorothy Day speaks—the banquet of heaven and the banquet of earth—is an inclusive feast. As she writes of it: "There is always room for one more; each of us will have a little less."

These two essays of mine, written forty years apart, sum up my own personal and public journey with the question, How to live well? How should we live? Theologian John Caputo expresses the depths of this question with exceptional power.

> God calls us before we call upon God, calling up what is best or highest in us. In that sense, God pursues us, preys upon us, or even prays to us, inasmuch as God calls upon, provokes, and invokes us. The name of God is the name of what we desire, of everything that we desire, but it is also the name of what desires us, of what desires everything of us. . . . We are called by God, which is our vocation, even as we call upon God, which is our invocation. We subsist in the space between these calls.[5]

We exist between God's desire for us and our responding desire for God, and as Caputo says, the name of God is the name of what we desire, of our deepest desire. (Everyone may not use the same name for this desire—we may not all use the term *God* for this desire, though as a Christian, I do use this term.) What we wish for most deeply is at the same time what we ought to do: respond to God's call to us. This journey is what human life is all about: finding fulfillment by doing God's will. We know deep within ourselves that we are not living as we ought, but what comes as a surprise is the discovery that our duty and our desire are one. We desire what desires us, and it is in the concrete living out of our response—our yes to God's Yes—that we become who we want to be and were meant to be.

Spiritual autobiography is the attempt to understand and strengthen our response to God's call, to the deepest call, which we experience as both delight and duty. It is an opportunity to see more clearly and to embody more fully the particular call made to each of us. How can my life be a reflection of divine love in this time and place? The classic Christian phrase for discipleship—the imitation of Christ—means that we were made by God to become like God, loving all others, loving universally. One's life story is never finished, for we are always in the process of participating in the goal of human life—to be made in God's image (as Genesis reminds us). Presumably, this process continues after death, when we shall be even more fully one with God. Attention to one's spiritual autobiography asks: What are you called to do? How are you to find fulfillment and happiness? The two questions are really one, for we exist between God's desire for us and our desire for God.

Hence, I have come to see in my decades of studying spiritual autobiography that this is not an avocation—a hobby or sideline—but the major task of our lives. Hence, for me, the goal of spirituality, spiritual autobiography, spiritual direction, and prayer is not primarily to achieve an experience of God; rather, we engage in these activities in order to understand more clearly what we are called to do in the world. Put as simply as possible, how do we "love the neighbor" appropriately, helpfully, fully, in our time and place? What does it mean, as privileged persons in developed countries, to do so at the beginning of the twenty-first century? Each of us lives out our discipleship, our response to God's call, in concrete, particular circumstances. For John Woolman, it was eighteenth-century American slavery; for Simone Weil, it was the oppression and hunger of World War II; for Dorothy Day, it was the slums of New York City during the Depression. To quote Caputo again: "The name of God is the name of a deed." Religion is not primarily about correct belief but about committed and appropriate practice. The vocation, the call, the context comes first. Not, Who is God—or, Who am I?—but, What does God require of me, of us, in this particular time and place? Spiritual growth begins with the call to live differently. Sometimes it is nothing more than the sense that things are not right, that I am not living as I should, as I want to. It is the sense that a different world is possible, a sense of disjunction between what is and what ought to be.

What needs to be done? What ought I do? What ought we to do? By grace, by God's love, we respond to the call—spirituality is allowing God to shape us so we can do the work we are called to do. How can we respond to the suffering of the world in our time and place? What are the practices that helped Woolman live a life of discipleship fighting slavery in eighteenth-century America? What is the understanding of God and the world that pressed Simone Weil to identify completely with those starving during World War II? What are the thoughts and actions that lay behind Day's life of total commitment to the poorest people of New York City during the Depression?

Spiritual Autobiography

More specifically, what theology and practices do we need in order to face the quintessential problems of the twenty-first century, epitomized in climate change and economic meltdown? How can spiritual autobiography be a useful source for answering these questions? It would seem that the personal, idiosyncratic, and often narcissistic style of autobiography would be the last place to look for insight on our major planetary crises. As Facebook and "reality" TV illustrate, much contemporary autobiography displays the worst of the individualistic, selfish, consumer orientation of our culture. Is autobiography not the very thing we most need to avoid? If the present spate of outlets like Facebook and reality TV and addiction and abuse memoirs were the only kind of autobiography available, this would certainly be the case. But since the earliest appearance of the genre, it has come in two major forms: the Rousseauean and the Augustinian. Jean-Jacques Rousseau's *Confessions* in the eighteenth century shocked his contemporaries with lurid descriptions of his "masturbation and masochism," which were the equals of Oprah-like confessions of present daytime television.[6] But a much older form of autobiography—the "vocational"—presents a radically different reason for telling one's personal story and the goal of doing so. Augustine's *Confessions*, written centuries earlier, was the answer to his agonizing question of who God is to him and who he is to God—"For Thy mercies' sake, O Lord my God, tell me what Thou art to me."[7] In addition to clarifying his own journey, Augustine states that it might also be of use to others as they attempt to do the same thing. (I read it in college, and to my delight and wonder, I found that the centuries-old questions of this African bishop spoke directly to my own "sophomoric" agonies, an experience that witnesses to the power of this book.) The Augustinian model of autobiography lies behind the myriad of personal, spiritual stories through the centuries—from those of medieval saints such as Teresa of Avila and Ignatius of Loyola to John Bunyan and hundreds of Puritan confessions lamenting sins and asking for God's grace. And behind all of these autobiographies lies the "confessional" practice of the Catholic Church: the recitation of sins and the search for forgiveness. Moreover, the vocational autobiography also served as the prototype of the Western novel, with its classic theme of young men searching for the meaning of their destiny—from Dickens to vampire stories. (Who I am and what I should be doing in the world finally crosses the species line!)

Both of these forms of autobiography focus on the self, but with radically different understandings—the Rousseauean is interested in the self because it is *my* self (who I am is important because it is about me), while the Augustinian model is interested in the self because the self must respond to a call (who I am is critical because it is the way I will know how to answer the question of what I should do). Both forms witness to the inescapability of the question that lies behind all other questions—it is not a "religious" or "secular" question, but a *human* question. As Annie Dillard puts it, "We wake, if we wake at all, to mystery, rumors of death, beauty, violence. . . . 'Seem like we're just set down here,' a woman said to me recently, 'and don't nobody know why.'"[8] Indeed, that says it all. The two types of autobiography suggest two very different answers to the question of "why we are here": the first says that we are here to fulfill our own desires, as insatiable and outrageous as they might be (as long as we stay within the law), while the second says that we are here to respond to a "call," to something beyond ourselves that is both our deepest desire and our most profound duty (though we may not realize how these come together).

If the second type of autobiography is, in fact, at the heart of human existence, then surely those institutions (often, but not solely, religious) that press the question of why we are here would do so, not at a lukewarm but at a radical level. The question is not marginal, easy to answer, or some combination of indifference and convention; rather, the only answers worthy of consideration are radical—they get at the heart of things, press us to the limit, lead us to extremes. It is also not surprising to find that one of the most widespread answers to the question of how we should live makes the shocking suggestion that self-fulfillment rests on self-emptying (a radical move, to say the least). We can also see here how this movement—from a lukewarm to a radical, self-emptying ethics—results in a public as well as a personal answer to the call. To see the self as part of a network that includes all other life and its well-being means that answering the call to who we are in the scheme of things is a public—indeed, a political—move. Finally, this understanding of the self is terribly difficult not only to "understand" but also to put into practice. In fact, one of the reasons for the existence of autobiography as a genre is the realization that life stories are more effective in moving people toward change than logical arguments. Most religious traditions depend on parables, stories, and confessions, which show lives lived in this radical, self-emptying way, rather than on essays advocating its acceptance. There is probably nothing more difficult in the world than change at this level, change at the level of what we think our lives are "about." Which is why the language of "conversion," of "rebirth" has been used to express it. We will do almost anything to avoid facing this question, and our advertising consumer culture reinforces this avoidance, shouting at us with thousands of ads daily telling us that "nothing is too good for you" and that "you owe it to yourself to have the very best" (the Lexus, the trip to Paris, etc.).

Whether one thinks of Augustine or Woolman or Day, each of their stories becomes a form of pedagogy, an illustration, a way of overcoming the chasm between belief and lifestyle. They become for us a version of the "lives of the saints," reflecting on the way great religious leaders and activists have incarnated the gospel in their own personal and public lives. "A saint is a person so grasped by a religious vision that it becomes central to his or her life in a way that radically changes the person and leads others to glimpse the value of that vision."[9] They see their own lives as instruments of God; hence, one sees in their autobiographies the paradox of self and selflessness—pointing away from the self through the self. The goal is to point *away* from the self to God—and to the reader. This brings us to the point of why read spiritual autobiographies, apart from the pleasure of reading some great classics. Here *we* are called into question; our personal and vocational lives, our public commitments, come under review. We read the stories of others—we pass over into their lives—in order to pass back into our own and reflect more carefully on them. Does one live according to one's beliefs? Is one only a private Christian (or religious adherent)? Is there in these stories a clue to how private passion and public social change might come together?

Conclusion

We have looked at the rise of interest in personal narratives of all sorts in our time—at the fascination and at times obsession with telling one's story in all its details, the more sordid the better, with instant technology like Facebook and Twitter. While it is easy to dismiss this phenomenon as yet another form of juvenile narcissism, we have seen that it masks a deep need in human beings to answer the most eternal and difficult of all questions: How to live well? From our ancestors huddled around campfires telling stories of coping with natural catastrophes and the death of children to contemporary teenagers contemplating suicide and grandparents rejoicing in yet another day to live on planet earth, people cannot avoid the question of how to live well at both personal and public levels. We do not arrive on earth with "instructions" (as most other animals do) on what we should do during our brief sojourns here; rather, we are "just set down here" . . . "and don't nobody know why." Moreover, what we, living in the twenty-first century, are coming to realize is that we are "set down" in an extremely dangerous and anxious time, as evidenced by massive economic and ecological issues, affecting us deeply at both personal and public levels. The question of how to live well cannot be now (if it ever was) a question of individual well-being; it is that, but it is also a public and a political question. Thus every field of study, every religion, every institution—as well as every individual—is called to marshal its best insights and proposals to address this multidimensional question. The religions have, I think, a special reason to do so, since time and again thinkers and writers have identified these economic and ecological issues as "spiritual" as well as technological, financial, and political.

Barry Lopez sums up the challenge facing us as a culture and as individuals. He also reminds us of the humility necessary as we attempt to answer that challenge.

> No culture has yet solved the dilemma each has faced with the growth of the conscious mind: how to live a more compassionate existence when one is fully aware of the blood, the horror inherent in all life, when one finds darkness not only in one's own culture but within oneself. . . . There are simply no answers to some of the great pressing questions. You continue to live them out, making your life a worthy expression of a leaning into the light.[10]

Notes

[1] Daniel Mendelsohn, "But Enough About Me," *The New Yorker*, January 25, 2010, 68.

[2] John Woolman, *The Journal of John Woolman and A Plea for the Poor* (New York: Corinth, 1961), 46.

[3] Simone Weil, *First and Last Notebooks*, trans. Richard Rees (London: Oxford University Press, 1970), 286.

[4] Dorothy Day, *The Long Loneliness* (New York: Harper and Row, 1952), 317–18.

[5] John Caputo, *The Weakness of God: A Theology of the Event* (Bloomington: Indiana University Press, 2006), 122.

[6] Mendelsohn, "But Enough About Me," 68.

[7] *The Confessions of St. Augustine, Books I-X*, trans. F. J. Sheed (New York: Sheed & Ward), 1.5.

[8] Annie Dillard, *Pilgrim at Tinker Creek: A Mystical Excursion into the Natural World* (New York: Bantam, 1975), 2, 12.

[9] Lawrence Cunningham, *The Meaning of Saints* (Mahwah, NJ: Paulist, 1987), 65.

[10] Quoted in F. Lynne Bachleda, *Blue Mountain: A Spiritual Anthology Celebrating the Earth* (Birmingham: Menasha Ridge, 2000), 118.

2

"Where Are We?": Living Well on Planet Earth

In Annie Dillard's reminder that we are just set down on the earth and no one knows why, she continues her reflection by making an intriguing suggestion: we *could* "explore the neighborhood . . . to discover where it is that we have been so startlingly set down, even if we can't learn why."[1] Would it make a difference *how* we should live if we understood *where* we live? The answer seems obvious—yes, of course. And yet when we ask the question of how to live well, we often limit our context to ourselves, or at most to ourselves and God. How to live well? is considered one of those big questions that religion or spirituality deals with; hence, it is a question about our "inner life," while economics, medicine, science, and technology deal with our "outer" or ordinary life.

I would like to suggest that this division of inner and outer lies at the base of much that is wrong with contemporary analyses of how to live well. *We need to look at the full context of where we live if we are to discover how to live well.* We will attempt to do this in three steps. First, what would a spirituality for the planet (and not just for human beings) look like? This is a necessary step in widening our vision of where we are as we try to determine how we should live—we cannot leave out 99 percent of the world in our search for the good life. Second, we need to take a hard look at "the state of the planet," especially in regard to ways we deny what is plainly before our eyes: the deterioration of the basics that support human and all other life. We do not need another reminder, full of facts and statistics, of the dire planetary status. Rather, we need to open our eyes and be willing to acknowledge "where we live." To do this we will look at four experiments to internalize the plight of the planet—experiments in thought, feeling, morality, and art. Third, what steps might the religions take in developing a spirituality for a planet in need? What particular insights do the religions afford that are both contrary to current interpretations of our place in the scheme of things and helpful in forming our response? We will suggest that kenosis, self-restraint, giving space to others, pulling back, saying "enough," recognizing the interdependence of all life-

17

forms: these are a few of the words that attempt to describe the special—and challenging—religious contribution to the economic and ecological crises of our time.

A Spirituality for the Whole Planet

The current fascination with "spirituality" versus "religion," with spirituality seen as inner and personal, while religion is institutional and traditional, is yet another indication of the narcissism of our culture. However, a 1977 definition of *spirituality* by the Scottish Churches Council claims it is "an exploration into what is involved in becoming human," and "becoming human is "an attempt to grow in sensitivity to self, to others, to the non-human creation, and to God who is within and beyond this totality."[2]

Spirituality is not about a one-on-one relationship with God, but about growing in relationship with others, including the natural world. Spirituality is *communal*, learning about and caring for the world. And what is our world like these days? If we were to answer the question, Where are we? two main crises would surface immediately: global warming and the economic recession. Since climate changes are happening much faster than thought even a few years ago,[3] the urgency of the situation is evident. In less than two decades the Arctic Ocean will be free of ice all summer, melting permafrost and releasing methane gas, which will further accelerate global warming. Researchers fear tipping points with irreversible temperature rise, and its terrifying effects.

The economic crisis has retreated a bit since the dire days of spring 2008, but the possibility of further global economic meltdown is still with us. And there is little optimism about finding a way forward to ensure that another Great Recession does not occur. These two crises point to a dilemma deep at the heart of where we live—we are living in la-la land, a place that has no relationship to the finitude of our actual home, planet earth. We are living beyond our means, both financially and ecologically. We are consuming with an insatiable, and unsustainable, appetite.

We need to change our minds and change our behavior. Thomas Friedman, writing in the *New York Times*, puts it this way: "What if the crisis of 2008 represents something much more fundamental than a deep recession? What if it's telling us that the whole growth model we created over the last 50 years is simply unsustainable economically and ecologically and that 2008 was when we hit the wall—when Mother Nature and the market both said: 'No more.' What if we face up to the fact that unlike the U.S. government, Mother Nature doesn't do bailouts?"[4]

One way we can begin to change our minds and our behavior is through a communal spirituality. The poet Robinson Jeffers says that we should "fall in love outward"; we should fall in love with the world rather than "inward" with ourselves.⁵ For some, spirituality is about the individual—how might I live serenely and happily? But what would a "communal" spirituality look like—one that was good for both the planet and all its creatures?

The religions—the wisdom traditions—might have something to teach us. They move us from individualism to community, for they are not just about "me and my well-being." Rather, they are tough-minded and objective, insisting on global kinship—that all creatures have the right to the basics of existence. How can you get more revolutionary than that? Such a revolution would involve immense changes in the lifestyle of us well-off North Americans. Some have suggested that the religions encourage people to be good "stewards" of creation, and I agree. However, most religious traditions suggest much more: most make the radical suggestion that to find your life, you must lose it, that sacrificing for others is not just for the saints but for all of us, that when the basic necessities of life are limited, they should be shared fairly. John Hick claims that the function of the main religious traditions is "the transformation of human existence from self-centeredness to Reality-centeredness."⁶ And Gandhi claimed that "worship without sacrifice" was one of the seven deadly sins.⁷

CAN WE LOVE BOTH GOD AND THE WORLD?

Pierre Teilhard de Chardin said that at seven years old he had two passions—for the world and for God—and he could not imagine giving up either one. Must it be beauty versus duty, an either/or, or is there another way? What is the character of the spiritual practice for just, sustainable living? What kind of spiritual practice is called for?

Both God and the world *call* to us to "fall in love outward" (Robinson Jeffers), not inward. One is not duty and the other love; rather, both call for our *attention* and do so primarily by focusing on the world. Spirituality is not a one-on-one inner relationship with God; rather, it is meeting God in the world, in both its beauty and its pain. An incarnate God directs our attention to what God loves—the world, all its creatures, human and otherwise. We are constituted by this call outward, this call to pay attention to the beauty and pain of the world. It is "who we are" (made in the image of God who loves the world). We are not first of all selves who then respond to a call to love the world; rather, this is *who* we are—world-lovers—which always means world-bearers, for both nature and the neighbor are the "new poor" in our time.

So, it is not God *or* the world, but the world *in* God. We must love nature as it is: physical, needy, interdependent, vulnerable. If we find God in the world, then we have set the context, the place, where we meet God. This perspective militates against an individualistic, spiritual relationship between God and the soul. It unites mystical spirituality—our personal relationship to God with the world—with the needy body, which must have the basics for flourishing.

Finding God in the world means as well that our use of energy becomes important, for nature and its many creatures can only live by energy. Hence, mundane things like transportation, heating and cooling systems, concrete for buildings and roads, food production (whether local or brought from afar) become the way we love God. Loving God and sharing energy are one and the same thing. This kind of spirituality leads not only to delight and joy in the beauty of the world but also to kenosis, limitation, self-restraint, ecological economics, a sense of finitude, the need to share space, as we come to realize who we are in the scheme of things.

KENOTICISM AND REALITY

Is this religious insight of the transformation from self-centeredness to reality centeredness simply wild, crazy idealism? Is reality anything like this? The evolutionary, interdependent story of reality that we are presently learning from the sciences suggests it is. Nature is the grandest, most intricate, most complex system of give-and-take, of debt and payback, of borrowing and lending, and of sacrifice (albeit unwilling sacrifice). Everything—from one-celled organisms to mosquitoes to whales to human beings—lives within a vast system of exchange, whether they know it or not, whether they want to or not. We give and take constantly at every level of existence, simply to exist at all. Every breath we take is borrowed, and our lives depend on being able to borrow more and more breaths every moment for the rest of our lives. Nature says this is the way the system works: if we live at all, we live off each other.

A good example is an old-growth forest. When I moved to Vancouver, I was introduced to them for the first time. I did not know anything like them existed. The forests back east do not have the complexity and bizarre qualities of old-growth forests, which are a mess—literally, a mess. On first view, such a forest strikes one as a tangle, a jumble of trees standing lying down or half-way down; caves, holes, and openings; ferns, mosses, and lichens; mushrooms, rocks, and epiphytes; springtails, crustaceans, and dragonflies; water dripping, running, standing; trees on top of other trees, trees with bushes growing out of them, trees with holes and knobs and twisted limbs like pretzels. An old-growth forest is seemingly chaotic, but it works, it sustains billions of different forms of life. Its haphazard quality is part of its genius: anything that is successful, that can find a way to live, is okay. Animals and plants live with, inside of, on top of, beneath, partly inside and partly outside one another. It is often impossible to tell what is what: where does this tree begin and this other one end?

The best example of this marvelous messy muddle is the phenomenon of the "nurse log." Nurse logs are lying-down trees—some would say dead trees—that, having lived several hundred years as standing trees, have now begun a second career as homes for other trees. The body of the nurse log provides a warm, nutrient-rich birthplace for young saplings of all sorts to grow. And it is not just seeds from the nurse tree that grow on a nurse log, but anything and everything. All are welcome! The nurse log can live another several hundred years as the giver of new life from its body. Sometimes one sees ghost nurse logs: big empty holes under the roots of trees where a nurse log used to be. The new tree stretched its roots around the nurse log and still retains this odd position after the nurse log disappears. With the hole between its roots, it is a visible sign of the tree that nurtured it.

Life and death are mixed up here. What is living and what is dead? Is the nurse log dead because it is no longer standing up straight? Scarcely. Is the sapling living because it has new leaves? Yes, but barely, and only because it is living off the nurse log. It all works by symbiosis—living off one another. Nothing in an old-growth forest can go it alone; nothing could survive by itself; everything in the forest is interrelated and interdependent: all flora and fauna eat from, live from the others. The nurse log is but a clear example of what occurs everywhere in such a forest.

A Communal Spirituality

The recognition that we own nothing, that we depend utterly on other life-forms and natural processes, is the first step in our "rebirth" to a life of self-emptying love for others. The religious insight that we should move from self-centeredness to reality centeredness is not contrary to the way nature works; rather, it is an intensification of it. In fact, self-centeredness and reality centeredness are not total opposites; rather, recognizing that all life is interrelated and interdependent is the basis for a new view of the self, one that does not try to hoard everything, one that recognizes that others beside oneself truly exist and need resources in order to live. The religions say that the self is found, is "reborn," when it acknowledges the ultimate nature of self-giving, by sharing space and food with others. Many call such sacrifice for others contrary to reality, but nature's brutal exchange system, in which everything is borrowed and payment exacted, is a preparation for the further, total step of self-emptying. What is distinctive about human beings is not we that we escape the economy of debt and payback, but that we can not only recognize that this is the way things work, but we can take it one step further and *give* when we see the balance sheet to be unfair to the weak, the oppressed, the needy. The debt-and-payback system is not merciful or fair or compassionate, but human beings have the capability of making it more so, of sharing when they have too much, of sacrificing for others, of limiting their wants so the needs of others can be met.

At the heart of most religions is a message, an invitation to a marvelous, messy, muddle where we must live in and with and off of one another—if we live at all. Like the plants and animals in an old-growth forest, we are interrelated and interdependent. We live or die together. Along the way we find some nurse logs, those people and places of exceptional warmth and nutrition, who give us the extra help we need. We also can become nurse logs to others. But like any forest, we can be clear-cut, made into a lifeless, sterile, straight superhighway; we, our world, can also become a desert, where few can thrive. Or we can welcome the good news that all of us, all human beings in our incredible and delightful diversity, as well as all other creatures and plants in their awesome differences, are invited to the feast table of planet earth.

In sum, we are not called to love God *or* the world. Rather, we are called to love God *in* the world. We love God *by* loving the world. We love God *through* and *with* the world. But this turns out to be a kenotic, a sacrificial love.

Opening Our Eyes to Where We Live: Four Experiments

The stakes for "climate change deniers" are high; if they can convince the world that global warming either is not taking place or is occurring at a reasonable pace, then we do not need to revise our complacent estimate of the state of the planet. A group of British climate scientists, who sent some ill-advised memos, learned how high the stakes are for the opposition. From these ill-advised memos the deniers were able to elaborate the myth that the entire 2007 United Nations Intergovernmental Panel on Climate Change Report was questionable and was not the "inconvenient truth" Al Gore had claimed. The falsity of these efforts has itself been denied in several carefully monitored studies, but the damage is done. Even though the substance of the UN report has been upheld, people who want to deny climate change (and who doesn't in their heart of hearts?) have found "evidence" to support their wish.

It is very difficult to accept what is now clearly before our eyes: study after study has shown that our planet is sick at the structural level, the level where health is necessary if the planet is to provide the resources for all life-forms to flourish. The authors of a 2009 essay titled "Planetary Boundaries Breached," published in *Nature*, mention nine key "planetary boundaries" that must be respected to avoid catastrophic environmental damage. Three of these boundaries (climate change, biological diversity, and nitrogen and phosphorus inputs to the biosphere and oceans) have already been breached, and since all nine are linked, the other six (such as land use and freshwater use) are already compromised.[8]

No matter how blue the sky may look or how green the grass is in our particular square mile of planet earth, we need to *see* that appearances are deceptive. What is necessary now is that we raise our vision beyond the superficial picture of planetary health that wealth, air conditioning, pollution controls, and zoning laws give to some privileged corners of the earth. And we must be willing to acknowledge what our brothers and sisters in developing countries see more readily—that extreme heat, unusual flooding, and violent storms are warning signs that the structural health of the planet is in danger. Our ability to "deny" what is before us lies in part with the inner/outer split mentioned earlier—we assume that how we live is not connected with where we live, except in the most superficial way. We do not think, deep down, that we are really and truly interrelated and interdependent with all other life-forms and that their health determines our own. At most, we imagine that while some people will suffer from economic and ecological meltdown, we special human beings, the ones with education and some wealth, can escape.

But what if this inner/outer, us/them kind of thinking is false? We have lived so long with this picture of ourselves—as subjects inhabiting a world that is our object and our resource—that it is difficult to imagine it might not be true. In this picture, each of us is the "center" of the world (at least to the extent we can make it so). But what would it be like to imagine the world differently, not as subject versus object, or us versus them, or superior versus inferior, but "all together"? But *how* are we all together? There have been many different ways of imagining this. Much of the Christian tradition has seen all spiritual beings (God, angels, the human soul) as together while the fleshly aspects of human life (and the earth as a whole) are excluded. But what if we refused this inner/outer, spirit/world split and imagined a "democracy of life"? Since all interpretations of the world at a level beyond mere description are necessarily based on models, what if we worked with the model of democracy rather than empire, or subject-object, or hierarchy, as the basis of our thought experiment?[9] There is good evidence from a wide variety of fields—philosophy, theology, the sciences, and others—that the old model is neither satisfying for human life nor beneficial for the planet, and that a new model is emerging. One way to summarize this shift is with Alfred North. Whitehead's well-known statement that "we find ourselves in a buzzing world amid a *democracy* of fellow creatures" (italics added).[10] We need to internalize the world as "process" not "product," a process of which we are a part, not the whole. I am not suggesting "deep ecology," a collapse of the human into nature; rather, I am attempting to imagine a more complex, nuanced, and profound relationship among all beings. "In short, an ecological politics of everyday life is about engaging in a form of 'feeling life' . . . where the boundaries between self, body and environment are made less certain."[11]

Contemporary ecological, evolutionary science is certainly telling us that this interdependence is the case, but it is very difficult to internalize. Let us engage in a thought experiment based on the proposition that there is no "environment" or "nature" surrounding us human beings, but simply one reality we all inhabit, whether we be caterpillars, leaves, camels, or people (rich or poor). One way to interpret the last three hundred years of Western consciousness—from the Enlightenment to postmodernism—is a growing awareness that the line between "us" and "them" has been stretching to include all of "them." When Immanuel Kant said that one should always treat another rational being as an end and never simply as a means, the moral circle was implicitly limited to men of status similar to Kant—the question of women, let alone children and primitive peoples, was not addressed. And certainly there was no whisper of concern for nonhuman life-forms (including the majestic red cedar, the glorious hummingbird, or the land and water). Ethics was limited to behavior between rational men. We are now approaching a very different limit—a time of no moral "limit." *Everything is interconnected.*

A THOUGHT EXPERIMENT

Philosopher Bruno Latour has imagined such a world. Its primary characteristic is that there is no "environment," no external world that is our playfield. Rather, there is "one world," a cosmos, a totality of things, all of which are "insiders," members of the collective who have voice. Hence, "we must connect the question of the common world to the question of the common good."[12] In other words, the two key moral questions are: "How many are we?" and "Can we live together?"[13] Here there is no nature versus human beings, but rather one world; here we must internalize the environment, which we used to think of as "another" world. In this view, when ecological crises arise, they do so as a result of what Latour calls "a generalized revolt of the means"; that is, those parts of the collective whose "voice" has not been heard, who have been utilized solely as means: "no entity—whale, river, climate, earthworm, tree, calf, cow, pig, brood—agrees any longer to be treated 'simply as a means, but insists on being' treated also as an end."[14] This is not sentimental embrace of the lowly creatures whom we have previously abused; rather, it is the hard-headed implication that the world really is one process, which will not work efficiently or productively if its parts are not valued as subjects (in some sense) rather than mere objects.[15] The deterioration of the "whales, rivers, and climate" taking place before our eyes is ample evidence that this way of imagining the world is anything but sentimental. It is horrifically factual. What Latour is attempting is a "political ecology," a common world of humans and nonhumans in which politics and ecology apply to *all*: a radical democracy in which all have a voice. Rather than making us "free" of our attachments to others, this view will deepen our acknowledgment of those "numerous crowds of aliens who have become full-fledged members of the collective," an attachment that is not sentimental, but one that is "always trembling because it has left outside . . . a spider, a toad, a mite, a whale's sigh . . . some unemployed person, some teenager on a street in Djakarta."[16]

Needless to say, this view of the world and our place in it is neither easy nor comfortable; it will demand not only the expertise of all fields of human endeavor, but also a change at the level of our most basic sense of who we are and where we fit in the world. This widespread acknowledgment that the imagination must help us entertain another alternative is well expressed by Václav Havel. "What could change the direction of today's civilization? It is my deep conviction that the only option is a change in the sphere of the spirit, in the sphere of human conscience. It is not enough to invent new machines, new regulations, new institutions. We must develop a new understanding of the true purpose of our existence on this Earth. Only by making such a fundamental shift will we be able to create new models of behavior and a new set of values for the planet."[17] At the very least, experimenting with new models of the human-world relationship plays *a* key role: it will not solve the economic and ecological crises we face (no one "solution" is at hand), but it opens up the possibility of "thinking differently," which plays a part in acting differently. The power of imagined constructions is all too evident in the enormous influence of the consumer model of the human-world relationship. So why deny that alternative models, were they to become deeply imbedded in our consciousness and our behavior, could play a similar role?

A Feeling Experiment

We have been imagining a different world, a world in which democratic practice rather than empire or subject/object describes its mode of operation. In this world, everything has a voice, humans are not set apart from all others, and the lines between "them" and "us" are fuzzy in intricate, sometimes de-lightful, sometimes scary ways. We live with, in, for, above, beneath, through all these others. How does that feel? Does our thought experiment result in something we would like—perhaps even love? Bracketing for the moment all the many ways that nature, the world, impinges on human desires and needs, does *not* please us, and can in fact threaten, harm, and kill us, is there also a dimension of the democracy model that is deeply appealing?

There is a considerable contemporary literature on what has been called "nature-deficit disorder," which is the result of what biologist E. O. Wilson calls our inability to fulfill a basic human need—"biophilia." He claims that human beings are hard-wired to pay attention to and delight in other forms of life. He says that "we are human in good part because of the particular way we affiliate with other organisms. They are the matrix in which the human mind originated and is permanently rooted. . . . To the extent that each person can feel like a naturalist, the old excitement of the untrammeled world will be regained."[18] Or as David Abram suggests, "nature-deficit disorder" is the ways "whereby the human mind came to renounce its sensuous bearings, isolating itself from the other animals and the animate earth."[19] What should be obvious is that our "roots," what makes us human (our peculiar ways of perceiving and communicating), come from the world in which we evolved. "The human mind is not some otherworldly essence that comes to house itself inside our physiology. Rather, it is instilled and proved by the sensorial field itself, induced by the tensions and participations between the human body and the animate earth."[20] Abram says we need to "turn inside-out," freeing ourselves from encasement within the human sphere, acknowledging that we are touched by and in turn touch our kin, other animals, and the earth itself at all levels of our evolution, including our minds. Unless we acknowledge this connection, we engage in what Gregory Bateson in 1972 called an "epistemological fallacy," thinking of the mind and nature as separate.[21] This is hardly a novel or radical statement, for since the Enlightenment and Cartesian philosophy, the West has thought mainly in terms of subject-object dualism, with humans not only out of "touch" with other life-forms but also claiming that these others are merely resources for our needs and entertainment. The basic link between mind and nature, however, is not only at the heart of many religions (Buddhism, Christian mysticism, native spirituality) but is evident also in the arts (Romanticism in poetry, painting, and music) and in some forms of present-day psychology (Theodore Roszak and the notion that personal health and planetary health are connected). In spite of the overriding hegemony of inner/outer, mind/body, spirit/flesh thinking, there is a strong undercurrent of alternative interpretation suggesting that we can and should entertain a different model for understanding where we are and what we should do. This would be a model closer to democratic process, in which we human beings and all other creatures and systems of the earth exist in a set of interrelationships and interdependencies so profound, so total, and so intricate that both the earth's continued sustainable existence and our health and well-being—as well as our joy and delight—rest on acknowledging this alternative.

The considerable support for an alternative model coming from the sciences, arts, philosophy, psychology, and religion also "feels right." Again, a little imaginative exercise: ask yourself, Where do you feel good, right, happy? My answer (one that I would have given when I was seven years old as well as now, in my late seventies) is "on a trail." Any trail will do—the ones in the Canadian Rockies are marvelous, but the ones in my neighborhood park (which I now navigate with walking sticks, given back injuries) are fine also. The minute I get on a little opening in some woods that leads around corners to more woods that await me, I feel a sense of both excitement and pleasure. I feel as if I "belong" here: I am the right size—not too big or too small, big enough so I am not overwhelmed but small in relation to the trees, which humble me and make me realize my relative insignificance. When I read that I evolved in and with the earth, I not only believe it but also *feel* it—yes, it seems right! I never feel this way in a city made of skyscrapers, swarming with people, and only decorated with nature—a few monoculture trees and flowers. Is there something primordial about my "trail" feeling? Is it perhaps biophilia? That hard-wiring in us causes children to reach out to pat a caterpillar (while ignoring the komodo dragon on the TV screen) and for us adults in our "second naïveté" to acknowledge that we too are more interested in the caterpillar than the TV dragon.

What I have been trying to do with these thought and feeling experiments is to loosen the hold of the predominant model of subject/object, human/nature, and to entertain the possibility that a different model—one in which all have a voice and the goal is sustainable well-being—might guide our actions. I have suggested that not only do the sciences support such a model, but so do our "guts," our sense of what is right and feels good. In a society that increasingly makes it more and more difficult to exercise our primordial biophilia—a society in which children are deprived of the chance to run free and feel the earth between their toes—is it any surprise that adults should feel nature-deficit disorder? Hence, what now appears, from our economic and ecological crises, to be a necessity—changing the basic model with which we understand ourselves and the world—is also something we *want*, that might give us joy at the deepest level of our personal existence. "Where we live" turns out to be "where we want to be"—in, with, for nature, the world, which is also in, with, and for us. We have been living as "misplaced persons" for several centuries; it is time for us to come home and rejoice in the comfort that only home can give.

A MORAL EXPERIMENT

However, the realization immediately follows that our new thinking and feeling involve new forms of behavior, of action. The acknowledgment that we might live in a democratic process with all other beings and planetary systems means that our former way of utilizing these others simply for our own benefit is impossible. It is not only immoral or unethical, but also unimaginable, because it does not fit with our current understanding of the world. We are trying to understand the world differently, not as subject versus object or superior versus inferior, but as all together. Our thought experiment from earlier—"a democracy of life," in which no part is only a means to other parts, but in which each and every creature and process has its intrinsic merit and place—implies that *no one* being, individual, or species is the *center*. In a democracy, there is no center; rather, needs and contributions are balanced for the good of the whole by all its parts.

How can people be helped to move from self-centeredness to reality centeredness? Does realizing that reality is put together differently than one supposed lead to changed action? Not easily, and certainly not totally, but a thought experiment can raise the possibility, open the question, invite alternative views. To say that reality is more like a democracy, where "everyone counts," than an empire, where only the king counts (and where all of us human individuals fight to be the king, the center, the Only One), raises radical questions. Morality in such a world is neither a spiritual nor a mental affair, but is a deeply physical and mundane matter. It is, first of all, about who gets to eat and who does not. (Recall Latour's questions, How many are we? and, Can we live together?) In other words, the moral question becomes one of space, place, and energy, for these are what bodies need in order to live and flourish: a place to build a dwelling, space to grow food, energy to raise the next generation.

Just as an earlier generation faced the Second World War as the quintessential issue of their day, so climate change is ours. During that war people all over the world mobilized, sacrificing their comfort and often their very lives in order to avoid what they believed was a threat of disastrous proportions. We are faced with another such threat, one perhaps even more dangerous in terms of the long-term health of the planet, for it involves the very basis of physical existence—space and energy, habitation and food, clean air and arable land, a viable climate for the flourishing of life.

In other words, the crisis facing us is one of geography, one of space and place and habitability. It is not about time and history and human meaning; rather, it is physical, earthly, worldly, fleshly—the basics of existence. Christianity has often focused on time, history, and human meaning; for example, salvation has been understood to be individual human beings' eternal existence in another world. But an "incarnational" Christianity, a Christianity that believes in an incarnate God who loves the world and inhabits the world, is radically mundane. It is not possible to imagine "every creature fully alive" (Irenaeus) on planet earth in the twenty-first century. If we continue living as we have been—and if more people join the high-energy lifestyle of us privileged ones—we are headed for disaster. Climate change is telling us loud and clear that the size of our population and its increasingly excessive energy use is raising the temperature of the planet to the point where disastrous effects will occur: excruciating heat, the melting of glaciers and the rise of the oceans, violent storms, the loss of arable land and clean water, the decline of biodiversity, the intensification of diseases, the increase of wars fought over food and water, and so on.

AN ARTISTIC EXPERIMENT

But, as with all serious alternatives for understanding and acting on a new view of ourselves and where we fit in the scheme of things, it is the internalization of the alternative that is difficult. Imagining a different world is one thing; acting on it is quite another. Often it is the artists, novelists, and poets who help us the most at this point. Margaret Atwood, the Canadian novelist and essayist, has attempted such an internalization of a democratic-versus-empire view of reality in her book *Payback: Debt and the Shadow Side of Wealth*.[22] In this book, she retells the Scrooge story for the twenty-first century, for now it is not only the poverty-stricken of England who cry out for justice, but the entire planet is making its cry heard through ecological disaster and economic meltdown. Atwood makes the astounding claim that not only are we not the center, the Only One, the kings of our domains, but we own nothing, not even our bodies. Her retelling of the Scrooge story begins with a curious event, which she recounts in the opening paragraph of her book.

> Canadian nature writer Ernest Thompson Seton had an odd bill presented to him on his twenty-first birthday. It was a record kept by his father of all the expenses connected with young Ernest's childhood and youth, including the fee charged by the doctor for delivering him. Even more oddly, Ernest is said to have paid it. I used to think that Mr. Seton Senior was a jerk, but now I'm wondering, What if he was—in principle—right? Are we in debt to anyone or anything for the bare fact of existence? If so, what do we owe, and to whom or to what? And how should we pay?[23]

At the close of the book, after the three spirits of past, present, and future have shown Scrooge horrendous pictures of ecological decay and financial greed, gradually raising his conscience, he exclaims: "I don't really own anything. . . . Not even my body. Everything I have is only borrowed. I'm not really rich at all, I'm heavily in debt. How do I even begin to pay back what I owe? Where should I start?"[24]

Atwood has told the story of a man who has a "conversion," a basic change in which he moves from seeing himself as an exceptional human being at the top of a pyramid of less-privileged human beings (as well as billions of life-forms that are simply resources for his lavish lifestyle), to realizing that he is radically and totally dependent on all these others. Scrooge comes to realize that the very world he thought he owned—the vast resources of nature—is the world from which he and all others receive the "gifts" that allow life to exist—the free services of nature that support the food that is grown, the homes we live in, the water that sustains us, the very air we breathe minute by minute. A complete turnabout has occurred in which subject versus object, superior versus inferior, make no sense *because* that is not the way the world is put together. As Atwood comments: "Maybe it's time for us to think about it differently. Maybe we need to count things, and add things up, and measure things, in a different way. In fact, maybe we need to count and weigh and measure different things altogether. Maybe we need to calculate the real costs of how we've been living, and of the natural resources we've been taking out of the biosphere. Is this likely to happen? Like the Spirit of Earth Day Future's, my best offer is Maybe."[25] Atwood leaves us with this question, having coaxed us into identifying with Scrooge as he experiences the lessons from the spirits of past, present, and future about the planet's ecological and economic deterioration. In her retelling, the old Scrooge has become Scrooge Nouveau. He has a corner office and owns a corporation, but his wealth is stretched by supporting four ex-wives as well as the lifestyle of his present wife. "But it's not his fault that he's a self-centred narcissist: he grew up surrounded by advertisements that told him he was worth it, and that he owed it to himself. He's on his fifth Mrs. Scrooge now. She's twenty-two, a stunning girl with very long legs. He owes it to himself because he's worth it."[26] Atwood sucks us into Scrooge's story, because, as she notes, while some people ask, What would Jesus do? we aren't very much like Jesus, but we are a lot like Scrooge. Indeed, that is the pedagogical power of art: to tell a story or paint a picture that draws us into the depths of the most difficult human questions through the delight of a well-told tale. So, we are left with the spirit's answer of "Maybe" to Scrooge Nouveau's question of whether there is any hope if he "makes amends," lives as if he owns nothing and begins to pay back all the gifts he has received.

A Summary of a Spirituality for the Planet

That scary "Maybe" should haunt us all. The future is not certain—maybe we will not wake up, have a conversion, realize that the way the world is put together is closer to a democracy than to an empire (of which each of us is ruler). We have entertained a thought experiment on an alternative interpretation, imagined how it might feel to live within such a construction, and considered the moral implications of this new view. So far our resources for such an alternative model have largely been the sciences, philosophers, ecologists, and artists. We have been looking at our present context, not to more fully describe the ecological and economic disaster, but to move us to the next stage of beginning to imagine, interpret, feel, and moralize within an alternative paradigm. And as we do these things, a narrative emerges in which words like *restraint, sharing, limits, boundaries* are central, and words like *limitless, expansion, growth, development*, which have ruled our personal, political, and market lives for centuries, move to the margins. What is happening? Are ordinary people as well as economists and business leaders beginning to question the individualistic, consumer-oriented, growth-obsessed model? Before turning to our final source for insight on our present context—the world's religions—let us make a brief detour into a few examples where this new language of restraint is beginning to be found.

Restraint and individualism are polar opposites: On the one hand, restraint insists that since there are many of us, all of whom need the basics for existence, we must restrain our own individual desires (the democratic-process model). On the other hand, individualism claims that each of us human beings is the center (the empire model), worthy of unlimited goods and services. People in high places have supported individualism: Margaret Thatcher famously claimed that "there is no such thing as 'society.'" There are just individuals and their families. (Presumably these "individuals" are all human.)[27] Larry Summers (former chief economist of the World Bank as well as president of Harvard University) wrote as follows: "There are no . . . limits to the carrying capacity of the earth that are likely to bind anytime in the foreseeable future. There isn't a risk of an apocalypse due to global warming or anything else. The idea that we should put limits on growth because of some natural limits is a profound error."[28] These absurd statements by the highest-placed political and academic leaders lend credence to what many would like to believe: that the carrying capacity of planet earth is boundless and that as long as "growth" occurs, all will be well. What they refuse to acknowledge, but which every householder knows who has to meet monthly budgets, is that you cannot live beyond your means: no matter how generous the credit card companies will be for a while, eventually you must pay. Curiously, however, contemporary market economists are in such deep denial that they fantasize about infinite growth for a planet of finite resources. The simple truth, which ecological economists insist on, is that population multiplied by lifestyle determines the carrying capacity of any ecological system. Since all life depends on exchanges of energy, the amount of available energy determines the number of life-forms that can be sustained. Moreover, the level of energy use (the amount of energy each life-form requires—the energy use by a well-off human being versus one at the poverty level) must be factored in.

In order for us to internalize the need to change from assuming unlimited growth to understanding the need for limits and restraint, we need to contemplate a few examples of the level of energy use involved in "growth." For instance, China's recent growth of infrastructure to accommodate rapid production of all levels of transportation is an instructive case.

All of these objects—the skyscrapers, highways, railways, subways, bridges, airports, planes, automobiles, and appliances—have one thing in common: They rely on a colossal hoard of raw materials and massive infusions of energy for their construction, operation, and upkeep. Every large building requires tons of steel and concrete, along with plywood (to hold concrete in place when poured), glass, and copper (for electrical wiring); every highway needs mammoth supplies of concrete and asphalt; every car needs steel, chromium, aluminum, and glass plus oil for propulsion; every computer and appliance needs a regular, reliable flow of energy.[29]

This description could be repeated for every massive building and production venture taking place in every corner of the world. Michael Klare, an expert on resource geopolitics, claims that a new chapter in the history of international politics has begun, "one in which the pursuit and control of energy resources would be the central dynamic of world affairs."[30]

Another way to help internalize our need for restraint is to consider the importance of "natural capital." While market economics focuses on financial and manufactured capital, it fails to appreciate the "capital" on which it all depends—the natural world.[31] "As biologist E. O. Wilson has commented, the multitudinous diversity of obscure species don't need us. Can we say with certainty the same about them?"[32] Natural capital is so present, so ubiquitous, so "invisible" that we forget it is our lifeblood. "Few if any human-made substitutes can truly supply the diverse array of benefits that flow from nature. We can't manufacture watersheds, gene pools, top soil, wetlands, riverine systems, pollinators, or troposheres, let along an entire ecosystem."[33] When we think of nature's "gifts," we often limit our thoughts to the obvious resources of trees, water, soil, minerals, and so on, but even more important are the "services" that nature supplies, such as climate. We cannot do without them. Climate, one of the most important nonlinear systems on which we depend totally, can maintain its dynamic equilibrium up to a point—but only up to a point. Then, as we are experiencing, even small shifts can throw the system into disequilibrium, causing immense disruptions. It turns out that natural capital is the sine qua non of existence—ours and all other life-forms. Moreover, natural capital is not interchangeable; that is, one factor does not compensate for another. "Drinking more water will not make up for lack of clothing if you are freezing, just as having more clothing will not satisfy hunger."[34] The basics of existence: clean water and air, healthy soil, food, forests, and so on, are "limiting factors," things we can't do without; and yet contemporary market economists do not even consider them in what they call "capital." Hence, a tax shift is needed in order to match price to cost. "The present system is dissociative. People now know the price of everything but the true cost of nothing. Price is what the person pays. Cost is what society pays, here, now, elsewhere, and into the future."[35] Again we see the disconnect between individualism and restraint: as long as only price is counted, the focus is on individuals (what particular individuals are able to pay), and restraint is not necessary. However, when society, the planetary community, the democratic process, is the focus, the true cost demands that we figure in what the others, now and in the future, must pay.

Our experiment with considering a different model for human presence on the planet has resulted in some sobering conclusions: individualism, the heart of the old model, turns out to be highly dangerous to the well-being of the planet. Is it also unsatisfactory for human beings in their own lives? What if it turns out that the new model of reality that we have been considering is not only better for the planet and all its life-forms but for human happiness as well? That might be a surprising turn, but one worth considering as we look now at what the religions have to offer our reflections on restraint, sharing, limits, and boundaries. In most of the major religions, one finds at least a whisper that one must lose one's life in order to save it. What an odd thought that is!

Where Are We? Religious Perspectives

"The bishop of London, Richard Chartres, once noted that St. Francis, the 13th century Tuscan advocate for the poor and a lover of nature, came from a wealthy family and was, by the standards of his day, a heavy consumer. A conversion experience convinced him to abandon the life of nobility and embrace a bare-bones lifestyle as a pathway to God. Chartres sees a lesson for people of faith. 'We move toward God by subtraction, rather than accumulation,' he says, a consumption ethic embraced by many world religions."[36]

This statement is radically countercultural—in fact, in our culture, almost heretical. And yet this "heresy" is at the heart of most religions traditions, as the following chart suggests.

Selected Religious Perspectives on Consumption[37]

Baha'i faith	"In all matters moderation is desirable. If a thing is carried to excess, it will prove a source of evil" (Bah'u'llah, Tablets of Baha'u'llah).
Buddhism	"Whoever in this world overcomes his selfish cravings, his sorrow fall [sic] away from him, like drops of water from a lotus flower" (Dhammapada, 336).
Christianity	"No one can be slave of two masters. . . . You cannot be the slave both of God and money" (Matt. 6:24).
Confucianism	"Excess and deficiency are equally at fault" (Confucius XI.15).
Daoism	"He who knows he has enough is rich" (Dao De Jing).
Hinduism	That person who lives completely free from desires, without longing . . . attains peace" (Bhagavad Gita ll.71).
Islam	"Eat and drink, but waste not by excess: He loves not the excessive" (Qur'an, :31).
Judaism	"Give me neither poverty nor riches" (Prov. 30:8).

Interestingly, none of these perspectives is ascetic, none calls for hair shirt and ashes, none demands fasting or starvation. Rather, they are recommending moderation, which, however, appears to be reached by being "free from desires." The path is by way of "subtraction," not "accumulation." What odd sort of logic is operating here? Flannery O'Connor, the American Southern novelist, commented that for people who are deaf, one must shout, and for people who are blind one must write in large letters. Our society certainly is in need of loud words and big letters when it comes to such things as moderation, restraint, and sharing resources. We don't know how to say, "I have enough."

To reach this place of moderation, however, involves a conversion, as the story of St. Francis illustrates. It involves a disorientation, a disruption, a shock that jolts one awake from one's slumber induced by the comforts of conventional, consumer culture to consider a different way of being. For example, Jesus' parables, his typical way of teaching, usually begin with an ordinary story of ordinary people doing ordinary things (like laborers in a vineyard who agree to a wage set by the landowner) who then find a disorienting shift (as the laborers do when the landowner gives the last person to appear for work the same payment as those who have worked all day). They grumble: "These last worked only one hour, and you have made them equal to us who have borne the burden of the day and the scorching heat" (Matt. 20:l2). The workers (and other listeners to the story) are left to figure out what has happened to the convention of "fairness."

Likewise, with the goal of restraint in mind, many religious traditions call for the logic of shock. Franciscan writer Richard Rohr notes that in order for people to undergo the conversion necessary to support a lifestyle of restraint, a kind of suffering, of self-denial, is usually necessary. He writes that "the bubble of order has to be broken by deliberately walking in the opposite direction. Not eat instead of eat. . . . Silence instead of talking, emptiness instead of fullness."[38] In other words, kenosis, self-emptying, is a way to get to the goal of moderation. A special gift that the religions bring to the conversation of how to live sustainably on our planet is not just to call for restraint but to show the way to get there. One of the most difficult problems we have encountered in responding to the economic and ecological crises facing us is the conundrum that while we know what we ought to do, we do not do it. And we do not know *how* to do it. The religions say that one way is to shock ourselves into a new way of being in the world. John Hick, an eminent student of religions, claims that "the function of post-axial religion is to create contexts within which the transformation of human existence from self-centredness to Reality-centredness can take place."[39] This succinct definition of religion is also a highly charged one: what is more difficult for most of us than such a transformation, a shift of focus away ourselves as the center of "Reality"? This is especially so if "Reality" is described as a response that "produces compassion/love towards other human beings or towards all life."[40] This seemingly innocuous statement, when translated, results in the universality of the Golden Rule: "to treat others as having the same value as myself."[41] Thus, at the heart of most religions is the simplest as well as the most difficult of all moral injunctions, and as Hick notes, we call someone a "saint" whose journey on this path from self-centeredness to reality centeredness is more advanced than the rest of us, sufficiently advanced that we marvel at them.[42]

Thus the heart of the religious contribution to our problem of how to live differently is attending to a different logic: the logic of self-emptying as the way both to personal fulfillment and to public restraint. As another student of religion, Karen Armstrong, puts is: "Above all, the habitual practice of compassion and the Golden Rule 'all day and every day' demands perpetual *kenosis*. The constant stepping outside our own preferences, convictions, and prejudices is an *ekstasis* that is not a glamorous rapture but, as Confucius's pupil Yan Hui explained, is itself the transcendence we seek."[43] She also notes, "Religion is not an easy matter," for it takes tremendous effort to "drive us out of ourselves."[44] Religion is a practice, what the Jewish rabbis called *migra*, essentially a program for action. One must engage this central teaching of gradually substituting reality centeredness for self-centeredness imaginatively, ritually, and ethically, becoming so involved with it that it effects profound change.[45] In Buddhism, the search for *anatta*, or no-self, "required Buddhists to *behave* day by day, hour by hour, as though the self did not exist. . . . By far the best way of achieving *anatta* was compassion, the ability to *feel with* the other, which required that one dethrone the self from the center of one's world."[46] This strange connection between self-emptying and personal fulfillment as well as public harmony and well-being is the key, I believe, to the special and perhaps unique contribution of the religions. Most religions do not emphasize belief in a distant, supernatural being, but rather recommend a practice of living differently than society usually supports and commends. The religions are saying, "There is a better way." But curiously, this better way involves giving up something—namely, the centrality of the self. As Armstrong summarizes the point: "The truths of religion are accessible only when you are prepared to get rid of the selfishness, greed, and self-preoccupation that, perhaps inevitably are ingrained in our thoughts and behavior but are also the source of so much of our pain [and could we add, "as well as the world's pain"?]. The Greeks would call this process *kenosis*, 'emptying.'"[47]

SOME CLOSING REFLECTIONS

The central thread running throughout my reflections so far is the gnawing question of how to live well on planet earth in the twenty-first century. As we go deeper into the question and its possible answers, we are struck by the necessity of looking at *where* we are living. It is necessary to realize the particular and grave situation that climate change and the economic meltdown have presented to us. Thus, in this chapter I have focused on a spirituality or practice of right living for the *whole* planet and not just for ourselves or our corner of the world. I have also looked at "the state of the world," not only in terms of the appalling facts and figures about our planet's resources and the needs of its inhabitants, but more particularly at what this information suggests for an alternative model of understanding our place in the scheme of things. I have experimented with this new model at the levels of thought, feeling, morality, and art, and concluded that it demands a different way of living from the conventional market model. Finally, I considered what the religions might offer us in our attempt to live differently in the world, and concluded that the overwhelming problem that faces all plans for living differently is the disconnect between belief and practice. That is, while we can imagine different and better ways of living in the world, we do not seem able to change at the fundamental level necessary to actually bring about a just, sustainable world for all. I have suggested that at the heart of many religions is the curious advice that to find one's life (and abundant life for the planet), one must lose one's life (as presently understood). Put most brutally, one must die in order to live; or at any rate, the narcissistic self, the greedy self, must die in order to find a new center for living.

Since right belief does not automatically lead to right action, what are we to do? The religions suggest that a radical disorientation is needed, and they attempt to express, to teach, this new way through parables, models, and especially lives lived. By following the clues in the lives of exceptional people—those called saints—one begins to understand, internalize, and perhaps to act in new ways. The saints "scream" at us, the hard of hearing, and become living parables of a crazy, revolutionary, countercultural response to the reality they see before them: the world as radically interrelated and interdependent (an insight that contemporary science is also telling us). Thus the small practices of the saints are inductive, empirical examples of the big picture—John Woolman's wearing white clothing as a protest against dyes shipped on vessels manned by slaves; Simone Weil's refusing to eat in order to identify with the starvation rations of the conquered French during World War II; and Dorothy Day's practicing "personalism," the ethical stance that required one to serve the needy who were directly on one's doorstep. Through these modest—and perhaps ridiculous and "unsuccessful"—practices, one gets a glimpse of how the kenotic way of being in the world contrasts the imperial, market-oriented, consumer way. Kenosis, self-emptying, is not an ascetic, world-denying practice of the saints; rather, it is a catchall term for the way the world works: it works at all levels through restraint, pulling back, sharing, reciprocity, interrelationship, giving space to others, sacrifice. This way of being in the world is the opposite of self-aggrandizement at every level, from the personal through the public to the planetary. Self-emptying at the personal level, democratic process at the public level, and interdependence at the planetary level are all from the same root, which claims that we owe our very existence to others, that the system works by a wide range of complementary terms ranging from payback to sacrifice, from restraint to gift, from death to new life. It turns out that looking at "where we are" is central to answering the question of how to live well on planet earth. Hence, how to live well at a personal level is commensurate with living well at the political and planetary level. *We live in one world*, all of us together, and there is one appropriate way of being, stretching from the simplest organism to us human beings.

I have asked in this chapter how we can develop a spirituality for the whole planet, a planet characterized by climate change and economic disparity. And we are all asking this question at the beginning of the twenty-first century. Then why turn to three individuals from other centuries with different issues and different personal stories, when our dilemma is public—indeed, cosmic?

As I have noted, the distinctive characteristic of human beings (in contrast to other animals) is that we not only "discover" the world in which we live but also consciously help "create" it. This is the case whether one lives in the fifth, the eighteenth, or the twenty-first century. We must always ask, Where are we? And the answer to that question is a combination of what the world is and what we would like it to be. The saints of each generation are those people who embody the deepest, most hopeful incarnations of how to live well on our planet at any particular time. In the details of their life stories lie hidden the aspirations of their fellow human beings. Their lives are capsules containing the most profound wisdom of their times in this strange human journey of discovery and creation to live well on planet earth. They do not tell us how to live but *show* in this and that particular case how someone did it in a different time and place, with different realities to discover about our planet and different creations to deal with the issues of their days. The lives of the saints are "case studies," wisdom in a nutshell, a microscopic instance of the macroscopic human problem of how to live well on planet earth.

Thus we turn to the lives of three individuals to glimpse some hints of the perennial human problem, as Barry Lopez states it, of how to live a more compassionate existence, blessed and cursed as we are with a conscious mind "fully aware of the blood, the horror, inherent in all life" but nonetheless "making your life a worthy expression of a leaning into the light."[48]

NOTES

[1] Annie Dillard, *Pilgrim at Tinker Creek: A Mystical Excursion into the Natural World* (New York: Bantam, 1975), 2, 12.

[2] Scottish Churches Council, "Working Party Report on 'Spirituality'" (Dunblane: Scottish Churches House, 1977), 3.

[3] United Nations Intergovernmental Panel on Climate Change Report, 2007.

[4] Thomas Friedman, "The Inflection Is Near?" New York Times, March 8, 2009.

[5] As quoted in David Abram, *The Spell of the Sensuous: Perception and Language in a More-Than-Human World* (New York: Vintage, 1996), 271.

[6] John Hick, *An Interpretation of Religion* (New Haven: Yale University Press, 1989), 300.

[7] Quoted in Gary T. Gardner, *Inspiring Progress: Religions' Contribution to Sustainable Development* (Washington, DC: Worldwatch Institute, 2006), 4.

[8] "Planetary Boundaries Breached," *Nature*, September 24, 2009.

[9] See my detailed descriptions of this point in various books, especially *Metaphorical Theology* (Minneapolis: Fortress Press, 1982); *Models of God* (Minneapolis: Fortress Press, 1987); *The Body of God* (Minneapolis: Fortress Press, 1993).

[10] Quoted by Michael S. Carolan, "An Ecological Politics of Everyday Life: Placing Flesh on Whitehead's Process Philosophy in Search of 'Green' Possibilities," *Worldviews: Global Religions, Culture and Ecology* 12, no. 1 (2008).

[11] Ibid., 69–70.

[12] Bruno Latour, *Politics of Nature: How to Bring the Sciences into Democracy*, trans. Catherine Porter (Cambridge, MA: Harvard University Press, 2004), 98.

[13] Ibid., 108.

[14] Ibid., 155–56.

[15] For further discussion of the subject/subject vs. subject/object models, see Sallie McFague, *Super, Natural Christians* (Minneapolis: Fortress Press, 1997), chaps. 4–5.

[16] Ibid., 158.

[17] Václav Havel, "Spirit of the Earth," *Resurgence* (November–December 1998): 30.

[18] Edward O. Wilson, *Biophilia* (Cambridge, MA: Harvard University Press, 1984), 139.

[19] David Abram, *The Spell of the Sensuous* (New York: Vintage, 1996), 261.

[20] Ibid., 262.

[21] Quoted in Daniel B. Smith, Is There an Ecological Unconscious? New York Times Magazine, January 31, 2010, 41.

[22] Margaret Atwood, *Payback: Debt and the Shadow Side of Wealth* (Toronto: House of Anansi Press, 2008).

[23] Ibid., 1.

[24] Ibid., 203.

[25] Ibid.

[26] Ibid., 176.

[27] Quoted in Bill McKibben, *Deep Economy: The Wealth of Communities and the Durable Future* (New York: Henry Holt, 2007), 98.

[28] Quoted in ibid., 24.

[29] Michael T. Klare, Rising Powers, *Shrinking Planet: The New Geopolitics of Energy* (New York: Henry Holt, 2008), 70.

[30] Ibid., 7.

[31] See Paul Hawken, Amory Lovins, and L. Hunter Lovins, *Natural Capitalism: Creating the Next Industrial Revolution* (New York: Little, Brown, 1999).

[32] Ibid., 151.

[33] Ibid., 147.

[34] Ibid.

[35] Ibid., 166.

[36] Gardner, *Inspiring Progress*, 123.

[37] Ibid., 124.

[38] Richard Rohr, "Giving Up Control in Life's Second Half," *National Catholic Reporter*, February 8, 2002.

[39] Hick, *An Interpretation of Religion*, 300.

[40] Ibid., 301.

[41] Ibid., 149.

[42] Ibid., 301.

[43] Karen Armstrong, *The Case for God* (New York: Alfred A. Knopf, 2009), 328.

[44] Ibid., 319.

[45] Ibid., 321.

[46] Ibid., 24.

[47] Ibid., 20.

[48] Quoted in F. Lynne Bachleda, *Blue Mountain: A Spiritual Anthology Celebrating the Earth* (Birmingham: Menasha Ridge, 2000), 118.

3

The Lives of the Saints

John Woolman, Simone Weil, and Dorothy Day

INTRODUCTION

Michel de Certeau, a postmodern commentator on sainthood, notes what he calls "the Franciscan dream"—"that a body might preach without speaking, and that in walking around, it might make visible what lives within."[1] Such integration is beyond our imagination—to actually live, to be, to embody what one believes. What integrity, what joy, what absence of guilt and anxiety—one imagines that such an existence would indeed be "salvation," full health and wholeness. Edith Wyschogrod, another commentator on sainthood, suggests the analogy of performing versus merely appreciating music: the difference between saints and most of us is that saints not only appreciate but also perform.[2] It is not enough simply to know and admire the good life; the goal is to do it. Moral theories, even the best ones, do not result in moral actions. Would it make a difference if we paid close attention to some stories of people who have actually "performed" the good life? Could such lives serve as parables, disorient our usual worldview, open up other possibilities? And could our study of their lives, with a focus on the process by which they came to be performers, help us become performers as well?

Fifty years ago, when I first began reading the lives of the saints, these possibilities both frustrated and fascinated me. I was frustrated because I sensed that, for people like Francis of Assisi, the process of turning belief into action was hidden within their bodies, within the daily and ordinary actions that made up their lives. The center of our contemporary dilemma—of turning belief into action with regard to the economic and ecological crises—appears seamless in the life of Francis. He does not agonize over "theory" and "practice," calculating the next steps in his journey toward total love of God and neighbor; rather, he embodies it. And yet, it surely must be a process: no one is born a saint, as Dorothy Day insists. And John Woolman, who remarked that "conduct is more convincing than words," actually *lived* his words of radical love. No one does this, we say, or at least we know that we do not.

And we also know that the embodiment of right thinking, of thinking that is good for the planet, is necessary if we are to survive, let alone prosper.

But my frustration with the saints is matched by my decades-long fascination with them. The way they communicate—by living rather than preaching—certainly holds a clue to our central problem of moving from belief to action. How can they do it when we cannot? What is the process whereby they overcome constant and overwhelming self-centeredness so that they can actually *see* the pain of others *and act on it*? Again and again, as I have noted, analysts of the economic and ecological crises come up against the solid wall of a worldview that puts each and every one of us at the center—a worldview supported by the institutions of our society, especially market consumerism, but one that we also embrace with a combination of delight and denial. How to break through this all-encompassing picture of ourselves so that we can imagine other possibilities and perhaps then act on them, at least in some measure? Can the saints help us here? Strangely enough, I believe they can.

In this chapter, I would like to suggest some of the important stages on this journey from paralysis to action, how the saints "walk" their beliefs. This is merely my reading of the lives of the saints; it is not meant to be a contribution to the scholarly literature on them. My focus is solely on how one moves from "here" to "there," from knowing the good to actually doing it. As I understand the lives of the saints, there are four main stages of this movement. First, parables, voluntary poverty, and other forms of "wild space" open up the possibility of something different; the "bubble" of conventionality is burst so that one might contemplate another way of being in the world. Second, this awakening allows one to practice paying attention to others, focusing primarily on their material condition, their bodily needs. Third, this practice results in a much broader view of the self, one that involves loving the neighbor as the self and thus calls for kenosis, sharing, restraint, self-sacrifice, and limits, as the sense of the self eventually becomes "universal." Finally, this new worldview is relevant at both the personal and the public level—the need for kenosis at the personal level (at least for the privileged) and restraint at the public.

My attempt to understand this process over many years has not resulted in clarity; on the contrary, I have become more amazed by the nuanced complexity of the process. There is no one path, no formula, no technique whereby we cut through the conventions of our society that keep us enslaved to selfish and unhealthy ways of seeing ourselves and our world. Rather, as I have studied these people, a number of characteristics have repeatedly emerged: saints are extreme, excessive, often "wild"; voluntary poverty appears to be a signature feature of these folks; they see things differently than the rest of us. This different worldview is related to an enlarged view of the self: They identify empathetically with all living things; they engage in both contemplation and action in a reciprocal way, seeing both as important; they pay careful attention to others, focusing on others' needs rather than their own desires; they appear to be egoless, empty of self; their primary concern is the material condition of others—that is, whether others have the basics for sheer existence; their love knows no bounds—it is universal; they often see themselves as "ordinary" and take small steps to practice their beliefs, incorporating belief into everyday affairs. I do not know how to "order" this collage of characteristics? What is cause and what is effect? What is theory and what is practice? What matters most and what least? Hence, by proposing some stages in the process of moving from belief to action, I am by no means suggesting a pattern one can follow to become a saint! The television gurus are in the business of such gimmicks; sainthood is light years away from such trivia. Hence, my modest analysis of four stages in the process of those who have attained some integrity of belief and action acknowledges the chaotic, complex, nuanced influences, coincidences, detours, regrets, agonies, and joys that create the mysterious muddle that is a life, any life.

Among many lives that we might consider, I have chosen a mere three—the eighteenth-century Quaker John Woolman, the World War II–era French philosopher Simone Weil, and the Catholic Worker movement founder Dorothy Day. I have chosen these three first of all because I love them. One should not study and write about people one does not love; so much work and time ought not be wasted on indifference or dislike. I have also chosen them because their lives, while infuriatingly elusive and challenging, are insightful and hopeful. I believe each of them speaks in particular and significant ways to our issue of practicing an alternative way of life, one of restraint, sharing, self-sacrifice, limitations, reciprocity, and interdependence.

In this chapter, we will consider the "stories" of their lives, focusing on the surprise of learning that comes from a story rather than an essay. The four stages that I see emerging in their lives will not dominate their stories. On the contrary, the stories, in all their complexity and sometimes chaos, will be our focus. However, in chapters 4 and 5 we will search more deeply for the pattern of basic change emerging from the stories—"wild space," a focus on the material well-being of the other, a kenotic rather than individualistic view of the self as universal, and the belief that this new paradigm is for both personal and public practice.

JOHN WOOLMAN: PROPHET OF ECONOMICS BASED ON UNIVERSAL LOVE

John Woolman, an eighteenth-century American Quaker, a tailor by trade and an itinerant minister, has been called the quietest radical in history. He was certainly a radical. While he lived during the Enlightenment, he was not a child of the rights of the individual or of the power of reason. Rather, like prophets and reformers, he had a vision of an alternative way of living; his vision was of a society built on universal love, which he arrived at slowly and meticulously, by a process of gradually embodying it in his own life. But his manner of embodying inner truth with action was anything but quiet. He was, in his personal oddness and eccentricity according to the world's standards, a walking parable of inversion. He grated on the commonsense conventions of his contemporaries, combining his quietism with radical performance. He wore only white clothing (hat included) because he objected to the use of slaves on the ships used to transport dyes from the West Indies. He sold his prosperous grocery business because he was making so much money that it clouded his vision of economic justice. As a guest in affluent homes he refused to eat with silver cutlery because of the oppressed workers who mined the silver. He would not ride post horses, walking hundreds of miles to conduct his itinerant ministry, because the boys who cared for the horses were treated cruelly. But Woolman was not just an eccentric; he was attempting to take every thought captive to Christ, and he knew and became increasingly convinced that such subjection involved an inversion of the world's patterns of convenience and convention. He realized that, like Jesus' parables, disorientation was often necessary before a new orientation was possible. His manner of pedagogy, like that of the parables, worked by indirection—in the daily details of his own life, he *was* a walking parable.

Was this effective in converting others to his gospel of universal love? It is impossible to say, but his journal, in which he recounts his life, has been in print for over two hundred years. During the fifty years that I have taught this book, students have invariably found Woolman's life, as he recounts it, to be one of the most compelling, challenging, and difficult of the saints' lives they encounter. We all agree with his casual statement, "Conduct is more convincing than language," but few of us actually practice it. The amazing— both frustrating and fascinating—thing about Woolman is that he *does* practice it. This is by no means an easy task, for it involved constant, agonizing, and detailed dissection of his conscience—what the Quakers call the "inner light"—to be convinced that his conventionally outrageous behavior was necessary. As a quiet radical, Woolman did not relish being out of step with his society; it pained him to upset people, believing that the wealthy, whom he insulted by refusing to eat with their silver cutlery, and even the slaveholders, whom he fought at every turn, were included in his vision of universal love. As commentator Thomas Slaughter comments on Woolman's method of reform: "It would be difficult to overstate the significance of this low-key almost invisible approach. In the history of the abolition movement there was no more effective advocate by virtue of submerging his ego to the interests of the cause. Woolman led by appearing to follow; he dissented with consensus in mind."[3]

Hence, Woolman's "conversion" was a lifelong realization of what the new orientation of universal love meant not only in the daily details of his own life but also for the social, political, and economic structures of his culture. His combination of radicalism and unswerving integrity combined with a sense of how the personal and the public intertwine makes Woolman a relevant figure for our twenty-first-century dilemma of "changing" our minds and our lives, at all levels.

AN ALTERNATIVE VISION

The beginning of Woolman's conversion was not a startling affair. At sixteen, he refers to love of "wanton company" and to "a plant in me which produced much wild grapes," but he was scarcely in the class of Augustine as a sinner.[4] Within a few years, he had begun to live, as he says, "under the cross," his denial of self for Christ well underway. He sums up his life in these words: "To turn all we possess into the channel of universal love becomes the whole business of our lives."[5] His credo, which he arrived at fairly early in his life, was as simple as it was disturbing.

> True religion consisted in an inward life, wherein the heart doth love and reverence God the Creator, and learns to exercise true justice and goodness, not only toward all men, but also toward the brute creatures; that, as the mind was moved by an inward principle to love God as an invisible, incomprehensible Being, so, by the same principle, it was moved to love him in all his manifestations in the visible world; that, as by his breath the flame of life was kindled in all animal sensible creatures, to say we love God unseen, and at the same time exercise cruelty toward the least creature moving by his life, or by life derived from him, was a contradiction in itself.[6]

The "logic" here is straightforward and, Woolman believed, ought to be obvious to all. God owns and loves every creature; therefore, those who love God will show justice and goodness toward all that lives and breathes. His inclusion of "brute creatures" underscores how inclusive Woolman's universal love was; Kant's extension of love to all "men" is far behind this fellow eighteenth-century thinker! In fact, few, if any, shared Woolman's logic that loving God meant loving *all* sensible creatures, no matter how humble. What in our time is still a huge task—to convince people that all life is interrelated and interdependent—seemed obvious to Woolman. In his journal, he recounts an incident as a young child, when in play he threw stones at a robin, killing the bird. He then realized that the young birds in the robin's nest were now his responsibility, for they would die without their mother. After painful consideration, he killed them as well, because killing them, he reasoned, was better than their dying slowly from starvation. This incident stayed with Woolman and was his first understanding of the interdependence of all life. The same reasoning persuaded him later to analyze the connections between excessive wealth and slavery. People with large landholdings "needed" slaves in order to care for their extensive property, while a more simple lifestyle would help the slaveholders to "see" (that is, to imagine and perhaps enact) a different way of living, one without slaves. Thus, early on, Woolman came to a form of reasoning that saw the widespread and inevitable connection between excessive possessions and violence. Since all life is interconnected, excessive possessions at the expense of the basic rights and needs of others results in violence. He saw these connections with slavery, with war, with the whites' treatment of the native Indians, and wherever possessions stood in the way of seeing clearly.

Such simple logic—and yet how revolutionary! The reasons that our eyes are not "single" and thus able to see how we perpetrate various forms of violence on others, Woolman claims, is that our own possessions get in the way. We then see "double"; we see reality through our own greed, and it masks the needs of others. Woolman's simple logic demanded that he give up his prosperous grocery business when he found the money he was making clouded his vision of the more basic necessities of his neighbors. He started with himself, making his own eye "single," and was meticulously sensitive to the ways in which "his will was unsubjected" because his sight was obscured by possibilities of personal gain and self-love.

What Woolman intuited in the eighteenth century, Wendell Berry expresses fully in the twenty-first century. In the statement below, we find the complex web of life that we ignore to our peril. Both the economic meltdown and the ecological deterioration are the result of refusing to acknowledge the interconnectedness of all our decisions.

> In an energy economy appropriate to the use of biological energy, all bodies, plant and animal and human, are joined in a kind of energy community. They are not divided from each other by greedy, "individualistic" efforts to produce and consume large quantities of energy, much less to store large quantities of it. They are indissolubly linked in complex patterns of energy exchange. They die into each other's life, live into each other's death. They do not consume in the sense of using up. They do not produce waste. What they take in they change, but they change it always into a form necessary for its use by a living body of another kind. And this exchange goes on and on, round and round, the Wheel of Life rising out of the soil, descending into it, through the bodies of creatures.[7]

Woolman came to this alternative interpretation of how the world works—alternative to the accepted exchange of money for slaves, guns, and personal possessions—through clarifying his vision by voluntary poverty. What we now recognize is the "Wheel of Life," to which all of us creatures, human and otherwise, are subject, whether we like it or not, Woolman arrived at slowly and painstakingly through the decisions he made in the concrete and seemingly insignificant decisions of his own life—whether, for instance, to use silver cutlery when invited to dinner at a wealthy person's house. Here we have an example of someone who links his personal spiritual journey with decisions of public—and indeed planetary—significance.

The long journey that started with the death of a robin, the journey that enlarges his sense of self to include all, ends with an extraordinary dream toward the end of his life. During a serious illness he had a dream in which he "forgets" his name: "Being then desirous to know who I was, I saw a mass of matter of a dull gloomy color between the south and the east, and was informed that this mass was human beings in as great misery as they could be, and live, and that I was mixed with them, and that henceforth, I might not consider myself as a distinct or separate being."[8] During the dream there came to his mind the words of Paul, "I am crucified with Christ, nevertheless I live; yet not I, but Christ liveth in me." The dream ends with the words, "John Woolman is dead," that the will he had journeyed all his life to subject to God and to open to all others had become a reality. Here we have the bookends of Woolman's life, and yet it remains for us to sketch the route he took from the robin event to the dream of his new self. How did he become the prophet of an economics based on universal love, an economics that twenty-first-century scientists would agree is not mere idealism but is necessary in light of what we know about how the world works?

Practicing Kenosis

At the heart of his story is a form of kenosis, of self-emptying, in order that he might live with and for others (all those in "great misery"). It is noteworthy that in the dream and Woolman's interpretation of it, he actually loses his sense of being a separate self, both by being mixed up with all those in misery *and* by being taken up into Christ's life. His entire journal is a recounting of the gradual process whereby this exchange takes place—the exchange of the life of an individual who could kill a robin for a life mixed with all suffering creatures by the power of new life in Christ.

Lest we suppose that this exchange was easy for Woolman, we need to look carefully at some features of the process. The kenosis or self-emptying that Woolman found necessary in order to achieve universal love started with one of the deepest and most important of all relationships—the love of parents for their children. In his criticism of slaveholders, he discovered that one of the reasons they gave for keeping slaves was to ensure their children a good inheritance. Here we see his keen sense of how even such a conventionally good virtue as a natural attachment to one's children and concern for their well-being could be used as a mask for evil behavior. Even as Jesus had warned against overattachment to family (Matt. 12:46-50), Woolman also saw how it can be a way to avoid concern for others—in other words, parents could love their own children too much, so much that universal love of all is neglected. Such love can be, in fact, a form of self-love, a "double vision" that distorts a person's perception of one of the greatest evils known to human beings—enslaving another human being. Woolman was aware of how unpopular such analysis was, especially among family-centered Quakers, and critics of his life and work have called him distant, impersonal, and lacking in concern for his own family. (In his journal, his wife and daughter are mentioned briefly only a few times.) Hence, the other side of universal love for all creatures was loosening of the ties to his own family as well as a critique of those who used such attachment to justify slaveholding and excessive wealth.

This example of Woolman's insight and practice illumines one of the notes of kenoticism that we will see in Simone Weil and Dorothy Day as well. One aspect of self-emptying is the discovery that what the self "naturally" or "conventionally" holds as important and good is not necessarily so; a more "impersonal" approach can actually be more appropriate in that it sees beyond one's narrow desires, is able to imagine what the good life would be for other human beings and creatures. While the word *impersonal* may seem distant and uncaring, it reminds us, as does the biblical statement that God sends the rain and the sun on the righteous and the unrighteous, that it is *our* "personal" perspective that is often in fact merely self-serving. One of the major features of our saints is that they "reason" differently than most of us; once the self-centered lenses have been removed from our eyes, the saints' crazy reasoning often seems not only possible but in fact eminently reasonable. How could anyone disagree with Woolman's assertion that the reasoning of slaveholding parents was faulty to the core: that they were accumulating wealth and land (which then needed to be serviced by slaves) only because of their deep love of their children? And how could anyone disagree with the statement from his credo of universal love that if one loved God one should also love all the creatures God has made? The only reason this is denied (and not acted on) is our amazing ability to reject what is "inconvenient" to the sake of our personal desires for self-aggrandizement. As Woolman shrewdly comments, "The love of ease and gain are the motives in general of keeping slaves, and men are wont to take hold of weak arguments to support a cause which is unreasonable."[9]

This feature of our three saints (which is also found in other religious traditions) is called *wild space*, a term anthropologists have used for the peculiar insight into alternative ways of living that some people seem to have. Often wild space occurs in those individuals who do not fit into the conventions of their own cultures due to differences (disability, skin color, gender, class, and so on) that allow them to "see differently." Such vision is not necessarily beneficial to them or to their society, but it could be and has been; at the very least, it suggests that alternatives are possible, and this in itself is a great gift, for most people in most cultures assume that the way things are is the way they must be. All people have the possibility to generate this wild space to one degree or another, as it appears to be a characteristic of all human beings (the ability to imagine something other than what is). While most of us do not live at the level of insight one finds in the saints, we do at least have the ability to respond to a new vision when it is presented persuasively. I am suggesting here that one of the most powerful ways of such presentation is *a life that is actually lived according to a new vision.*

In Woolman's case, his living out of the vision was accomplished principally through prayer and experience—deep, searching prayer focused on the self-abnegating crucified Jesus and experiencing the lives of the most oppressed of miserable humanity. He saw these two directions—inner and outer, contemplative and active—as inextricably interrelated, undercutting any notions that saints are concerned only with the spiritual life, especially their own. Woolman could not be further from this misconception: his prayer life, which was constant, painful, and meticulous, was for the sole purpose of trying to read God's will for every next step on his journey. The Quaker attention to purity of intention and will was highly developed in Woolman and honed his conscience until it was like a finely sharpened blade, able to cut out the most subtle areas of greed, hypocrisy, and rationalization of which human selfishness was capable. He used himself as his first test case before applying the same scrutiny to others. This made for a painful prayer life. He speaks often of wrestling with God, of his oneness with Paul in filling up the sufferings of Christ, and of the office of ministry as a weighty one. Prayer did not bring peace, but discomfort, for through it he saw what few others have seen with such clarity—the way in which following God's universal love for all creatures demands sacrifices in one's outer life that are agonizing to contemplate. He writes that "every degree of luxury has some connection with evil," and he arrived at this simple but revolutionary insight only by putting himself through the refiner's fire and purging himself of his own forms of selfishness. This personal practice became the basis of his application of the insight to the principal evils of his time—excessive wealth and slavery. It does not stretch the imagination to see how his statement could be rewritten for the twenty-first century: Every degree of luxury has some connection with the economic meltdown and the climate crisis.

To increase his own wild space, his ability to see outside the conventions of his day, he constantly put himself in positions to actually experience the oppression that some of his most afflicted neighbors underwent. As his vision of God's will for exercising universal love became clearer through prayer, he developed deeper empathy for others by experiencing what they experienced. Realizing that his middle-class privilege could keep his vision clouded and not "single," he did what few people in his time did—voluntarily exited his own life to enter that of the less fortunate.

His concern for the treatment of Indians is a case in point. Woolman felt that the whites were mistreating the Indians by swindling them out of their land through the lure of liquor and useless trinkets, but in order to really understand their dilemma, he undertook an arduous and potentially dangerous journey to visit their villages. The visit had an astounding effect on him, drawing him to these strangers as to a brother. "As near sympathy with them was raised in me, and my heart being enlarged in the love of Christ, I thought that the affectionate care of a good man for his only brother in affliction does not exceed what I felt for that people."[10] This visit not only involved considerable physical discomfort but also a rather alarming encounter with an Indian grasping a tomahawk. Nonetheless, Woolman comments enthusiastically that "people who have never been in such places have but an imperfect idea of them," which is his modest understatement of an experience that was critical both in his own spiritual development and in his ability to make an empirically based critique of the public shame of governmental and business treatment of the Indians.

A similar motivation caused Woolman to refuse to use post horses in his itinerant ministry, as he objected to the way the boys who cared for them were treated. This daily and arduous practice of walking many miles between the Quaker meetings that he visited on the East Coast became a constant reminder of his identification with the physical and mental suffering that made him one with the oppressed and with Christ. It fitted his sense of his own life as a journey, in which every step he took had to bring him closer to the will of God. Walking allowed the inner reflection to simmer slowly as he contemplated his life as a sojourner attempting to imitate the self-emptying life of Christ.

Another example of Woolman's pedagogy by experience was a trip to England late in his life, to meet with English Quakers. He decided to travel steerage so he could experience what the sailors underwent living in cold, wet, and very crowded conditions. He also mentions the suffering of some fowl who were on board (as potential food) who were as susceptible to miserable living conditions as the sailors. After a lifetime of prayer and action attempting to follow the self-abnegating crucified Christ, he summed up his decision and its hoped-for consequences with these words: "I was now desirous to embrace every opportunity of being inwardly acquainted with the hardships and difficulties of my fellow-creatures, and to labor in [God's] love for the spreading of pure righteousness on the earth."[11]

It was shortly after his trip to England that Woolman had the dream in which he heard the words, "John Woolman is dead," dead to his own will but alive to the will of God in Christ. I have tried to indicate some of the major features of the long process by which he reached this place, to give some sense of the extraordinary exchange by which Woolman traded in his own self for a new self, one that saw and acted differently from the selfish and violent ways of a world that enslaved black Africans and dispossessed the Indians. Woolman faced two of the most appalling public issues of his day by illustrating in his own life the kind of exchange necessary for alternative responses to these issues to become, if not "conventional," at least possible. Is a similar exchange possible for us as we face the economic meltdown and the climate crisis? Is it possible to imagine a new anthropology, a new image of human life, one in which the well-being of others becomes our practice as well as central concern, a practice in which restraint, sharing, self-emptying, and limits for those of us who have too much is accepted so that the oppressed, both human and nonhuman, might live? In the closing pages of his journal, Woolman sums up his long journey with these words.

> I have sometimes felt it necessary to stand up, but that spirit which is of the world hath so much prevailed in many, and the pure life of truth hath been so pressed down, that I have gone forward, not as one travelling in a road cast up and well prepared, but as a man walking through a miry place in which are stones here and there safe to step, but so situated that, one step being taken, time is necessary to see where to step next. Now I find that in a state of pure obedience the mind learns contentment in appearing weak and foolish to that wisdom which is of the world; and in these lowly labors, they who stand in a low place and are rightly exercised under the cross will find nourishment. The gift is pure; and while the eye is single in attending thereto the understanding is preserved clear; self is kept out. We rejoice in filling up that which remains of the afflictions of Christ for his body's sake, which is the church.[12]

I have read and reread the journal of John Woolman for decades, and it continues to amaze, confound, and instruct me. Is this man saintly or unreal? Is he crazy or eminently sane? Should we all be "John Woolmans," or is it enough simply to take him as another example of an astounding life (but not one that we could lead)? As I read him once again, I find myself still asking these questions but with some more insight than I had fifty years ago. On one point, I think we should pay strict attention: What would it be like if our eyes were to become "single"? What does a life of self-emptying, of daring to say, "I have enough," of realizing that the sharing of basic resources is not only a necessity but perhaps leads to "contentment," that *limit* is not a bad word but perhaps a life-giving one for all—what does such an exchange hold for us personally and publicly? Maybe it is more than we could ask or imagine.

SIMONE WEIL: PHILOSOPHER OF PAYING ATTENTION TO THE OTHER

We turn now to a very different "saint," one so extreme, tortured, and demanding that some have written her off as neurotic, if not psychotic.[13] Toward the end of Simone Weil's life, her mother is said to have remarked to an inquirer about her: "Monsieur, if you ever have a daughter, pray to God she isn't a saint."[14] Living in France during World War II, Weil decided to limit her food intake to what her fellow citizens were enduring under Nazi occupation. She eventually died of starvation, which made it easy for her to be criticized as anorectic, dismissing her life and message as delusional. It is certainly "convenient" to do so in our age of insatiable appetites of all sort—appetites that lie at the core of our current planetary crises. I have been reading Weil for many decades, and of all the saints whose lives I have encountered, hers has been the most fascinating and the most challenging. I spent an entire summer reading her *First and Last Notebooks*, not because I was preparing for a class, but simply because I could not resist. Her vision of human life as I have gradually come to understand it is the one most instructive for my personal spiritual journey—and I believe one that holds great riches for our public life today.

In the subtitle introducing Weil, I have called her a "philosopher" rather than a theologian, in part because she refused baptism into the Catholic Church on the grounds that the church's *anathema sit*, its exclusion of parts of the world, was a false understanding of the radical inclusiveness of the incarnation. She says, "The love of those things that are outside visible Christianity keeps me outside the Church."[15] Hence, it could be argued, and I will attempt to do so, that Weil is calling for a more radical understanding of Christian incarnationalism, one that is so inclusive, so materialistic, so grounded in the reality of her time (starvation of whole populations), that "food" became for her the central illuminating metaphor for the radicalism of Christian faith. Her central vision is as simple as it is radical: God empties God's self in creation, incarnation, and the cross so that others might live, and we, the imitators of God, must also empty ourselves of ego, all forms of self-aggrandizement, so that others might live. Just as God is our creator, literally the "food" that allows us to exist, so also we love our neighbors by giving them "food," our attention and our material goods, so that they might live spiritually and physically. Christ, the incarnation, is the focus in this vision, for here we become acquainted with the true nature of God—self-emptying love for the other. The nature of reality is epitomized by the total self-giving of the crucifixion, which is not a substitutionary atonement for the forgiveness of sins, but is the truth about the way things work in the world. Reading "back," then, to the creation, we see the same pattern of self-emptying: God pulling back, giving space, restraining the divine power, so others might have space to live. Creation is not an act of the all-powerful God, controlling all things, but a radically different paradigm for both divine and human action: self-emptying love for others. Hence, discipleship, the role of human beings, is to do likewise, giving life to others, sharing our "food," the basics of life, with those who suffer from lack of it. The story of the good Samaritan is Weil's central narrative: the Samaritan is good because he did the two things necessary for a needy other: he paid attention to him, restoring him to the human community, and he did so at the most basic level of the other's needs, food and medical care.

LOVING GOD BY LOVING THE NEIGHBOR

While this radically incarnational interpretation of the Christian faith is not the reigning one—and certainly not a comfortable one—I believe it is a plausible reading of the tradition. (And I will try to show that it is a subterranean view that both has been neglected in our time and is necessary for us to consider.) While it came to Weil gradually in living her own life, it is deep in Christianity. What is powerful about Weil's radical incarnationalism is the way it arose through living in a time of extreme suffering and deprivation. It is truly, in her case, "pedagogy in practice," the amazing story of the life of someone who saw that Christianity must take into itself the most tragic, tortured, and despairing of circumstances if it is to be truly incarnational, truly inclusive and total. Starvation during World War II was the context and the opportunity for digging into the Christian tradition, beyond the comforts of institutional inclusion and individual salvation, to its deepest and most challenging insight: to love God is to love the neighbor, as one loves oneself. Taken literally, this simple dictum contains all we need to know, says Weil. As she writes: "I think . . . our obligation for the next two or three years, an obligation so strict that we can scarcely fail in it without treason, is to show the public the possibility of a truly incarnated Christianity."[16] This "truly incarnated Christianity" turns out, in her understanding, to go beyond anything most of us could imagine, both in its overwhelming depth of divine love and total implications for human life.

In order to grasp the depths of her understanding of neighbor love, it is necessary to unfold the literal meaning of "to love the neighbor as one loves oneself," a phrase that Christians have recited glibly for centuries. But what this means at the simplest level, says Weil, is that we feel our neighbor's hunger as we feel our own. What if we understood one's "self" not to stop at the edges of one's own body, but to extend without limit to include everything that is? What if the "neighbor" is not only the person next door, but all of creation, everything that exists? What would it mean to love this neighbor as one loves oneself? To begin with, it would be a total reversal of what a post-Enlightenment, market-oriented culture means by "self" or "individual," the narrow interpretation of "me and my desires." Weil's view of the self, and of what loving the neighbor as the self means, is so alien that most people don't "get it"; they simply don't understand what she is saying. As one commentator notes, "Many who attempt to read Simone Weil for the first time have the experience of feeling strongly that there is something important there to understand, yet not actually understanding a word of it."[17] This same commentator goes on to recall Wittgenstein's comment that if a lion could talk, we wouldn't understand him, not because we wouldn't know the meaning of individual words, but because its world and life would be too different from ours.

This, strangely, is the experience many of us (including myself) have in reading Weil. This strangeness is epitomized in the famous and much criticized "paralytic prayer," which ends with the following request: "And let me be a paralytic—blind, deaf, witless and utterly decrepit."[18] What could possibly have prompted someone to make such a request? Was she insane or suicidal? Some have suggested she was one or the other or both (which of course is an easy way to dismiss uncomfortable people), but she gives another answer. Directly prior to her request to be a paralytic, she pleads with God to make her love of God so all-consuming that she literally gives her body for others in total obedience. "May this love be an absolutely devouring flame of love of God for God. May all this [her mind, powers of sensation, and experiences] be stripped away from me, devoured by God, transformed into Christ's substance, and given for food to afflicted men whose body and soul lack every kind of nourishment."[19] As one commentator interprets her plea, "In other words, to be stripped of our own will, sensibility, and thought, in order to have none but God's for good of the world; to die to self so that God may live in us."[20]

A number of things could be said about this prayer and its interpretation. First, it is nothing but a literal reading of loving one's neighbor as oneself, if we take the whole world to be our neighbor. What it means practically is another matter, but the logic is clear and irrefutable. Second, the principal metaphor of the prayer is "food": her own body (and all its parts, physical and mental) as nourishment to those who lack spiritual and physical sustenance. The food metaphor is one of the most important means by which she understands both her own journey from self-will to utter obedience to God, as well as the most basic service we can give to needy others. Third, giving one's body for others is what Weil understands salvation to be: God empties the divine self in solidarity with the most despised human beings. This is good, standard, classical Christian theology as manifest in the many passages in the New Testament, especially the Pauline Letters, which speak of self-emptying for others as the pattern for both divine and human action (see, for instance, Phil. 2:1-11). Thus the prayer of the "paralytic," as absurd as it seems initially, holds in a nutshell Weil's entire theology, which is the self-emptying God, who in all the divine acts—creation, incarnation, and crucifixion—reveals a pattern of total self-giving in clear opposition to the hierarchical, power-hungry, individualistic paradigm of contemporary culture. From the humble words of "love your neighbor as yourself," we have moved to an interpretation of the way the cosmos works (in utter, albeit mechanical, obedience to God) to the way we should also function—in utter, though conscious, obedience to God, signified by the way we treat the neighbor.

Pedagogy in Practice

We shall now see, in detail and through her own life, what Weil means by this unnerving though very simple vision. The facts of her life are both ordinary and extraordinary. They were ordinary in that, born in 1909, into a French middle-class family, with Jewish ancestors but nonpracticing parents, she received an outstanding education in philosophy and literature, taught in various secondary schools, suffered from several illnesses, including severe migraine headaches, and died at the age of thirty-four in England, exhausted by her limited diet. They were extraordinary in that this thumbnail sketch reveals little of what set her apart: at the age of five she refused to eat sugar since the soldiers at the front did not have any, the first of a lifetime of absurd efforts to identify herself with the most oppressed groups in society. At fourteen, she experienced a dark spiritual crisis with an acute sense of her absolute worthlessness, brought about in part by comparison with her math-genius brother. An outstanding student, she was deeply influenced by both Plato and Marx, a combination central to her mature thought.[21] The materialism of Marxism prompted her to desire the experience of the most oppressed: she thus set off for Spain as part of her revolutionary spirit and worked in an auto factory and on farms in order to share the degradation of manual work. Toward the end of the war, she volunteered to be parachuted into France to engage in espionage. The extremism of these decisions was of a piece with her earliest behavior: besides not eating sugar, another of her childhood decisions was to go without socks since the children of workers didn't have any. Add to all of the above the fact that she was an excruciatingly shy, rather homely young woman, who at times was not sensitive to the burdens her "vocation" put on other people—certainly she was not sensitive to her beleaguered parents, who feared for her safety, but others also often found her actions not only useless but sometimes absurd.

So what do we make of such a person? Why has she attained increasing attention and fame? David Tracy writes that she was "a thinker who articulated better than anyone else of her time why Christianity must be a mystical-political religion of and for the oppressed."[22] I cannot imagine a better description of a saint than this one. As I wrote earlier, my focus in this study of the saints is solely on how one moves from knowing the good to actually doing it. This involves a form of wild space, opening up the possibility of living differently; it suggests a self-emptying view of the self that allows one to pay attention to the needs of others; it results in a view that focuses on the material needs of others; and finally, it is a view, while starting at the personal level, is also relevant at the public. "A mystical-political religion of and for the oppressed": this sounds like a radically incarnational understanding of Christianity, inclusive of the entire world, demanding deeply spiritual roots, and resulting in action at all levels. Too often, Christianity has been one or the other: contemplative (recommending a deep prayer life) or active (focusing on social progress). Simone Weil, the odd little woman who annoyed some and infuriated others, is such a saint, displaying in her life and writings a vision for personal and planetary well-being that begins with self-emptying and reaches to universal relevance.

And it is the *incarnation* that is at the heart of it all. Here Weil discovered both the mystical and the material. A mystical event opened up her vision. She began to read the seventeenth-century British metaphysical poets, especially George Herbert. While reading his lovely poem "Love (III)," she experienced "a presence more personal, more certain, more real than that of a human being, though inaccessible to the senses and the imagination."[23] The poem is a highly intimate conversation between a "sinner" and God, the sinner bemoaning her utter worthlessness and God, the gracious host, inviting the sinner to "sit and eat." Here is the last stanza.

> Truth Lord, but I have marr'd them: let my shame
> Go where it doth deserve.
> And know you not, says Love, who bore the blame?
> My deare, then I will serve.
> You must sit down, says Love, and taste my meat:
> So I did sit and eat.[24]

In this poem, mysticism and food unite to provide an experience of God and materialism that was to be the center of Weil's mature thought. The experience is gentle, inviting, personal, and hospitable (sharing food with God!); it is revealing that not only did Weil learn the poem by heart, but she also recited it to herself at the moments of her greatest suffering from migraines. She writes that it was during one of these recitations that "Christ himself came down and took possession of me."[25] She comments further that "in the midst of my suffering the presence of a love, like that which one can read in the smile on a beloved face," came to her.[26] In light of her demanding perfectionism—of herself and others—as well as her strong sense of obligation, rather than rights, both religiously and politically, this "smile on a beloved face" comes as a surprise. What it illustrates, I believe, is a profound *experience* of God's love, love for the most wretched of human beings (which she considered herself to be), which was to serve as a grounding for her tough-minded, no-consolation view of Christian faith. It was not so much her own experience that mattered, but the fact that it served as the basis for her radically incarnational view of Christianity—her personal experience was a witness to the universal, total, self-emptying love of God for the entire creation.

PAYING ATTENTION

At the base of Weil's mature insight that God's love is manifested in our love for others is her conviction about the importance of "paying attention." From her earliest days to the height of her career as a writer, "attention" is at the heart of what she values most and how she learns. Writing to a correspondent to whom she sent an essay, she says: "I was very moved to see that you had paid real attention to some pages I had shown you. . . . Attention is the rarest and purest form of generosity. It is given to very few minds to notice that things and beings exist. Since my childhood I have not wanted anything else but to receive the complete revelation of this before dying."[27] And as she says to the same correspondent: "The root of all evil . . . is daydreaming."[28] These two quotes sum up Weil's understanding of knowledge—the kind of knowledge that really matters, the knowledge that allows us to see things as they are and not simply as we wish them to be. The way we wish things to be is daydreaming, what flatters our egos, but to *see* otherwise is almost impossible for us, Weil claims. We do not "look" at something or someone; we "eat" it: we are like "cannibals" consuming the world for our own benefit. "The only people who have any hope of salvation are those who occasionally stop and look for a time, instead of eating."[29] Here we have Weil's version of changing from a position of egocentrism to egolessness, the central movement that we are focusing on with our three saints—how to change at a deep level from one root paradigm of how to live in the world to another paradigm. Weil is claiming that it all starts with *paying attention to the other*—any other—as the way to form our appropriate stance toward the world and all its creatures. Her essay titled "Reflections on the Right Use of School Studies with a View to the Love of God" joins what appear to be opposites—a child's concentration on working on a math problem and training for loving God. From her own earliest days, she saw the value of studying math and science, disciplines that demanded an openness and patience to a subject outside of oneself and whose truth did not rest with one's own interpretation. Weil believes that the joy in learning for its own sake helps to form "the habit of that attention which is the substance of prayer."[30] It develops in us the possibility of withdrawal for a critical moment, so that we can look rather than eat. What is true of a child's attention in solving a problem simply for the joy of doing so is the beginning of an epistemology that goes all the way to knowing God and neighbor without our own sense of exceptionalism clouding our perception. As is clear in the title of her book *Waiting for God*, attention is a passive, open, receiving attitude, the opposite of imposing our will, power, and interpretation on the "other," whether the other is the beauty of the world, God, or the neighbor. Attention is radical openness, not control.

The route, however, from attention to one's studies in childhood to attention that is itself prayer is long and arduous. It involves, Weil says, a form of decreation of the self and a reorientation of our deepest desire from self to the well-being of the neighbor. One of the most interesting aspects of Weil's theology, in spite of her own mystical experiences, is that the final test of whether one is "saved," whether one has moved from self-love to love of God is not how much we love God but how much we love the neighbor. Do we, in fact, love the neighbor *as ourselves*? In other words, would I give my last piece of bread to a starving person as if that other person were myself? Weil puts it clearly: "To die for God is not a proof of faith in God. To die for an unknown and repulsive convict who is the victim of injustice, that is a proof of faith in God."[31] Or, as she writes, "It is not the way a man talks about God, but the way he talks about things of the world that best shows whether his soul has passed through the fire of the love of God."[32] The end goal, therefore, is radical incarnationalism: loving God means loving the neighbor, all neighbors, in their most material needs.

THE PROCESS OF DECREATION

The growth of this insight, from Weil's childhood until her death, was a complex journey of putting herself in situations where paying attention to the other would yield the greatest fruit. She wanted to know what paying attention would really yield, and she did everything she could to deepen her grasp of it. The key players in this complex are paying attention, the beauty of the world, the ego and decreation, God, suffering and affliction, and the neighbor. My best one-sentence summary of this vision is as follows: By paying attention, especially to the beauty of the world and to the suffering of others, we open the possibility for God to reach us, beginning the process of change whereby we allow ourselves to be decreated from egotists to lovers of God by loving the neighbor as ourselves. Weil sees this as a lifelong process, given how strong and determined our egos are to defend our exceptionalism at all costs. My summary may give the false impression that her vision was a theory; actually, it was anything but. It was the hard-won insight worked out in her own life through her experiences as a student in which she developed her understanding of attentiveness: As a factory worker, in which she underwent the demoralization and dehumanization of mechanical, repetitious work; as a farmer, from which she developed an appreciation for natural beauty as well as bone-wearying labor; as a participant in the Spanish Civil War, which introduced her to the horrors of bloody conflict; as a fellow citizen on starvation rations during the German occupation of France. From all of this she gradually developed her belief that the way to change at a deep level, change that would involve a reorientation at the level of action, was to get herself out of the center of all of her perceptions of the world, much as John Woolman realized that to have a "single" eye he needed to dispossess himself of excessive worldly goods. Both came to the conclusion that the ego, the sense of entitlement at every level (possessions, reputation, power, control), was false, and only a reversal in which the self retreats will permit us to *see things as they are.* In neither case, Weil's nor Woolman's, is this an ascetic move for individual purity or salvation; rather, it is a renunciation or self-emptying in order to live a more abundant personal life as well as a more just public one. In both cases, the first step appears to be breaking out of the conventional world, which supports the satisfaction of individual egos, by some "wild" action, something that allows one to see differently, such as factory work or selling one's prosperous business. As we shall see with our third saint, Dorothy Day, moving from middle-class comfort into the poverty of New York ghettos was her "wild space." The point is not that deprivation is good, but it appears to be necessary to burst the bubble of egotism.

The intricacies of Weil's mature position on basic life-changing action are very difficult to summarize, in part because her reflections on this matter are scattered over numerous publications. However, for our purposes, a simplified version would go something like the following. Starting with attention—the radical open, passive, receptive attitude—which can be as simple as solving a math problem, Weil mentions two main routes to change: beauty and suffering. While some have criticized Weil for being abstract and otherworldly, her love of the world, its beauty and its diversity, is central. Like the good Augustinian that she is, she sees all desire for beauty, all longing, as an implicit longing for God. She sees beauty as the easiest and most natural way to God; God uses beauty as a "snare." "The beauty of the world is the mouth of a labyrinth," trapping us by attraction until we reach the center of the labyrinth, where "God is waiting to eat him. Later he will go out again, but he will be changed, he will have become different, after being eaten and digested by God."[33] The shocking language of consumption is in keeping with Weil's belief that since *we* eat the world (rather than looking at it), our salvation lies in decreating the egotistic self, by being "eaten" by God. "Only beauty is not a means to anything else. It alone is good in itself, but without our finding any particular good or advantage in it."[34] Like math and science, beauty is a lesson in appreciation for something outside of oneself and in no way useful to the self. It is a lesson in impartial, impersonal love. The English novelist Iris Murdoch sums up this position on such love: "Love is the extremely difficult realization that something other than oneself is real. Love . . . is the discovery of reality."[35] Beauty is not just an aesthetic category for Weil: it is one of the ways to the decreated self.

The other principal way is suffering. "Joy and suffering are two precious gifts. . . . Through joy, the beauty of the world penetrates our soul. Through suffering it penetrates our body."[36] Suffering, Weil believed, gives us contact with the implacable order of the world, the impersonal laws of nature, which counter our desire to the center, to be exceptional. God does not play favorites; all are open to the slings and arrows of misfortune, and unlike many interpretations of Christianity, being a believer for Weil does not lessen one's suffering. In fact, our suffering (not just the suffering of Jesus) is the heart of her theology. "The extreme greatness of Christianity lies in the fact that it does not seek a supernatural remedy for suffering but a supernatural use for it."[37] What is the "use of suffering"? Suffering, and especially the depths of suffering, which she calls "affliction," is necessary to erase our illusion of power and our doubt that God can reach the depths of suffering. "Affliction" involves extreme physical pain, distress of soul, and social degradation, epitomized by slavery and by Christ on the cross: here we see the depths to which human suffering can sink.[38] On the one hand, affliction undercuts all human illusions about controlling life; on the other hand, it is the ultimate witness to the fact that no suffering is beyond God's love. This double movement of Christ and his disciples—downward in solidarity with all possible dimensions of human despair and degradation and upward to include all possible affliction within God's compassion—is the heart of Weil's understanding of both divine and human action. Weil's witness to radical and total divine oneness with human beings in suffering and in joy is what "salvation" means, and also sets the pattern for all of our actions. Thus "compassion" for the whole world (in imitation of Christ's life and death) becomes our mode as well, if we see the whole world as our body, if our ego does not stop with the self, but extends to all. We then find ourselves called to feed other human beings with the same compassion with which we would feed ourselves. "Self-compassion is what a pure soul feels in affliction. A pure soul feels the same compassion for the affliction of others."[39]

Thus the two routes opening oneself to God—beauty and suffering—both of which demand the first step of *paying attention*, have brought us to the pivotal moment: the decreation of the ego. In an important passage from *Waiting for God*, Weil points to the goal of decreating the ego: "The soul does not love like a creature with created love. The love within it is divine, uncreated; for it is the love of God for God that is passing through it. We can only consent to give up our own feelings so as to allow free passage in our soul for this love. This is the meaning of denying oneself. We are created for this consent, and for this alone."[40] We human beings were created to be open vessels of divine love, love that is focused on the neighbor and is unlimited. This simple description of human existence, which is merely the unfolding of the dictum to love God and neighbor without limit, is the most difficult to understand, let alone follow. Blinded as we are by our insatiable, self-centered egos, we deny that loving God means letting God's love flow through us to the needy neighbor in limitless ways. What "decreation" meant to Weil was the process of acknowledging this state of affairs, acknowledging what is the case, that our true status is not as autonomous selves at the center of the universe but as obedient creatures in conformity with God and God's actions. God allows us to exist as creatures, but we have one thing of our own—our free will—to give back to God in acknowledgment that all life and love come from God. One does not "decreate" others (though the autonomous, imperialistic ego constantly does this to others), but oneself, for willing to be obedient to God is the one act of which we are capable and is the beginning of becoming the open channel of God's love to others.

Thus we see that for Weil all human action is an imitation of divine action and always takes the form of deprivation of one for the other, a self-emptying so that others may benefit, whether it be at the physical level (food) or the spiritual (paying attention to the afflicted other, giving them new life). Weil writes: "The crucifixion of Christ is the model of all acts of obedience."[41] God's acts are all acts of self-emptying: creation, the incarnation, the crucifixion. "God is not all-powerful. Creation is abdication. . . . God has abandoned God. God has emptied himself. This means that both the Creation and the Incarnation are included in the Passion."[42] Unlike most understandings of God and of creation, self-emptying rather than power is at the center of all God's acts. This is a critical departure from much conventional theology and means that Weil's presumably "outrageous" suggestion about self-denial at the center of both human and divine life is perhaps not so outrageous as many have wished. It might be that "emptying oneself" is at the heart of reality, contrary to our presumption of both divine and human power. "The Creation, the Passion, the Eucharist—always the same movement of withdrawal. This movement is love."[43] So love, not power, is at the center of things—how different everything would be if we believed that were the case! Then Weil's "outrageous" suggestions seem eminently sensible: "God emptied himself of his divinity and filled us with a false divinity. Let us empty ourselves of it."[44] In other words, we die to self in order to live in and toward God. Let us recall our earlier discussion concerning the nature of reality as currently understood by the scientific community, summed up nicely by a poet (!), Wallace Stevens: "We are not our own. Nothing is itself taken alone. Things are because of interrelations and interconnections."[45] The lone, insatiable ego doesn't have a chance in either religious, scientific, or poetic interpretations: we live with and through others—our only choice is to do so through controlling power or self-emptying love.

LOVING THE NEIGHBOR AS GOD LOVES

I began my reflections on Simone Weil with the topic of loving God by loving the neighbor, and we now come, after the decreation of the ego, to loving the neighbor as God loves. In both cases, God is the behind-the-scenes player, but in neither case is the focus on God—and especially not on our mystical experiences of God. Weil did have such experiences, but they were not the center of her understanding of the God-human relationship. Rather, God is the secret, invisible player who begins the process of decreation by planting in us seeds of beauty and suffering to draw us into participation in God's own life through the long and painful process of dying to our own ego, that we might live within and for God. "Loving the neighbor as God loves" involves some strangely non-Godlike characteristics: detachment, impersonality, powerlessness, and materiality. The silent God beyond "God" is not the comfortable God who rewards good behavior, supports institutional power, or allows for "exceptionality." God is not like this, and neither should we be. Rather, the God who demands our decreation, our dying to our own egos, is the one who loves the entire creation with "impersonal" justice for the material well-being of all creatures. God "decreates" the divine self as our paradigm for imitation, as we see in the creation, incarnation, and crucifixion. Surprisingly, Weil believes our best image of the invisible, silent God is "friendship," specifically the friendship of the Trinity. "Pure friendship is an image of the original and perfect friendship that belongs to the Trinity and is the very essence of God."[46] Weil had the highest regard for friendship as the most perfect of all human forms of love: it is intimacy without assimilation. "Friendship is a miracle by which a person consents to view from a certain distance, and without coming any nearer, the very being who is necessary to him as food."[47] It is the opposite of the way humans "naturally" love each other—as fulfillment in one form or another of their own needs, whether physical, emotional, or spiritual. The total intimacy among the persons of the Trinity and at the same time their "respect" for the otherness of the other is, like friendship, a clue for us to the character of the decreated, or we should say, the "re-created" life.

Hence, to love the neighbor as God loves means doing so with impersonal and detached love, open to all who need one's help without regard to their "worth" or "usefulness" (imitating God, who loves impersonally, as the sun shines on the good and the bad). It also means that this impersonal, universal love is not fueled by power but by compassion for the material well-being of the other and total respect for their intrinsic worth. While some might call this distant, impersonal, cold, and even mundane, Weil believed it to be the highest possible form of love, for it is radical *attention to the other*. Recall the story of the good Samaritan, which shows these characteristics: impersonal (the man lying in the street could be anyone), universal (probably the Samaritan would have acted to help a dog), material (the Samaritan attended to the man's need for food, medical care, and shelter), and respect for intrinsic worth (the Samaritan acted anonymously, paying no attention to his own reward for doing a good deed, but simply because the "neighbor" needed help). Moreover, the Samaritan's deed cost him something: he emptied himself—of goods and reward—in order to give another "bread" and "respect," the two basic things Weil believed we all need.

Hence, in summary, to love the neighbor as God loves means giving one's own body for the material well-being of others, anonymously, and without regard to the neighbor's worth. As Christ became bread for us, feeding us with the love of God, so we in imitation of God through Christ should offer ourselves to others in need. While this summary may suggest that we win our salvation by imitating Christ, Weil's understanding is the opposite: the grace of God, which has planted seeds in us and which leads to our decreation and hence our new life in God, allows us now to give in turn. The imitation of God in Christ is not a matter of our *will* to conform to God's image. If so, we could never do it. Rather, it is that we sin in God's light, love in God's love, see with God's eyes. By self-emptying, we take away the blinders that keep us from seeing with God's eyes, we open ourselves to be conduits of God's love, we eliminate our own egos so we can shine with God's image. It is not a matter of *will*, but of waiting, paying attention, opening ourselves to God's will—first for ourselves (we are "coming home" when we open ourselves to God, as Augustine's "restless hearts") but also for others. Grace precedes action: this is not an ascetic program but one of abundance and fulfillment for all. Woolman, Weil, and Day all see it this way: to empty the self is to find God—for oneself and as a source for others. God's love shines *through* us for the well-being of others. Here the self is radically open in two directions—toward God and toward the neighbor.

Thus Weil never supposes that "our" love is anything but God's love: we are now empty conduits through which the divine love, the only love that is, can flow through us. One of the principal results of this new paradigm for living in the world is the complete overturning of power, divine or human, as the center of reality. Just as God emptied the divine self in creation, incarnation, and the cross, renouncing power as the force for change or for good, so we too are called to lives of radical love as the way for fulfilling personal and public life.

Is it practical? Probably not. Is it right and true? Probably yes. Weil shows us in an extreme way, by attempting to live such a life, how ridiculous, dangerous, and questionable it can be, but nonetheless something in us (at least, something in me) says that it is good. If renunciation for the good of others is at the heart of the universe, then maybe there is a way for it to work, in some fashion, for us. Eric Springsted writes, "Weil would argue [that] sacrifice that renounces the use of power as a solution may be the only way any true and lasting change may be effective. Therefore when Weil extends her insights about Christ's cross to embrace all of creation, she does it because the cross reveals a fundamental truth about our condition and a way of finding out what is truly good."[48]

DOROTHY DAY: PRACTITIONER OF PUBLIC PERSONALISM

Admittedly, "practitioner of public personalism" is a daunting title for some-one who claimed to practice the "little way" of Thérèse of Lisieux, small acts of compassion for the nearest needy neighbor. And yet, in a curious way, Day's "personalism," her soup kitchens in the ghettos of New York City during the Depression, was a statement of her radical commitment to fairness for the oppressed workers of the world. That she took the gospel "literally" was her way of joining the revolution, initiated by Communism, for economic justice. "St. Francis of Assisi was one of the most important models for the Catholic Worker because of his radical commitment to the Gospel. The heart of the Worker movement, expressed in love and service to the poor, personalism, voluntary poverty, pacifism, and participation in manual labor, had been brought to the world in a dramatic and unique way by St. Francis many centuries earlier."[49]

The connection between small acts of mercy and public good is mar-velously illustrated with the "onion" story by one of Day's favorite authors, Dostoevsky. In *The Brothers Karamazov*, one of the characters tells the story of a selfish old woman who did only one good deed in her whole life—giving an onion to a beggar. While on her way to hell, the woman's guardian angel reminded God of the onion gift, and immediately an onion appeared by which the old woman could climb up to heaven. However, others also grabbed the onion, which caused the woman to kick and scream, "Only for me! Only for me!" These three words were hell itself, and she and all the others fell back in. As Day commented many times, "Hell is not to love anymore." She meant this at every level, from finding clean socks for a homeless woman to helping organize strikes for fair wages. There is no individual joy or salvation. At the end of her autobiography, *The Long Loneliness*, she writes: "We have all known the long loneliness and we have learned that the only solution is love and that loves come with community."[50]

That simple statement, coming at the end of a long journey of both personal and spiritual loneliness, sums up the genius of Dorothy Day: personal fulfill-ment and public well-being are inextricably intertwined. Just as Woolman and Weil felt that they were part of "it all," so did Day. Just as Woolman's dream in which his own self is "mixed up" with the mass of human beings in misery and Weil's notion of decreation, in which she dies to herself that she might be a channel of God's love to the needy, so Day found that "Heaven is a banquet and life is a banquet, too, even with a crust, where there is companionship."[51] To be a "practitioner of public personalism," then, is nothing more (or less!) than finding one's own happiness in self-emptying for the good of others, with the proviso that "the good of others" has no limits. All "neighbors," of whatever sex, race, age, nationality, economic class, or species, are included.

This extraordinary woman, who lived for over forty years in New York's slums, organizing soup kitchens and workers' strikes, was born into a middle-class family in Brooklyn in 1897. She came of age during World War I and the radical workers' movements, initiated by Communist organizations, that followed. While a student at the University of Illinois, she participated in such movements and was soon moving in sophisticated intellectual left-wing circles, becoming a journalist for radical publications. During the following years, she was imprisoned for protesting on behalf of women's suffrage, became a nurse probationer at a New York hospital, began a relationship that ended in an abortion, briefly married Berkeley Tobey and traveled to Europe with him, was imprisoned again as a result of a raid on a house of prostitution (where she just happened to be), and wrote her first book, *The Eleventh Virgin*, an autobiographical novel detailing the abortion incident. She identified those years with Augustine's confession of his youthful sins; and indeed, she was living a high-flying, heavy-partying and protesting life, parts of which she later regretted. Nonetheless, it provided her with training, both in identifying with experiences of oppression and in writing about them. She wrote with a novelist's concern for precision in conveying both vividness and empathy. She notes that from early childhood she loved to observe people and hear their stories. Not only did these skills make her a fine journalist in her polemics against poverty and war, but she also found herself through writing: "The germ of Dorothy's writing lay in her hunger, present from very early on, to communicate and by communicating to find community."[52] For her, street life (strikes, jailings, protests) and fiction (her own story and the stories of others) illuminate each other; thus she is a "theologian" whose deepest beliefs and practices emerge from her own experience in the light of her understanding of others' stories.

In 1925, she fell in love with Forster Batterham and moved to a cottage on Staten Island. This move proved to be a major junction in her professional life and her own spiritual journey. Batterham was an introverted naturalist whom she deeply loved and whom she credits with bringing her to God: "I have always felt that it was life with him that brought me natural happiness, that brought me to God."[53] Some of the most moving passages in her autobiography describe her love for him.

> Fall nights we read a great deal. Sometimes he went out to dig bait if there was a low tide and the moon was up. He stayed out late on the pier fishing, and came in smelling of seaweed and salt air; getting into bed, cold with the chill November air, he held me close to him in silence. I loved him in every way, as a wife, as a mother even. I loved him for all he knew and pitied him for all he didn't know. I loved him for the odds and ends I had to fish out of sweater pockets and for the sand and shells he brought in with his fishing.

I loved his lean cold body as he got into bed smelling of the sea, and I loved his integrity and stubborn pride.[54]

It was also during this time that Day began to become open to the Catholic Church. Raised an Episcopalian, she was interested in God from her earliest years, but the time on Staten Island with Forster and the birth of her daughter brought her desire for God to a head. And, as she insisted, with "a whole love, both physical and spiritual, I came to know God."[55] This is an important note in Day's personal faith and public work: unlike Woolman, who led an ascetic life, and Weil, whose life at times verged on dualism, Day was a lover of the natural world in all its joys—sex, food, parties, nature, fellowship—and saw the love of God as the fulfillment, not negation, of these other loves. She was a true sacramentalist while at the same time being a prophet for voluntary poverty: to truly love the world, one must identify with the most oppressed of its creatures. This time onward—after the baptism of her daughter and her own baptism, as well as her separation from Forster, who would not join her in her move to the church—marks the second phase of her career. It was at this time that she first met Peter Maurin, who was the inspiration for the Catholic Worker movement. For the next forty years, she lived and worked in places of extreme poverty and discomfort. As she said many times, poverty is not romantic or attractive: it is smelly, noisy, uncomfortable, and lacks privacy. Yet she became a world-renowned speaker for worker's rights both in the States and around the world, a person who exclaimed late in life when people called her a saint, "Don't dismiss me so easily"—meaning, "Don't let yourself off the hook so fast." She claimed that her work did not require great talent but mostly hard work: "I have done nothing well, but I have done what I could."[56]

THE TWO "TERESAS"

Perhaps the best way to give a thumbnail sketch of Dorothy Day is to compare and contrast the two "Teresas" whom she claimed as major inspirations: Teresa of Avila (1515–1582) and Thérèse of Lisieux (1873–1897), both Carmelite nuns, but with very different personalities, one encouraging Day's activist side and the other her contemplative side. Teresa of Avila founded numerous convents, traveling in a time that involved brutal discomfort. In *The Long Loneliness*, Day writes that she has "fallen in love" with Teresa of Avila, in part for her feisty spirit in the face of the miseries entailed in God's service: "Once when she was traveling from one part of Spain to another with some other nuns and a priest to start a convent, and their way took them over a stream, she was thrown from her donkey. The story goes that our Lord said to her, 'That is how I treat my friends.' And she replied, 'And that is why You have so few of them.'"[57]

One can see the sparkle in Day's eyes as she recounts this anecdote, for it was typical of her ironic, unsentimental attitude toward the daily discomforts associated with activism on the ground. One of her favorite quotations by Dostoevsky expresses the depth of how hard true activism is: "Love in practice is a harsh and dreadful thing compared to love in dreams." What she had in mind were the forty years spent in smelly soup kitchens; breaking up disagreements among the volunteers at the Catholic Worker movement houses; traveling long distances to speak at local groups across the country; standing at street corners handing out copies of the *Catholic Worker* for a penny a copy; enduring life without privacy in a small, crowded room; dealing with suspicious members of the press who found her work either irrelevant or Communistic. She was an educated, somewhat introverted intellectual who enjoyed good music and good books, but spent the second half of her life living in voluntary poverty. What could this mean? At the very least, it showed that she had discovered something that shook the foundations of her earlier life and that she embraced as both the road to her own personal fulfillment and the public good.

But the other side of Dorothy Day is symbolized by her even greater love for the other Teresa—Thérèse of Lisieux—who was adored by the masses as their saint, the practitioner of "the little way," but also canonized with remarkable speed and one of only three women ever to be made a Doctor of the Church.[58] She was a shy, sickly woman who died at age twenty-four, but already renowned around the world because of her simple, heartfelt piety. "Love proves itself by deeds, so how am I to show my love? Great deeds are forbidden me. The only way I can prove my love is by scattering flowers and these flowers are every little sacrifice, every glance and word and the doing of the least action for love."[59]

It is not immediately evident why Day would be drawn to such simple, rather flowery nineteenth-century prose or the sentiments they convey. Thérèse lived a life of enclosure, not doing much to "change the world," yet as Day matured in her own activism and prayer life, she came increasingly to appreciate "the little way." Day apparently "once spoke of Therese as a saint we should dread."[60] A fascinating comment, but why would she think this? It seems that a strong case can be made that Day's understanding of "the little way" lies at the heart of her special and powerful linking of the contemplative and active parts of her own life. Thérèse is a saint we should dread because she doesn't let any of us "off the hook." As one commentator remarks, "In Therese's understanding, no act, however apparently insignificant, is without meaning when done within the awareness of God's loving presence. The Little Way is the ordinary way we can all become saints."[61] If, as Day believed, God has achieved victory over evil on the cross, then *we* are not in charge of outcomes, regardless of appearances. The nihilism that overcomes so many social activists, believing that changing the world is on their shoulders, did not overwhelm Day. Like Paul, she found that the failure of Christ in the world's eyes did not undermine her confidence that following the path of Christ in a literal way, in small acts of mercy for those in need as well as protest strikes for justice, was the right path. However much we succeed or fail, victory over evil is achieved by Jesus, giving us hope beyond hope (the hope of God) for our paltry efforts. "Participating in the folly of the cross made it possible for her and her followers to find religious meaning in working with the poor and the destitute . . . and in taking an absolute stand against the war. . . . The absurdity of the cross dovetailed with, yet transformed, the absurdity of life as seen by social nihilists."[62] The reason, then, that we should all "dread" Thérèse of Lisieux is that she squashes all our attempts to avoid taking action because it won't "succeed," and she forces us to look at the small things at our feet that we can indeed do. She cuts off all escape roots for inaction: since the results are not in our hands, anyway, but lie with God, we can and should, says Day, be saints in the little way. With great wisdom, she knew as she said, "The battleground of the spiritual life is in the small things."[63] She believed, as Gandhi did, that *satyagraha* ("truth")—and for Day, Christ, the power of truth—will prevail not only in the small things but also in public change. This is not a popular position, but it is a common one in the depths of many religions, which place personal actions and public outcomes on the same continuum. Of course, if it means, as it did for both Day and Gandhi, living in the midst of the poorest and most oppressed people, sharing their minimal food, crowded and uncomfortable living quarters, and disdain by better-off people, not many will choose it. But it makes a *statement*, loud and clear, that hypocrisy, half-way measures, and compromises are not allowed. If one wants to change the world, one must start with oneself.

THE WILD SPACE OF VOLUNTARY POVERTY

But we are getting ahead of ourselves, for Dorothy Day was not yet the "saint" she eventually became for so many people. Rather, the second phase of her life, beginning with her baptism into the Catholic Church, began with a sense of malaise and lack of direction. She was living on Staten Island, enjoying quiet reading by the sea, her books and music, exclaiming, "How little, how puny my work had been since becoming a Catholic, I thought. How self-centered, how ingrown, how lacking in sense of community!"[64] But all of this was soon to change: "And when I returned to New York, I found Peter Maurin—Peter the French peasant, whose spirit and ideas will dominate the rest of this book as they will dominate the rest of my life."[65] Maurin would introduce Day to "personalism," the central intellectual and religious impetus in her life and work, but the way *to* her mature practice of public personalism lay in another of Maurin's insights: the necessity of voluntary poverty. Quoting Maurin, Day claims, "Voluntary poverty is the answer. We cannot see our brother in need without stripping ourselves. It is the only way of showing our love."[66]

Day's relationship with poverty was long, deep, ambivalent, and realistic: "No, it is not simple, this business of poverty."[67] Voluntary poverty is not destitution; it is *chosen*, and it emphasizes a baseline of necessary material needs (food, shelter, clothing, as well as community and some leisure). It is not an ascetic choice, but principally a spiritual one, as we have also seen in Woolman and Weil, both of whom chose to eliminate all superfluous goods from their lives, so that, as Woolman puts it, his eye could be "single," so he could see the needs of others now that he had "stripped" himself. St. Francis of Assisi is the model for this kind of poverty, whose goal is the death of one's own ego, so that one can see clearly. Weil claimed that, through decreation, we should become open channels for God's love to flow to those in need; and Day knew that you could not reach this goal without *living with the poor*, because anything less allowed us to retreat to the comfort of our own egos, our own warm, quiet, spacious, and private homes. Voluntary poverty is not "simple," in part because it is very difficult to maintain, if there is any possible escape. Day notes that the church itself over and over again has emphasized voluntary poverty, but then, as with the monastic movements, became wealthy again. She notes that "it is hard to remain poor," for not only do we desire all the comforts of luxury (in her case, good books and music, stimulating conversation, and privacy), but also defrauding the poor is part of government practice, as hidden taxes indirectly go to support the wealthy and to war. She claimed that "precarity" or "precariousness" is necessary if an individual or institution wants to remain poor: this entails consciously living on the edge, refusing tempting invitations to live more comfortably (as with the offer of a new building for the Catholic Workers, for instance).[68] The temptations to slip out of voluntary poverty are many: "You can strip yourself, you can be stripped, but still you will reach out like an octopus to seek your own comfort, your untroubled time, your ease, your refreshment."[69]

Voluntary poverty was not an "idea" for Day; it was not a once-for-all decision that she then lived out without difficulty; it was not a solution to the world's ills. Rather, it was a practice that had to be renewed every day in order for her to do her work of public personalism, attending to the needs of others at her doorstep. She contrasts giant strides, such as "kissing a leper" (which she did, twice!), with the small, daily steps necessary to maintain the clear vision given by voluntary poverty: "To give up our own possessions and especially to subordinate our own impulses and wishes to others—these [and not kissing the leper] are hard, hard things; and I don't think they ever get any easier."[70] "Not to hold on to anything," even one's "reputation," one's opinions, one's simple desire for privacy—this is a discipline beyond the imagination of most of us. We can imagine "poverty" (at least in the abstract as bad food, homelessness, insufficient clothing), but giving up one's "self" (and all its reasonable desires for comfort and esteem) is beyond us. Yet this is the reason for dwelling on voluntary poverty as Day's "wild space," for it is what made everything else she accomplished possible. She did not do it for ascetic reasons; in fact, unlike Augustine (with whom she often compares herself), she did not see nature as inferior to supernature, for she believed that the exquisite natural happiness she had with Forster and the birth of her daughter brought her to God. Supernature was a *deepening* of nature, not a denial of it. Like Woolman and Weil, she was a materialist in the incarnational sense: doing the work of God meant giving bread to the poor. Moreover, as she exclaimed during a retreat from the city into the country, "I truly love sweet clover and thank God for it."[71]

THE POWER OF PERSONALISM

If voluntary poverty was the wild space that opened up a new way of seeing for Day, "public personalism" was the mature position for both her personal life and her public actions. "Christian personalism" is associated with the name of Emmanuel Mounier, who in 1932 criticized the bourgeois spirit that had contributed to the Depression: "Comfort is to the bourgeois world what heroism was to the Renaissance and sanctity to medieval Christianity: the final value, the reason for all actions."[72] On the contrary, personalism recognizes the dignity of the human person both as an individual and as a member of human society—the "both/and" unites the well-being of the individual and the well-being of society in a fashion that Day was never to relinquish, and it formed the uniqueness of her position in contrast to her critics who found personalism sentimental and ineffective. According to Mounier, the link between the personal and the public was irrevocable, with the goal being "a personalist communitarian civilization," influenced not only by the Christian focus on concrete works of mercy but also by Marxism and contemporary existentialism.[73] Day was introduced to personalism through Peter Maurin, the peasant philosopher whom she met in 1932 and who was to be her partner in founding and guiding the Catholic Worker movement. While the movement was accused at different times of being both Communistic, ineffective, and heretical, it rested on a simple—though for the bourgeois world, shocking—assumption, summed up by William Miller: "Personalism was first a disposition to grow in 'active' love toward all creation."[74] Hence, contrary to critics who claimed that personalism focused on giving soup to the hungry, it *started* there, but included "all creation."

How could such an economic vision, which rested on both personal and public action, be credible? It differed from Marxism in being personal and from capitalism in being socialist. It was grounded in voluntary poverty and meant to influence economic policy at all levels of society. For Maurin and Day, the freeing of the self lay in the action of freeing others; the world must be changed, but the change must begin with the person. "There could be no quick or revolutionary leap to the good society that could ever put aside, even for a moment, personalist action. Mass political and social pressures that ignored the poor at one's doorstep were false. The action of love came before the action of the world."[75] It may seem like a big stretch from soup kitchens to antimilitarism, but Day believed that the same hedonistic, materialistic cultural values underlay both issues. Cultural values of self-love, material consumption, and violence can never serve as the basis for personal or public flourishing. There must be continuity between the personal and the public, starting with a radical notion of personal hospitality and reaching to public hospitality: just as the homeless person is welcomed into our house, so food, clothing, medical care, and housing should be provided for all.

The classic works of mercy are not an ascetic practice for the souls of the saints, but are the basis of a public policy of well-being for the planet. Is radical hospitality a clue, as most of the world's religions suggest, to both personal fulfillment and social justice? Day agrees with St. Paul's uncanny psychological insight: "As St. Paul says, it is by little and by little that we are saved—or that we fail."[76] All of us would rather think our lives are determined by some great event rather than the small, but telling, decisions we make every day and that then make us who we are. In Day's eloquent words: "We were taught in the Gospel to work from the bottom up, not from the top down. Everything was personalist, we were our brothers' keeper, and we were not to pass by our neighbor who has fallen by the wayside and let the State, the all encroaching State, take over, but we were to do all we could ourselves."[77] This observation recalls Day's words when asked if she was a saint: "I have done nothing well, but *I have done what I could*" (italics added). The heart of personalism is being able to say that—and how radical it would be if we did!

For Christians, personalism can be seen as a form of God's incarnation. At the most immediate level, incarnation means that Christ is everywhere, hidden in every needy person we meet. In giving hospitality to the needy person, that guest is always Christ. "What a simplification of life it would be if we forced ourselves to see that everywhere we go is Christ, wearing out socks we have to darn, eating the food we have to cook, laughing with us, walking with us, silent with us, sleeping with us. . . . *He [Christ] made heaven hinge on the way we act towards Him in his disguises of commonplace, frail and ordinary human beings*" (italics added).[78] Thérèse of Lisieux's little way becomes the heart of Christian discipleship. Moreover, for Day the widest and deepest understanding of the incarnation does not limit it to the life of Jesus of Nazareth, but sees both creation and discipleship as "invisible" forms of God's taking on flesh in the world. In the beauty of creation, God's invisible form is recognized for those who have eyes to see, just as every homeless and hungry person is Christ incognito—we see in their suffering the suffering Christ. To say that God is with us and that we live and move and have our being in God means that God is incarnate in the beauty of creation and in the pain of our fellow creatures. Seeing the presence of God in these places is only possible if the ego is out of the way, permitting us to see clearly what is the case; namely, that God is at the center of all things, both beauty and pain. Thus, for anyone who embraces an ethic of our radical obligation to the "face" of the other, as well as for Christians who embrace an incarnational God, "personalism" is not some strange, sentimental do-gooding. Rather, it responds to the way things are.[79]

PERSONALISM, PACIFISM, AND WORKERS' RIGHTS

Personalism leads directly to pacifism and nonviolent action. Just as there is a spiritual immediacy in giving hospitality to the needy person, so there is a political directness in personalism's refusal to wait for government or someone else to take action. Direct-action politics has several characteristics: it is unmediated; it relies on protest, noncooperation, and resistance; and it arises from hospitality in the broadest sense. The Catholic Worker movement was the public face of personalist action and the *Catholic Worker* publication was its mouthpiece. The movement and the newssheet were among only a few organizations, apart from Communism, and the only voice in the established Catholic Church, that protested the myth of American Manifest Destiny, which provided a cloak for the country's complicity with militarism and materialism as well as disregard for the poor and marginal. The unnerving ideology of the movement was its insistence on consistency between means and ends: just as one has an obligation to do the right thing for the individual neighbor in need, so also one has such an obligation to act in a similar hospitable manner regarding political issues. A favorite quote of the movement by St. Catherine of Sienna sums it up: "All the way to Heaven is Heaven," which is a poetic way of saying that the end does not justify the means. If violence is wrong toward the person on one's doorstep, it is wrong to fight wars, for whatever reason. Another way to express this unnerving idea is that love is universal; personalism does not mean that our responsibility stops with the concrete works of mercy in one's immediate surroundings, but its *intention* is universal, even if one's own action cannot bring about universal results. Needless to say, this view has been accused not only of ineffectiveness but also of sentimentality.[80] It raises the whole issue of the usefulness of "fools for Christ" and can make personalism easy to dismiss.

A reflection by Robert Ellsberg, a member of the Catholic Worker movement and a longtime close associate of Dorothy Day, is helpful in understanding the importance of activism by "fools for Christ."

> The Works of Mercy could not be separated from the Works of Peace. We were told to feed the hungry, while war destroyed crops and caused starvation. We were told to comfort the afflicted, while war brought misery and ruin. And whatever was done "to the least of these"—whether kindness or violence—was counted as

done directed to Him. These too were His words. We were called to recognize Christ in the disguise of our neighbors. He came disguised as a crucified Jew, and this was a scandal. He came disguised in the body of the poor, the diseased, the unwanted, and this was a stumbling block. It was certainly hard to see the face of Christ in the body of a sick, unwashed, lice-ridden old woman. It was harder still to see Him in the face of the one called "enemy." This was true folly in the eyes of the world. But we are not told to love up to the point of reason, prudence, or personal safety—but to love unreasonably, foolishly, profligately, unto the Cross, unto death.[81]

What is the point of such activist witness? Success is obviously not its goal, and the Catholic Worker movement admitted as much. As one worker described the movement: "We really are mosquitoes on an elephant."[82] So, what is the role of "mosquitoes"? Actually, mosquitoes have a central role: they cannot be ignored. One of the amazing things about our three people—John Woolman, Simone Weil, and Dorothy Day—is that they began their lives as very ordinary folks who engaged in direct action for the needy and for justice, patiently, persistently, relentlessly, and who are now widely acclaimed as "saints." It is not the sainthood of miraculous cures that allow the sick to be made well; rather, the lives of these saints are studied by others for possible clues to the mystery of why we are here and what we should do. We feel that their lives hold secrets to the most basic questions of life and how we should live. The life stories of Woolman, Weil, and Day as indicated by the mosquito metaphor do not comfort us so much as challenge us. As one commentator on the Catholic Worker movement says, "Prophetic and saintly people do for society what the Gospel does: *they reveal a truth which makes it impossible to keep forgetting what myth exists to help us forget.* It was in the face of the powerful myth of American exceptionalism and Manifest Destiny, supported by prominent Roman Catholic leaders, that Day made her nonviolent stand."[83] Why should such witness be dismissed as useless and sentimental when its chief task is to remind us that the life we take for granted hides behind the myth of Americanism? And that is the heart of the matter. There are many different forms of activism, some only personal, some only political, and all only achieving relative levels of success. So the question remains, What is the contribution of an activist ideology that is both personal and public, that is grounded in hospitality, and that is focused on direct action and consistency— what is this position worth? As Day recounts in her book *Loaves and Fishes*, one day late in her life, she sees yet another homeless man coming down the street and sighs, "Is this what the Catholic Worker *means*?" She poses the question to Peter Maurin,

"Is this what you meant, Peter?" I asked him once about an over-crowded house of hospitality.

"Well," he hesitated. "At least it arouses the conscience."

Which is something.[84]

As we come to the end of Dorothy Day's story, the thread that stands out is the one that weaves its way between personal and public activity. In a unique way, Day wove together what is often torn apart: individual acts of mercy and public acts of protest. In one of her pithy statements, she demonstrates the inextricability of the individual from the social: "We cannot live alone. We cannot go to heaven alone. Otherwise . . . God will say to us, 'Where are the others?'"[85] Indeed, where *are* the others? This is a question Day always had on her mind and was so embedded in the Catholic Worker movement that one scholar describes "conversion" according to the movement in the following way. "Traditional conversion, particularly as described in evangelical rhetoric, calls for a turning away from personal sin, often sins of the flesh, and a turning towards the God of forgiveness and salvation. I noticed little of this in analyzing the CW interviews and heard instead about a turning away from complicity with the sins or ways of the world with its militarism and materialism and disregard for the poor and marginalized."[86] In Day's own telling of her spiritual journey, significantly titled *The Long Loneliness*, she experiences personal fulfillment in the community of the Catholic Worker movement, which she movingly expresses in the closing page of the book: "Heaven is a banquet and life is a banquet, too, even with a crust, where there is companionship. We have all known the long loneliness and we have learned that the only solution is love and that love comes with community."[87] Day's peculiar genius was to unite the personal and the public in a way and to a degree that few others have accomplished: on the one hand, her practice of love was direct, concrete, and immediate, doing the small things at hand; and on the other hand, this practice extended all the way to the most public, national, and critical issues of her day. What she practiced on a small scale in the intimacy of the hospitality houses of the Catholic Worker movement—the works of mercy for the needy—was translated into a practice at the public level of nonviolence, universal inclusion, protest, and perseverance. The heart of her practice at all levels and at all times was the cross of Jesus Christ. "The Cross is the law of our life. If we wish to live, we must die. . . . Christianity is not a religion of mortification but it is one of the love of Christ. Yet both go together. In order to love Christ, one must deny oneself."[88] Kenosis, self-emptying, was the rule of life for Day; it was not watered down, not reserved for the "saints," not practiced now and then. Rather, the wild space of voluntary poverty that came to her midlife, when she began to practice giving up at all levels—not only gourmet meals and good music, but also privacy and comfort—changed her so that she could *see* not only her own life differently, but also the myth of

American militarism and materialism behind which the masses were suffering and dying. The call to self-denial for people like Day (and many of us, who, like her, are educated, well-off, and comfortable within the conventions of our society) was the catalyst for deep change, allowing her to preach and practice "public personalism" as a counter to American exceptionalism. The seamlessness between the personal and the public, between rhetoric and practice, between what one says and what one does, makes the words and actions of Day's life an extraordinary story for reflection and perhaps—change.

SUMMARY AND REFLECTIONS

In this chapter, we have been reflecting on Michel de Certeau's enigmatic statement that sainthood is "the Franciscan dream"—"that a body might preach without speaking, and that in walking around, it might make visible what lives within."[89] Can we gain some clues for our own time by looking at the stories of three saints, people who perform rather than merely appreciate the good life, the life in which they attain a deep level of personal spiritual maturity while at the same time suggesting practical action for the crises facing their times? If one were to attempt a very broad sketch of Woolman, Weil, and Day, it might sound something like the following. All three, while Christian in different ways, share a vision based on an almost "literal" reading of Scripture (especially teachings on poverty), and a sense of the immediate vocational demand to embody the gospel—which involves a way of living opposite to the lifestyle of contemporary consumer culture. Their visions (or new readings of our situation) demand radical actions, beginning at the personal level but deeply and broadly affecting all of society. They realize that one must "see" differently, and for this to take place they need to prepare the ground, with voluntary poverty being a main means of opening oneself up to new possibilities. This is not an ascetic action for purification, but is an outward sign of the ego's inner emptying of its strategies to avoid change at a basic level. Which comes first—the seeing or the doing? It appears to be a subtle mix of each, with voluntary poverty removing the blinders—our constant attempt to keep our own ego in the center—from our eyes. Poverty allowed them to recognize how interdependent we are on the most basic level—the level of food, clothing, and habitat. Once one is opened up (made empty), one sees the world not from one's own center (ego) but *as it is*— interrelated, interdependent, with all creatures needing the basics of existence. Seeing differently demands acting differently, and saints actually do this, at the personal level and with implications for public life as well. The lives of Woolman, Weil, and Day embody this broad pattern in very different ways, ways that in their particularity can be instructive for us. As we have seen,

Woolman is the prophet of an economics based on universal love; Weil is the philosopher of total attentiveness to the other; Day is the practitioner of public personalism, an ethic that includes both the needy at one's doorstep as well as workers' rights. At the heart of each of these lives is the relation between egolessness and a form of public ethic that begins at the physical, basic level of each living creature's existence and extends to the planet itself. Kenosis, in the form of self-emptying poverty, is the opening to a vision of sustainable and just planetary living.

So, what does this say to us in the twenty-first century, when one fears that humankind will not succeed given its present trajectory? What does one do in light of the fear that our end (or at least our downfall) will be nasty and barbaric? Something like Day's and Gandhi's faith is necessary: be a fool for Christ, or follow *satyagraha*, because success is not ours in the first place. Day did not mind that people called her public personalism ineffective. What mattered was that she do the *right* thing, whether it be finding socks for someone or carrying a protest sign in a workers' strike. *We are not in charge*: so we can relax about outcomes while doing the work for the needy that is right before us. This is both a relief *and* marching orders: we have no excuse ("It won't work," etc.), so we do what we can. The lives of our three saints as well as many others (Gandhi, Mandela, King) influenced millions of people. They did not do what they did because they knew it would succeed, but because they felt called to do it, called both as a response to an obligation—and as an attraction, whereby they found personal fulfillment.

And at the heart of "doing the right thing" for these folks was voluntary poverty. It is the "wild space" that is especially relevant for our time, for it helps to keep us disoriented, apart from the consumerist assumptions of American culture, on edge against one's own willingness to give in and give up, to refuse the "stripping" that alone permits us to really pay attention to the other. There is no limit to our sneaky attempts to hold on to *something*: As Day plaintively comments: "The thing is not to hold on to anything. The tragedy is, however, that we do, we all do hold on. We hold on to our books, radios, our tools such as typewriters, our clothes; and instead of rejoicing when they are taken from us, we lament. We protest when people take our time or our privacy. We are holding on to these 'goods' also."[90] What is Day suggesting here? It appears that the "holding on" to anything is what matters, and voluntary poverty, certainly for people like Woolman, Weil, and Day (and many of us are similarly blessed with education, good taste, middle-class comforts, etc.), is about as wild a space as we could find. It is a constant reminder that we surround ourselves with seemingly infinite protective mechanisms to avoid facing the obvious: that we are living, both individually and collectively, far beyond our means to the detriment of our poorer brothers and sisters, as well as the health of the planet. In his biography of Day, William Miller writes: "It has been one of the central traditions of

Christian history that the free choice of poverty is the most direct route to freedom."[91] Why such emphasis on voluntary poverty? It appears to be at the heart of our three saints, Woolman, Weil, and Day. Poverty shocks us out of our denial, our insistent denial, that all is well and that we are not to blame. It appears to be the one thing that can wake us up, because it strips us of all our protective armor and makes us ready to say with Day, "Let us rejoice in poverty, because Christ is poor. Let us love to live with the poor, because they are specifically loved by Christ. Even the lowest, most depraved, we must see Christ in them, and love them to folly. When we suffer from dirt, lack of privacy, heat and cold, coarse food, let us rejoice."[92]

At the very least, why should this new way—a way that insisted on personal responsibility *all the way up*, from beds for the homeless to subsidized social apartments, be laughed out of court? Does it not deserve a hearing? When one reflects on what the capitalist, militaristic, greedy ideology based on individual desires has given us—economic collapse and ecological deterioration—what is so absurd about considering a vision that is based on human responsibility? Emmanuel Levinas's notion of an ethic based on the absolute call of the "face" of the other is very similar. Like our saints, he insists that reform starts at the lowest level, the insistence that right action is right action at all levels, that the absolute call to respond to the homeless person on one's doorstep is the basis for all public ethics, including all forms of nonviolence, and especially war.

It is no accident that people who claim to follow Jesus' teaching literally, those who believe in doing the task before their eyes (regardless of its "importance"), those who are moved to action by the simple feeling of compassion for another's pain, find in the parable of the good Samaritan their touchstone. From Levinas and John Caputo to Woolman and Day and others of their persuasion, this story says it all: Do the *right* thing that is before your eyes! It does not matter if it will succeed, is sensible or even sentimental, is a detour from one's more "important" business: it is *right* because it is the response of one subject, who is in a position to help, to another who needs it. That is all it takes to "love the neighbor as oneself." Everything else will follow from that—or not, as the case may be, but that is not up to us.

As an example of how this might apply to one of the most daunting of public issues—international negotiations on levels of greenhouse emissions allowed to different nations—what if the countries that were in a position to do the right thing actually took the lead, what might happen? Presently, the developed nations, especially the United States and Canada, refuse to take any steps in reducing emissions (even though they were major contributors to past greenhouse growth) unless China and India agree to the same standards (even though they have not contributed many emissions to date and have much larger populations). If emissions were divided justly, with every person on the planet getting the same level of pollution, the United States and Canada would have no case. In this instance, doing the right thing for those who have the money means giving to those who do not, so that the basics (food, water, clean air, and so on) can be fairly distributed. The parable of the good Samaritan is relevant all the way, from the personal gesture toward the fellow human being in the gutter to the hospitality demanded of those of us in a position to take the lead on the climate change crisis. The public personalism of Woolman, Weil, and Day turns out not to be absurd or sentimental, as proponents of market capitalism would claim, but the necessary and sensible policy for planetary well-being.

I suggest that such self-emptying may be the special role the religions should be playing in the twenty-first century in the face of economic meltdown and climate change, both of which are greatly influenced by the lack of conscience that rich individuals and nations are presently displaying. The continuing denial of climate change's serious consequences, for instance, provides a cover-up for anemic responses to the attempts to negotiate international agreements on greenhouse emissions reductions. Perhaps the special role of religions is to refuse to comfort us by congratulating merely rhetorical responses to our crises, to insist that some self-emptying on the part of the well-to-do is absolutely necessary, to state the obvious: that we have insatiable appetites that are eating up our planet and its poor inhabitants; in other words, to be the "conscience of the planet" when no one else is willing to take on that role. It is certainly not the only thing that needs to be done—every field of endeavor, every area of expertise—is needed, but the special niche of the religions may be as the "mosquito" that will not leave the elephant alone to roll comfortably in the mud of its own making—a deteriorating planet.

If something like this is one of the special roles of the religions in our time, then Christianity of the sort our three saints have preached and lived is equipped to make a contribution. In order to do this special task, Christianity needs to retain its "fool for Christ" ideology, one that calls its members to lives of self-denial, of hospitality at all levels, and of direct action, not because we know this method will be successful, but because we want to make a statement that a "different world is possible" (to quote the NGO slogan and the tradition's hope in the "kingdom of God"). We may not arrive at that world, but it should not be hidden behind masks of denial and exceptionalism, claiming that we have done all we can, when in actuality—with a case like climate change—we have done little but talk.

It is critical to remind ourselves that the wild space of voluntary poverty need not and should not mean the same thing in all times and places. Should we well-off, middle-class folks follow our three saints and do exactly as Woolman, Weil, and Day did—wear white clothing, eat starvation rations, serve soup to the needy? Scarcely. Of course, a critical step should be a significant reduction of energy at the personal level toward the practice of simplicity in our daily lives. This must involve a radical reduction in our energy use at all levels, but our basic calling as middle-class people is not to imitate St. Francis or Dorothy Day. Rather, those of us with money, influence, and various forms of expertise should harness our specific and considerable gifts to help change minds and legislation to reverse and control global warming. In other words, the saints show us a new paradigm, a new way of living in the world that is based on simplicity, restraint, sharing, and compassion. Our goal, however, is not to follow exactly what they did, but to interpret the wild space of voluntary poverty for our time and our own assets and talents. Twenty percent of us have considerable power, influence, and money, and we should use it to change legislation at public levels as well as practice simplicity in our personal lives. We middle-class (and wealthier) folks must be willing to "stand in the shoes" of the poor in order to develop a degree of empathy with the suffering of others (both oppressed human beings and other life-forms) deep enough that our circle of concern becomes radically inclusive. The aim is to develop a "universal self," an understanding of who we are in the scheme of things, that includes every living being—even such lowly ones as caterpillars! Occasional fasting or even large charitable gifts are not likely to be such wild space for us, but rather the "poverty" of sacrificing our exceptionalism, our prestige, and our money to bring about *systemic* changes at the levels, for instance, of assuming responsibility for greenhouse emissions as well as a more just distribution of wealth. What really hurts us and matters to us are the reputations and status that money and influence bring to those who have "made it" in the market capitalist system. Those who protest (the 99 percent versus the 1 percent) sense that the system itself needs to be changed toward just distribution and sustainability—and who else can do this except those of us who have, at least until recently, benefited from the injustices of present-day economics?

In summary, voluntary poverty for folks like myself is the wild space that will cause us to use *all* our considerable assets, at personal, professional, and public levels, to seriously reduce energy use and bring about a new way of being in the world, a way that moves away from the narrow, individualistic understanding of the self to a wide-open, inclusive view of who we are, a view that has no limits.

NOTES

[1] Quoted in Paul Lachance, "Mysticism and Social Transformation According to the Franciscan Way," in *Mysticism and Social Transformation*, ed. Janet K. Ruffing (Syracuse: Syracuse University Press, 2001), 71.

[2] Edith Wyschogrod, *Saints and Postmodernism: Revisioning Moral Philosophy* (Chicago: University of Chicago Press, 1990), 59.

[3] Thomas P. Slaughter, *The Beautiful Soul of John Woolman* (New York: Hill and Wang, 2008), 159.

4 *The Journal of John Woolman and A Plea for the Poor*, ed. Frederick B. Tolles (New York: Corinth Books, 1961), 4.

5 Quoted in Frederick B. Tolles, introduction to Woolman, *Journal*, v.

6 Woolman, *Journal*, 8.

7 Wendell Berry, *The Unsettling of America: Culture and Agriculture* (San Francisco: Sierra Club Books, 1977), 85–86.

8 Woolman, *Journal*, 214.

9 Ibid., 56.

10 Woolman, *Journal*, 152.

11 Ibid., 197.

12 Ibid., 222.

13 See the various levels of critique in J. P. Little, "Simone Weil's Concept of Decreation," in Simone Weil's *Philosophy of Culture: Readings Toward a Divine Humanity*, ed. Richard H. Bell (Cambridge: Cambridge University Press, 1993); J. M. Perrin and G. Thibon, Simone Weil as We Knew Her (London: Routledge and Kegan Paul, 1953).

14 Simone Petrement, *Simone Weil: A Life*, trans. Raymond Rosenthal (New York, Random House, 1976), 411.

15 Simone Weil, *Waiting for God*, trans. Emma Craufurd (New York: Harper and Row, 1951), 95.

16 Ibid., 76

17 Henry L. Finch, *Simone Weil and the Intellect of Grace*, ed. Martin Andic (New York: Continuum, 1999), 113.

18 Simone Weil, *First and Last Notebooks*, trans. Richard Rees (London: Oxford University Press, 1970), 244.

19 Ibid.

20 Finch, *Simone Weil*, 126.

21 "Hers is an exceptional and powerful Christian vision, and one that can be understood partly as a revised, that is, tragic form of Christian Platonism." David Tracy, "Simone Weil: The Impossible," in *The Christian Platonism of Simone Weil*, ed. E. Jane Doering and Eric O. Springsted (Notre Dame: University of Notre Dame Press, 2004), 233.

22 Ibid.

23 Quoted by Leslie A. Fielder, introduction to Weil, *Waiting for God*, 24.

24 *The English Poems of George Herbert*, ed. C. A. Patrides (London: J. M./Dent & Sons, 1974), 192.

25 Weil, *Waiting for God*, 69.

26 Ibid.

27 Quoted in Petrement, *Simone Weil*, 462.

28 Ibid., 465.

29 Weil, *First and Last Notebooks*, 286.

30 Weil, *Waiting for God*, 108.

31 Weil, *First and Last Notebooks*, 144.

32 Ibid., 145.

33 Weil, *Waiting for God*, 163–64.

34 Ibid., 167.

35 Iris Murdoch, "The Sublime and the Good," *Chicago Review* 13 (Autumn 1959): 51.

36 Weil, *Waiting for God*, 132.

37 As quoted by Eric O. Springsted, *Simone Weil and the Suffering of Love* (Cambridge, MA: Cowley, 1986), 42.

38 The French term *malheur* does not have an equivalent in English. "Affliction" may come the closest, but it must carry the sense of inevitability and doom. An afflicted person loses the ability to be a full human being; Weil writes that "a man loses half his soul the day he becomes a slave" (*Waiting for God*, 117). The immensity of blind, brutal force of affliction is "a more or less attenuated equivalent of death" (118).

39 Weil, *First and Last Notebooks*, 94.

40 Weil, *Waiting for God*, 133–34.

41 Ibid., 194.

42 Weil, *First and Last Notebooks*, 120.

43 Ibid., 81.

44 Ibid., 140.

45 Wallace Stevens, *Opus Posthumous: Poems, Plays, Prose*, ed. Milton J. Bates (New York: Vintage, 1990), 163.

46 Weil, *Waiting for God*, 208.

47 Ibid., 205.

48 Springsted, *Simone Weil and the Suffering of Love*, 130.

49 Mark Zwick and Louise Zwick, "Roots of the Catholic Worker Movement: Saints and Philosophers Who Influenced Dorothy Day and Peter Maurin," in *Dorothy Day and the Catholic Worker Movement*, ed. William Thorn, Phillip Runkel, and Susan Mountin (Milwaukee: Marquette University Press, 2001), 68.

50 Dorothy Day, *The Long Loneliness* (New York: Harper and Row, 1952), 317–18.

51 Ibid., 317.

52 Markha G. Valenta, "The Last Word Is Love: Activism, Spirituality, and Writing in the Life of Dorothy Day," in Thorn, Runkel, and Mountin, *Dorothy Day and the Catholic Worker Movement*, 342.

53 Day, *The Long Loneliness*, 153.

54 Ibid., 169.

55 Ibid., 160.

56 Ibid., 11.

57 Ibid., 161.

58 See http://en.wikipedia.org/wiki/Therese_of_Lisieux.

59 Ibid.

60 Zwick and Zwick, "Roots of the Catholic Worker Movement," 71.

61 By Jim Allaire in the Houston Catholic Worker, quoted by ibid.

62 Carol J. Jablonski, "The Radical's Paradox: A Reflection on Dorothy Day's 'Legendary' Resistance to Canonization," in Thorn, Runkel, and Mountin, *Dorothy Day and the Catholic Worker Movement*, 327–28.

63 Quoted by William D. Miller, *All Is Grace: The Spirituality of Dorothy Day* (New York: Doubleday, 1987), 67.

64 Day, *The Long Loneliness*, 188.

65 Ibid., 189.

66 Peter Maurin, as quoted in Dorothy Day, *Loaves and Fishes* (San Francisco: Harper and Row, l963), 82.

67 Day, *Loaves and Fishes*, 80.

68 See By *Little and By Little: The Selected Writings of Dorothy Day*, ed. Robert Ellsberg (New York: Alfred A. Knopf, 1983), 108.

69 Ibid., 110.

70 Day, *Loaves and Fishes*, 79-80.

71 Quoted by Miller, *All Is Grace*, 130.

72 Quoted in Brigid O'Shea, *Searching for Christ: The Spirituality of Dorothy Day* (Notre Dame: University of Notre Dame Press, 1994), 53.

73 Ibid.

74 William D. Miller, *A Harsh and Dreadful Love: Dorothy Day and the Catholic Worker Movement*, 2nd ed. (Milwaukee: Marquette University Press), 64.

75 Ibid., 24.

76 Day, *By Little and By Little*, 105.

77 Dorothy Day, as quoted in Fred Boehrer, "Diversity, Plurality, and Ambiguity: Anarchism in the Catholic Worker Movement," in Thorn, Runkel, and Mountin, *Dorothy Day and the Catholic Worker Movement*, 98.

[78] Dorothy Day, "Room for Christ," *Catholic Worker* 12 (December, 1945): 2.

[79] See, for instance, Emmanuel Levinas, *Totality and Infinity: An Essay on Exteriority*, trans. Alphonso Lingis (Pittsburgh: Duquesne University Press), 1961.

[80] See, for instance, Michael J. Baxter, "Blowing the Dynamite of the Church: Catholic Radicalism from a Catholic Radicalist Perspective," in Thorn, Runkel, and Mountin, *Dorothy Day and the Catholic Worker Movement*, 79–94.

[81] Robert Ellsberg, introduction to Day, *By Little and By Little*, xxxii).

[82] Patrick G. Coy, "Beyond the Ballot Box: The CW Movement and Nonviolent Direct Action," in Thorn, Runkel, and Mountin, *Dorothy Day and the Catholic Worker Movement*, 177.

[83] Stephen T. Krupa, SJ, "American Myth and Gospel: Manifest Destiny and Dorothy Day's Nonviolence," in Thorn, Runkel, and Mountin, *Dorothy Day and the Catholic Worker Movement*, 196.

[84] Day, *Loaves and Fishes*, 193.

[85] Day, *By Little and By Little*, 91.

[86] Rosalie Riegle, "A Long Loneliness: Metaphors of Conversion Within the Catholic Worker Movement," in Thorn, Runkel, and Mountin, *Dorothy Day and the Catholic Worker Movement*, 563.

[87] Day, *The Long Loneliness*, 317–18.

[88] Quoted in Miller, *All Is Grace*, 90.

[89] See n. 1.

[90] Day, *Loaves and Fishes*, 85.

[91] Miller, A Harsh and Dreadful Love, 97.

[92] Day, *By Little and By Little*, 231.

4

The Practice of the Saints 1

Voluntary Poverty in Order to Pay Attention to the Material Needs of Others

INTRODUCTION

We turn now to an analysis of our saints, looking at the four steps that emerge from the reflections on their life journeys: the wild space of voluntary poverty, attentiveness to the material needs of others, the development of a universal self, and its application at personal and public levels. The first two steps focus on preparation for the goal of the universal self, and the last two expand on the meaning of such an understanding of the self and its action in the world. Thus, in this chapter, we will follow the beginnings of a new way of seeing through the catalyst of the wild space of voluntary poverty, a step that opens a person to think outside of the controlling model of our culture, in order to move from desires of the narrow, consumer self to attentiveness to the basic needs of the universal self, the self that includes all others and says, "The world is my body." We will especially trace the value of disorienting experiences of voluntary poverty for middle- and upper-class members of the human community in order to wake us up to seeing the world with new eyes, eyes that are schooled to pay radical, genuine attention to such basic issues as "food" for all human beings and for other life-forms. In the next chapter, we will continue investigating the "practice of the saints" by focusing with more depth on the nature of the universal versus the market view of the self, two radically different paradigms of what it means to live on planet earth. And we will finish the fourth step by attempting to apply this new vision of our place in the scheme of things at all levels of our life—personal, professional, and public. In contrast to the current, narrow, market notion of the self that forms the substratum of all our actions, both local and global, pretending to be the one, "true" way to interpret our role on the planet, our new paradigm of the universal self will claim, not that it is the true or only way, but that it is the best and most appropriate view, as evidence from both the sciences and the religions suggest.

As we begin this process, let us step back for a minute and frame our four steps within the long history of people who have attempted such a process—those we call "saints."

What is a saint? I have been using the term freely in these pages, assuming a commonsense understanding of the term, but the range of definitions is wide, ranging, for instance, from the well-known children's hymn to the carefully defined limits of the Roman Catholic Church. The children's hymn is all-inclusive and upbeat.

> I sing a song of the saints of God, patient and brave and true,
> who fought and lived and died for the Lord they loved and knew.
> And one was a doctor, and one was a queen, and one was a shepherdess on the green;
> they were all of them saints of God, and I mean, God helping, to be one too.[1]

The Vatican has a very different view, which, while allowing the general use of the term *saint* for all who are "in heaven," reserves its specific use for those who have been officially canonized by the church, a process that usually takes years of investigation by experts with a required minimum of two posthumous miracles.[2] In between these extremes are many other definitions. Elizabeth Johnson has a wide-ranging set of criteria for the use of the term *saint*, picking up on the children's hymn, but with more nuances.

> Our interpretation parses the communion of saints into five rudimentary elements: the community of living, ordinary persons as "all saints," in particular as this designation is used to characterize members of the Christian community in their relationship to the triune God; their working out of holiness through creative fidelity in ordinary time; their relation to the circle of companions of who run the race before, who are now embraced in the life of God and accessed through memory and hope; the paradigmatic figures among them; and the relation of this community, living and dead, to the whole community of the natural world.[3]

Lawrence Cunningham provides a midrange definition that captures the common view: "A saint is a person so grasped by a religious vision that it becomes central to his or her life in a way that radically changes the person and leads others to glimpse the values of that vision."[4] All of these definitions are helpful, but fail to capture the extraordinary passion for self-emptying love in my three examples, John Woolman, Simone Weil, and Dorothy Day. However, recent studies, suggested by some comments by Emmanuel Levinas, indicate a deeper direction: "Goodness consists in taking up a position in being such that the Other counts more than myself."[5] What Levinas is suggesting here and what lies at the heart of the saintly life is a move from ontology to ethics as the "first philosophy," a move from describing human existence primarily in terms of being to describing it in terms of action: "Ontology as first philosophy is a philosophy of power."[6] To "be" a human being is not based on sheer existence (with a presumed hierarchy of power as the measure of value), but rather to "be" a human being is to respond to the other *as* other. What we see in the saints is the actual incarnation of this criterion, the reduction of the ego and the fulfillment of the self. These comments move the discussion from saints as mystics who attain a special relationship with God, allowing them to perform miracles, to saints as altruists who through a lifelong process of ego reduction and attention to the other incarnate radical self-emptying for the good of others, all others. It moves the discussion of ethics out of the realm of the conceptual, where we can always justify inaction in favor of more (and more sophisticated) arguments, to the level of stories of extraordinary self-giving, calling our own lives into question, apart from or beyond argumentation. Concepts domesticate the call of the oppressed other; lives lived in service of the other question our own lives in ways that make them more difficult to rationalize. The writings of Edith Wyschogrod and Andrew Flescher, among others, stress these characteristics of saints with some pithy comments. "The saintly response to the Other entails putting her/his body and material goods at the disposal of the Other."[7] "Self-renunciation to the point of effacement is the mark or trace of saintly labor."[8] "Saints are 'native speakers' of the language of alterity, poets of the imperative."[9] "Their ability to transcend the pull of their own ego constitutes their primary defining feature."[10] "What is important about saints . . . is their complete and uncompromising devotion to promoting the welfare of others."[11] These uplifting quotations also have the impact of separating these icons of virtue from the rest of us moral peons, "letting us off the hook," as Day remarked. But careful attention to the *lives*, the stories of saints such as the ones we have been considering, diminishes the distance and helps us to realize that while we may not be "saints," we need not be "slackers," which most of us settle for.

We will now consider the stories recounted in chapter 3 from a more analytical perspective, attempting to follow the *process* whereby these folks became what they were. I am not attempting to explain their lives, and I certainly do not wish to reduce them to a system or stereotype; rather, I am asking, What are the practices that moved them along their journey from the ordinary, self-absorbed people they were at the outset to where they arrived at the end of their lives? I am suggesting that there are four practices, which I see in somewhat of a pattern of progression, although the stories of their lives we have just rehearsed undercut any linear dominance. First, the practice of wild space, that phenomenon whereby an event, an insight, an experience disorients a person from the conventional world that they, along with all others, have come to accept as natural, as inevitable. Wild space is the opening that occurs when "worlds" overlap, when a new reading of reality encounters the old reading and one questions one's assumptions. For our three saints, *voluntary poverty* was that wild space. It served the function that Jesus' parables serve: inviting another perspective that can change one's life. It did so for our folks, and I will suggest it might well serve a similar function for us well-to-do, insatiable consumers for whom the experience of poverty may be our sine qua non.

Second, the experience of voluntary poverty caused Woolman, Weil, and Day *to pay attention to others* in a radical and focused way, specifically, attention to their material needs. Having been disoriented by living differently, they woke up to the enormous chasm between the resources they enjoyed versus the destitution of most others. As Iris Murdoch says, such attention makes us realize that others beside oneself *really exist* and need (and have the right to) the basics of existence. This radical awakening is like a conversion, a deep change of mind, which calls into question one's own exceptionalism and undermines the power hierarchies of family, political, and economic life. One sees things "the way they are," in which interrelationship and interdependence operate at all levels of biological and cultural life, demanding different structures if we are to live just, sustainable lives. Rather than power as control of others, the world needs to be run more by radical hospitality, in which the sharing of food with friends becomes the paradigm for planetary justice and sustainability. Needless to say, if some measure of egalitarianism and just sustainability is to be sought on our planet, it will involve deep changes on the part of us who have so much. Thus the appropriate response to paying attention to others' material needs is to cut down radically on our own excessive desires: restraint, limitation, sharing, and even self-emptying must become part of our language and our practice, replacing excess, abundance, riches, and self-fulfillment (understood in a narrow sense).

The third practice, which we will consider in chapter 5, emerges from paying attention to the others' material needs: it involves a changed understanding of self-fulfillment: from egocentrism to ecocentrism, from seeing the self as limited by one's physical body (and its immediate family and friends) *to imagining ourselves as "universal selves,"* the self as stretching to include all of creation. But this new view of self-fulfillment calls for self-emptying. Woolman's dream in which he heard the words "John Woolman is dead," followed by the experience of being mixed up with all of humanity (and now we would add all of creation), is the direction of saintly self-identity. Fifty years ago, when I began reading these saints (and others like them), one of my earliest realizations was that their sense of self kept growing. The line of who "counted" kept getting pushed further back, so that Martin Luther King Jr., for instance, who began his journey concerned with the rights of African

Americans, ended with his magnificent speech calling on "all God's children" to join together to reach the promised land. Deep ecology is right in stressing our profound relationship with everything that lives—imagine swimming with dolphins and stroking the fur of a bear! But the joys of belonging to a larger community carry the responsibility of taking care of all its members.

Finally, *practicing kenosis at both a personal and a public level* is the goal of the saintly process. Stated baldly, this may sound like a grim substitute for the life of material plenty that we privileged folks now live. But our saints discovered otherwise: one of the countercultural secrets of most religions is the unnerving dictum that to find one's life one must lose it: detachment from attachment, giving up, giving over, saying enough, saying no. This language *is* the language of self-fulfillment, real, satisfying self-fulfillment, but for many this is all it is. That is, religious disorientation has often been understood to apply only to individuals and their salvation; what is different with our saints is that they apply it all up and down the line, from the smallest acts of personal hospitality to issues of slavery, warfare, and planetary sustainability. Religion is not a personal matter, or rather, it is not only a personal matter: it is, or should be, implicitly revolutionary and subversive in that it questions the basic power relations whereby privileged people and nations conduct their affairs, especially regarding economic issues.

I will now focus on the wild space—voluntary poverty—that awakens us from our narcissistic dreams, allowing us to pay attention to the material needs of others, resulting in a new view of the self as universal and calling us to the practice of kenosis at all levels of life. I will be assuming that highlighting these stages can serve as a mirror to reflect back on ourselves as privileged persons in a privileged culture the steps we need to take to move us from paralysis to action that will at least dimly image the paradigm of radical hospitality.

The Wild Space of Voluntary Poverty

Something wakes us up—some disorienting event, story, or experience allows us to step outside the conventions of our culture, the egocentric, consumer, individualistic model that results in personal despair as well as public deterioration and injustice. I have been calling this waking up "wild space," a place to stand and to interpret one's culture from the "outside," as it were. This opening allows us to *see differently*, to imagine other possibilities, to pay attention to others. It is often associated with moments of beauty or suffering, moments that "take us out of ourselves" and open our eyes to others—something, someone, valuable in itself apart from its utilitarian importance. It is a movement that most religions find to be essential to change, real deep change, change of mind and of behavior. Many call it "conversion."

It is the beginning of a long process of discipline, patience, and self-emptying that allows us to recognize that something outside of ourselves is real and has needs. However, this wild space, this disorienting experience, must be *seized*; it must be acknowledged and used rather than rationalized and avoided. It is tempting at times of disorientation to force the experience to fit the conventional patterns of interpretation, rather than to seize the opportunity it provides to think and thus to act differently.

The attention to the needs of others that disorientation provides results in acknowledging at the simplest level the material needs of others, their right to the basics of existence and, as a partner insight, their intrinsic merit or right to self-esteem. In the Christian tradition, the good Samaritan is the classic story of someone caring for the physical and emotional needs of a stranger. The goal of this process is a different understanding of the self—an ecocentric versus an egocentric view—a gradual expansion through attention to others that gives a new view of the nature of the self, a "universal self," in which all others, including other species, fall within the circle of one's regard. The process of bringing our own wills into line with reality (now understood as inclusive of all beings, the great web of interdependence and interrelationship that composes the cosmos) is a slow one. But through it, we realize that nothing is itself alone, and that the process of self-emptying allowing us to pay attention to others has resulted in a new sense of who we are: *the world is my body*. In this process, attention comes first, with the new view of the self emerging as a result of daily, persistent, and long-term practice of attention to others. "Attention to others" is not an idea that one puts into practice; rather, it is a practice that results in another practice: attention to others results in the practice of living as a universal self.

As voluntary poverty is the wild space that begins the process for the three saints we have been studying, let us look at a few definitions of *poverty* before we continue. Before we do so, let us look at a few definitions. "'Poverty' is the lack of basic human needs, such as clean water, nutrition, health care, education, clothing and shelter, because of the inability to afford them. This is also referred to as absolute poverty or destitution. . . . About 1.7 billion people live in absolute poverty."[12] No religious tradition celebrates absolute poverty; what they do support is voluntary poverty because of various virtues it allows and promotes. Thus Roman Catholicism supports poverty of its clergy so as to devote themselves to God—to free themselves from extraneous diversions in order to focus on the saving of souls. Protestant sects have a long, rich tradition of poverty, simple living, and frugality, as do various Buddhist traditions in order to restrain desires, promote detachment from things, and develop virtuous living. Hence, "voluntary poverty" is a very different matter from "destitution." "Among some individuals, such as ascetics, poverty is considered a necessary or desirable condition, which must be embraced to reach certain spiritual, moral, or intellectual states. Poverty is often understood to be an essential element of renunciation in religions such as Buddhism (only for monks, not for lay persons) and Jainism, whilst in Roman Catholicism it is one of the evangelical counsels."[13] Certain religious orders, such as the Franciscans, recommend extreme (though not absolute) poverty.

As we turn to Woolman, Weil, and Day on voluntary poverty as wild space, what do we find? It is difficult to overestimate the importance of voluntary poverty in the lives of these three individuals. It is almost the sine qua non that allowed all the rest to happen. It was indeed wild space for all three: three middle-class people living in very different times and situations—one an eighteenth-century American Quaker troubled by the slave question; another a twentieth-century French philosopher surrounded by the Nazi occupation; and the third a twentieth-century American intellectual living in the New York ghettoes during the Great Depression. None of these people had to accept poverty; none was a clergy person or monastic; in fact, each of them embraced voluntary poverty against the wishes of their families and their culture. Theologian Dorothee Soelle, writing in the twenty-first century, when economic disparity and ecological damage has reached ominous levels, finds the wild space of voluntary poverty to be necessary for us. She writes of a new asceticism, not one of the body, but an asceticism that "must start from the existing dependency of the ego on the world of consumer goods, a dependency hailed as autonomy; and free choice. The issue today is a different relationship to things, not the mortification of the body."[14] Of course, our three saints never did see poverty as associated with bodily mortification; rather, like Soelle, they saw the connections between voluntary poverty—asceticism of the insatiable ego for middle-class people—and involuntary poverty of others. "Ego-lessness, propertylessness, and nonviolence belong together. They are the cornerstones of the change of life that comes from the spirituality of mysticism."[15] The linkage of these three—ego, money, and violence—is a trinity with deep and deeply problematic implications, as we shall see in our three stories.

As we consider voluntary poverty as wild space for twenty-first-century well-off people, Soelle's comments are suggestive, for they remind us to look at the most critical public issues of our day in order to interpret the kind of disorientation we need. I have suggested that the most effective and appropriate issue is climate change and the poverty that accompanies it. Hence, for us middle-class people, focusing our attention not on acquiring more consumer goods but rather on using our expertise, gifts, and assets to change the paradigm within which we understand ourselves and act on the planet is the call we need to answer. "Voluntary poverty" for us means giving up our exceptionalism, our status, our separation from those who will suffer the most from climate change: "ego-lessness, propertylessness, and nonviolence belong together." Hence, since the way we experience the trinity of ego, money, and violence in our culture is the perpetuation of a limitless consumer, high-energy lifestyle, we need to use all our considerable power and influence (and our possessions) to change both the model within which we live and the ways in which we live in it. This will entail serious limitations in our personal lives, new energy-efficient methods of practice within our professions, and radical restraint and sacrifice at the public and systemic levels. It is not sufficient for us to fast in solidarity with the poor; rather, we need to change our way of living "with the poor" in every dimension of our lives.

John Woolman

John Woolman was a walking parable of voluntary poverty. He wore white clothing, including a white hat, at a time when his fellows were dressed in sober grays, blacks, and browns. He did this to call attention to the fact that slaves were used on the ships bringing the dyes to New England cloth markets. Woolman had seen the intricate relationship between possessions and violence in the large estates of slaveholders who claimed they needed workers to tend their vast holdings. Without the possessions, Woolman reasoned that the slaves would not be needed—or at least they would not provide a rationale for the slaveholders. By garbing himself in white, he had ample opportunity to answer questions posed by his fellow citizens and thus to instruct them on the relationship between money and violence. Woolman chose the indirect route of parables—teaching by story, example, disorienting experience—in order to encourage others to question their conventional acceptance of the horrendously violent practice of enslaving other human beings. A "white hat" becomes pedagogy in practice.

Such indirect pedagogy is only possible, of course, if one actually *lives* the parable one is trying to teach. Woolman's entire life was one of gradual but increasing realization of what he needed to "give up" in terms of possessions in order to keep his eye clear and to continue to see the connections between ego, possessions, and violence. Thus he gave up his prosperous grocery business, riding post horses, using silver cutlery, and so forth not to purify himself or for ascetic reasons but solely to enable himself to pay attention to others and their needs. He found that he needed to create situations in which his wild space—the insight he gained from voluntary poverty—stayed fresh in order to continue his work of prophetically reforming the injustices of his day: slavery, cruelty to the Indians, inhumane conditions for sailors on passenger ships to England. Hence, he purposively sought out experiences that would increase his clarity of vision by living with, participating in, the suffering of those less fortunate. He developed his empathy, his clarity of vision regarding the suffering of others, by experiencing what they experienced. He believed that he must *feel* what others felt in order to keep his ego at bay and his vision "single." He was an early, albeit unknowing, practitioner of "emotional intelligence," the current theory that we develop empathy and hence willingness to act on behalf of others when we feel what others are feeling.[16]

For Woolman, this process was a dialogue between prayer and action, seeking the "inner light" from God and practicing its direction in concrete, physical ways. In this process, the ego diminishes while the self, the true self, emerges, the self grounded in God and imitating the cross of Christ, who suffered with others in their deepest needs. The first step, and an absolutely necessary one for Woolman, was the dispossession of his own ego, getting himself and his monetary desires out of the center of his vision, so he could even begin to see others as they are with their needs. Woolman was not a member of our consumer culture; he was not inundated with thousands of advertisements for products to enhance his ego or his well-being. And yet, in the limited context of an eighteenth-century New England village, he realized that the process of self-denial, of kenosis, at the level of material goods, was a necessary first step toward his eventual goal of oneness with God through Christ. The dream at the end of his life, when he heard the words "John Woolman is dead," is the realization that he was now not only one with God but had become so because he had allowed himself to be mixed up with the "mass" of "human beings in as great misery as they could be." He had lost his separate self and gained a "universal self," the self whose will is one with Christ crucified. This was not only ultimate personal fulfillment but also a public strategy for current social injustices—he gained his soul and he fought slavery at the same time. Woolman, as a teenager, realized the interdependence of all life both in flourishing and in violence when he killed a mother robin, but this realization began with the death of his ego through dispossession of goods, which was the wild space giving him the chance to pay attention to others—in this case to baby robins.

SIMONE WEIL

Just as Woolman was a walking parable with his white hat linking slavery and violence, so Weil, with her history of personal starvation, literally embodied the voluntary poverty that she embraced. One of the distinguishing marks of our three saints is that they "walk the talk," living in extreme and, often in others' eyes, foolish, absurd, and ridiculous ways, ways, however, that make a statement that no words can. From the time Weil was a child, she practiced voluntary poverty, refusing to wear socks because other children did not have any and eating only as much as the poorest fellow Parisians during the Nazi occupation. These people make statements with their bodies; as Edith Wyschogrod says of such people: "Compassion, renunciation, sacrifice, generosity are not values added on to a person; the saint's corporate existence *is* these properties."[17] The body of the saint becomes the principal signifier of the message; here we see the movement from ethics as language about the good to ethics as embodiment of the good. This movement—from thought to action—is the main goal of our focus on the stories of these exceptional persons: the power of *lives as lived* versus instruction by precept or concept. Woolman's modest comment (as well as colossal understatement) says it all: "Conduct is more convincing than language." Like Woolman (and Day, as we shall see), Weil lived her ideology or, more accurately, arrived at her ideology through living it.

What we see here is the first step that we are tracing in our three figures: the wild space of voluntary poverty that awakens us from our egotistic dreams, allowing us to pay attention to the real needs of others. Like Woolman, Weil did not preach voluntary poverty as the way to love both God and neighbor; rather, she experienced it, and kept her wild space of voluntary poverty alive by continuing to put herself in situations where she renewed her conviction of its importance and the insights it gave her. In the same spirit as refusing to wear socks as a child, she undertook tedious factory and farm labor, so that she, a privileged middle-class person could actually undergo the suffering and degradation of such labor at both the physical and emotional level. One must *feel* what it is like to be physically hungry on starvation rations and emotionally degraded as a worker on an assembly line in order to appreciate a theology of radical incarnationalism. She claimed that it was the duty of her generation to "show the public the possibility of a truly incarnated Christianity."[18] And by "show the public," the real meaning of radical incarnationalism, she meant beginning with her own body and the bodies of others like her to imitate God's self-emptying in Christ. She claimed that we see the heart of the divine action on behalf of the world in our own time: action so inclusive, so materialistic, and so grounded in concrete experience (the starvation of whole populations) that "food" became both the reality and the symbol of her understanding of Christian faith. Christian faith is not principally a substitutionary atonement for the sins of the world; rather, it is *showing* through the radical self-emptying of God in creation, incarnation, and the cross that the nature of reality is self-emptying love for others. Just as God is literally our "food" (from our very existence in creation through our re-creation in the incarnation and the cross), so we are called to be imitators of God in being "food" for others, both literally (sharing our last crusts with the hungry) and emotionally (doing so in a way that preserves their self-esteem).

Food is the major metaphor for her life and her thought. In a way not unlike her mentor, Augustine, food tells the whole story. Augustine's *Confessions*, from his censure of himself as a greedy baby at his mother's breast to his recognition of his gluttony at table, is a story about food, food as a primary symbol of longing and desire, which only the bread of heaven can finally satisfy. His spiritual journey goes from being "an infant suckled on Thy milk and feeding upon Thee, O Food incorruptible," to hearing God say to him,

"I am the food of grown men; grow and you shall eat Me. . . . [and] into Me you shall be changed."[19] It is hard to imagine stronger language for profound change: you are what you eat—eat Me and you will become like Me. Weil shared with Augustine this visceral symbolic understanding of food: we "cannibalize" others, literally eat them by our egotistical, insatiable hunger for fulfillment. Likewise, as she insisted, the only people who have any hope of salvation are those who do *not* eat others, but pay complete attention to the hungers of others, including for food.

For incarnational theologians such as Augustine and Weil, it is not odd that food should play such a crucial part in their stories and their work, since the Eucharist is the major Christian ritual of spiritual renewal. Through the embodiment of God in the flesh of Jesus Christ, God offers food for us to eat, thus changing us into new beings living in Christ.[20] But Weil takes the food metaphor further than Augustine, and in a different direction. For Weil, material food never disappears into its symbol—she does not come to Augustine's conclusion of dismissing ordinary hunger in preference for "the food which is not lessened by eating" (the "Food incorruptible"); rather, through her experience of starvation, she retains the power of the thing itself, bread as ordinary food. I believe this emphasis opens a window for her relevance to us: the contemporary food crisis, an effect of both economic injustice and climate change, is one where Weil's insights into food ring true for us.

From the beginnings in voluntary poverty, Weil arrived at self-emptying as a theology of the incarnation. Which came first? It is impossible to say, but it is certainly the case that her persistence in voluntary poverty throughout her whole life kept her in the wild space, alive to new insights. Her theology is the product of her life and her learning. When we ask what relevance her story has for us today, I think we cannot avoid her witness to a lifelong practice of voluntary poverty as the beginning of insight for people like us. Her concrete context—daily starvation—is similar in micro fashion to our macro situation: increasing lack of basics for the world's populations of both human and other beings because of the excess of the privileged. Climate change and gross economic disparity and chaos are the result of excessive human cannibalism of other people and the planet itself. We are literally "eating ourselves out of house and home," as the old phrase puts it. What would a form of voluntary poverty be for people like us? Could it be the first step in waking us out of our insatiable dream of more, more, more?

DOROTHY DAY

Of our three saints, Day is obviously the one closest to us, not only in time but in a number of other ways as well. She is also the clearest about the central importance of voluntary poverty as her wild space, opening her up to her life's vocation. She writes, "Voluntary poverty is the answer. We cannot see our brother in need without stripping ourselves. It is the only way of showing our love."[21] Why is voluntary poverty the "only way" we can show our love? Is it because "without stripping ourselves," we cannot *see* the need of others? This appears to be the case for Day and, I suggest, probably for us as well, given the similarity of our situations. Day was a middle-class, educated, American journalist who loved good music, good food, and privacy. She lived in Chicago and New York City during the Depression and could easily have escaped the poverty and despair that it brought to so many. She chose not to, however.

All three of our folks found it necessary to create situations that moved them out of their comfort zones so as to actually *experience* the suffering of others. We have been analyzing the way that people change at a deep level, a level deep enough so that action changes as well. Day understood the psychological deception that people like her—the ones who like good music, good food, and privacy (and assume access to the necessities of middle-class life)—are prone to. The pull of the American Dream is so strong that she compares it to an octopus, reaching out with all its tentacles to hold onto "your own comfort, your untroubled time, your ease, your refreshment."[22] She claims we will do anything necessary to avoid looking at the reality before us: in her case, the despair and degradation of millions of workers reduced to standing in bread lines daily and sleeping on the streets. The reality facing us is similar and no less dramatic: a deteriorating planet, which the scientists are telling us is already in an irreversible pattern of rising temperatures, certain to result in destroying many other species and reducing our species to constant warfare to attain diminishing arable land, fresh water, and breathable air. And yet, our ability to deny this reality is everywhere around us; it is the elephant in the room—our planet—that no one will notice.

Dorothy Day and our other saints give us some simple but very difficult advice for this dilemma: seek the wild space of voluntary poverty. Each of them lived voluntary poverty *literally*: Woolman gave up his grocery business; Weil ate the same rations as her fellow starving Parisians; and Day lived in Catholic Worker hospitality houses, eating their bad food, listening to their loud noises, sleeping in their crowded corners. Must we do the same in order to *see* the stark reality of our time? Must we visit (and perhaps live with) the Inuit, where the polar bears are disappearing, the Australians in their flooded lands, the starving millions in Africa where drought is devastating food harvests? Probably not—"visits" are often mere tourism, and even living with the oppressed is not necessarily what middle-class people should be doing. It may be more helpful to use the wild space of voluntary poverty in order *to change ourselves and our actions in the places where we live*. Because of Day's similarity to us—both to our backgrounds and our context (middle-class North Americans facing economic—and in our case, ecological—disaster), her linkage of the personal and the public becomes centrally important. The lesson this saint has to offer us is in her practice of Thérèse of Lisieux's "little way" as the foretaste to systemic, public, political action. It is the connection between the local and the global, as we would say today, the connection between the daily and the long-term, between the micro and the macro, that is important. She unites the "personalism" of the soup kitchen with political organization for workers' rights. In three interesting ways, she suggests some clues of how to use the daily discipline of voluntary poverty—a spiritual as well as a physical discipline—to provide insight, stamina, courage, and perseverance for the long haul of action for social justice at both the political and planetary level.

Her dictum, we recall, is *stripping ourselves so we can see the needs of others*. The three clues that emerge from a study of Day's practice are (1) that charity and justice go together; (2) that even relative freedom from the wage system of capitalism can provide the detachment necessary for action; and (3) that "living on the edge," or "precarity," is a useful practice for keeping one's vision clear. We shall look at each of these approximations of voluntary poverty to see the practices they encourage, but first we should note that all of them are not actually, literally, the thing itself. We are not *stripping ourselves*. As mentioned earlier, the American novelist Flannery O'Connor made an interesting comment when she answered a question regarding the extreme situations of the characters in her stories, stories that painted good and evil in outrageous and often grotesque ways. She said that for the hard of hearing, you must shout, and for the blind, you must write with large letters. Our situation is similar: we are definitely hard of hearing and short-sighted when it comes to the reality of our planetary crisis. The lives of the saints are salutary tales writ large so that we can begin the get the point. Even if we cannot be a Woolman, Weil, or Day, we can, as Day pointed out several times, do considerably more than we are doing. Hence, as we consider the clues that Day's voluntary poverty suggests, we should keep in mind what is possible for us unsaintly ones, rather than what is impossible.

Our first clue for how voluntary poverty became a wild space for Day— opening her to seeing differently—was her linkage of charity and justice, the personal and the political. While many have settled for one or the other— charitable acts for the poor to compensate for systemic injustice or political action while ignoring the needy people on one's doorstep—Day insisted on the necessity of both. She speaks of "the heresy of good works," the comfortable settling for philanthropy when what is also needed is a change in public policy. "To feed the hungry, clothe the naked and shelter the harborless without trying to change the social order so that people can feed, clothe and shelter themselves, is just to apply palliatives."[23] While the works of mercy set forth in the Sermon on the Mount form the foundation for all other ways of loving the neighbor, including both political-protest movements and dry, arcane legislation for workers' rights, that is not sufficient. There is also "the heresy of social action," making the big speech for the rights of the oppressed while passing by the destitute person in the ditch. Day's "little way" never wavers: no matter how famous she became, speaking internationally on issues of nonviolence and peace, she continued to live in her cramped quarters, bemoaning the bad food and smells. Her wild space demanded constant attention: voluntary poverty was a daily practice necessary to fight the "octopus" of exceptionalism.

Likewise, our second clue shows us that voluntary poverty can help free a person from the hegemony of capitalism's wage system, which keeps all workers in bondage, enticing them to work longer and harder in order to gain more consumer goods. Peter Maurin felt strongly that voluntary poverty (living more simply) could help break capitalism's stranglehold on one's freedom and one's time. If we are constantly absorbed in the consumer rat race, we are not free to give our labor to others as a gift, even if we wish to. For Day and the Catholic Worker movement, voluntary poverty, even if only practiced at the level of reducing one's "needs" and "wants," could result in both more freedom and more time. If one were satisfied with basic support (food, habitat, education, medical service, and so on), one would have more freedom and time to engage in both charitable and political work for others. "The voluntary poverty of the Catholic Worker movement is not simply living simply, but living simply in order to freely serve."[24] The pragmatism of the Catholic Worker movement is poignant advice for middle-class folks who claim they want to help, but don't have the freedom or the time. There is a way, and it involves one important aspect of voluntary poverty: reducing your desire for more, more, more.

Finally, a third clue comes from the Catholic Worker's notion of "precarity," or "living on the edge." To live in a precarious way means to choose funding the basics for others rather than ensuring all desires for oneself. On an institutional level, this meant for the Catholic Worker movement foregoing expensive fire insurance for its own buildings in order to keep the bread lines moving and the newspapers published. If we are constantly making our possessions secure against earthquakes or other disasters, we will not have enough money to feed the hungry. On a personal level, it means a careful assessment of one's own desire for (excessive?) security for one's nearest and dearest in preference for others who need the basics. Precarity is a sensibility developed by voluntary poverty in which one agrees to live with a degree of uncertainty in regard to one's own level of comfort in order to allow for a minimum level of necessities for others.

These three clues only touch the surface of deep insight that voluntary poverty brought to Day and to others. While they lived an extreme version of it, voluntary poverty has a wide range as well as great depth. It certainly means giving up possessions, but also giving up one's will—refusing to be "exceptional" in either physical or spiritual ways. As Day wrote toward the end of her life, "Voluntary poverty means daily, hourly to give up our own possessions and especially to subordinate our own impulses and wishes to others; these are hard, hard things and I don't think they ever get any easier."[25] The various ways we can free ourselves from both possessions and exceptionalism permit us the freedom to love God by loving the neighbor.

It is difficult to overestimate the importance of voluntary poverty as wild space for our three saints. It necessarily disrupted their conventional, middle-class lives, and it allowed them to see the world differently. It was also a gradual, lifelong practice that demanded daily recommitment in order to avoid the temptations of backsliding into the comforts most of us take for granted. But probably of even more importance is the underlying dispossession of the ego that it eventually brought about. Francis of Assisi is the iconic figure in Christian history of voluntary poverty and its profound possibilities for change. For him, in order to live differently, one must dispossess the ego of *all* possessions—not just excessive goods and comforts, but all forms of power. "Indeed, what distinguishes the Franciscan path from all others in the history of spirituality is poverty conceived as a process—that is, a therapy for the liberation of desires and their mimetic entanglement in conventional culture or the world.[26] "Poverty conceived as a process" to free one from the conventional satisfactions for ego glorification sums up very nicely how our three saints saw the importance of voluntary poverty. Thus one must give up not only money and other material possessions, but more importantly, all "spiritual goods" such as power and authority over others. In other words, whatever blocks communion with God and others must be denied, especially the most subtle forms of power and ownership, such as envy of others, refusal to accept criticism, the glorification of the self rather than God. For Francis, voluntary poverty was not an ascetic exercise in bodily purification but a call to embody the perfection of the gospel, as summarized in the order's rule "to follow the most high poverty of our Lord Jesus Christ."[27] Voluntary poverty epitomizes the kenotic or self-emptying path of Christ. In sum, the goal of voluntary poverty was to create in its practitioners a sensibility, a way of being in the world, that "had to do above all with the quality or being or a manner of relating that was humble and dispossessed, that was without pretense and that made no claims to rights and privileges for themselves."[28] This is not the description of raving revolutionaries, but rather of quiet reformers, who first of all reformed themselves before attempting to change others. The Franciscan way (and the way of our three saints) was "the royal road that led to the riches of God and the key to brotherhood and sisterhood, communion with all creatures, true peace and joy."[29]

Does this way of self-emptying at all levels have any relevance for today's twin crises of climate change and poverty? It needs to if it is to speak to our times, for these two are inextricably linked in current assessments of the critical issue of our time: "The impact of climate change and poverty is one of the greatest areas of human impact, and proposes a burden on a global scale"; "The majority of adverse effects of climate change are most experienced by poor and low-income communities around the world"; "According to the UNDP, developing countries suffer 99% of the casualties attributable to climate change."[30] There is little doubt about this linkage; hence, it is with great interest that we raise the question of how one of the deepest and most powerful means of personal transformation—voluntary poverty—might also be of planetary relevance. This question cannot be answered fully until we have completed our study of how personal change can affect public actions; in other words, how the other aspects of the process we are following— attention to the other and imagining ourselves as universal selves—can result in forms of personal fulfillment as well as planetary flourishing. However, with the wild space of voluntary poverty, we have made a beginning: we have raised the possibility of disorientation to the current paradigm of insatiable individualism that is both crushing our personal spirits and ravaging the planet.

Moreover, we see, especially in the Franciscan insight that voluntary poverty is a deep change in how one understands "power," a major clue to the twenty-first-century middle-class use of the concept. As we have suggested, the practice of kenosis is a fundamentally different paradigm for living and acting in the world: one in which we give up *all forms of privilege*, whether these have to do with economics or our reputation. Kenosis points to an understanding of power as facilitating the well-being of others rather than control of these others: from the evolutionary level of give-and-take, reciprocity, death before new life, to the dynamic dance of self-giving love in the Trinity, we see not the power by control of market individualism but the empowerment by self-sacrifice for the flourishing of creation. Hence, when we consider the role of voluntary poverty as wild space for us twenty-first-century well-off folks, we imagine what we have and could offer to this network of well-being. We are privileged by our personal, class, and monetary power; hence, offering these assets is our form of wild space that can disorient us to move from the conventional, destructive model to a fulfilling one for oneself and the planet.

ATTENTION TO THE OTHER'S MATERIAL NEEDS

The fourfold process of acting differently for the fulfillment of the self and the well-being of the planet—the process involving voluntary poverty, attention to the material needs of others, the growth of a universal self united compassionately with all others, and the application of this process at both personal and political levels—is mysterious and complex, and lies at the heart of most religions. As Buddhist scholar Donald Swearer notes, "The ideal of spiritual and material poverty and the correlative value of selfless action has been especially prominent in the teachings of the major world religions in conjunction with saintly or heroic attainments, although less demanding or extreme formulations of these moral ideals are nearly universal."[31] But what is the mysterious connection between voluntary poverty and self-less action? The process that we have been probing, involving poverty, attention, and an expanded view of the self, has no beginning or end: voluntary poverty does not *cause* us to be aware of the needs of the other, nor does it *result* in a sense of the universal self. And yet, from a wide range of sources, including religion, secular ethics, as well as recent scientific studies of the plastic brain, *paying attention* appears to play a major part in the possibility that we might change our behavior.[32] John Woolman believed that possessions clouded his vision, causing him to see "double," with himself always in the center; whereas, when he freed himself of possessions, his vision became "single," and he could, for instance, clearly see the connection between large landholdings and slavery. We cannot "pay attention," really see things the way they are, unless our own ego is out of the way. As Gandhi puts it, "If you would swim on the bosom of the ocean of Truth, you must reduce yourself to zero."[33]

For folks like us, some movement toward voluntary poverty is probably the most powerful wake-up experience possible, for it has the ability to undercut our sense of privilege and power in a way few other things would do. In a consumer culture, we define ourselves by our possessions: they are the physical and spiritual defense of our exceptionalism. Once that fortress is breached, we are open to other ways of interpreting the world in contrast to the conventional one, for it is paying attention to this alternative awareness of self and others that is essential to the process of changed behavior. If one accepts that action is grounded in disposition, which most religions and Aristotle's virtue ethics assume, then "waking up," coming to awareness of the true nature of reality and one's place in it, is crucial. While it is never possible to be certain about "the true nature of reality," as the deconstructionists persistently and correctly remind us, the most responsible interpretation of this thorny issue surely takes seriously what science is telling us about it. With overwhelming agreement, all the sciences are painting a picture of a radically interrelated and interdependent cosmos, of which human beings are a unique part, given our self-awareness, but by no means an independent part.[34] This interpretation of reality as inextricably, inexorably, profoundly, and totally interdependent must provide the "background" for our emerging attention to the place of the human self in the nature of things. What the Buddhists call "dependent origination," or the codependent arising of all phenomena, meaning that no thing or event can be construed as coming into or remaining in existence by itself, is now the mantra of science as well. As the Dalai Lama claims, "Individual well-being is intimately connected with that of all others and with the environment within which we live."[35]

As we probe more deeply into this multilayered process of mindfulness and behavior, or paying attention to others' needs and action in order to address them, we begin to see something interesting emerging: *the distinction between "self" and "others" is an exaggeration.* The Western paradigm of political and economic theory has built itself on this exaggeration, not only of individual human beings as radically separate from each other (especially from those less fortunate) human beings, but also of human beings as separate from all other creatures and the cosmos itself. This exaggeration therefore has allowed for the meanest, most unjust form of capitalism to reign as the formula for all behavior toward other human beings and other life-forms. Our fourfold process of moving toward a changed paradigm of thought and action suggests that the accepted view is not only a lie, but a cruel lie—and that we are capable of better. But to become "better," we need voluntary poverty. It provides the opening, the chink in the wall, the tiny peephole in our well-guarded "separate self" that might allow us to *pay attention to others' material needs.* They are not our brothers and sisters to whom we owe a work of charity; rather, they are the others who make us who we are.

JOHN WOOLMAN

Woolman's deep desire to see with a single eye, to be *able* to pay attention to the material needs of others rather than his own, was also a lifelong struggle. The importance and the difficulty of clear sight cannot be exaggerated in the Quaker tradition. The "inner light," the light of Christ within, was the central goal of Quaker discipleship, and it was attained only through daily prayer and practice. Quaker faith is not a vague mysticism, an individual's experience of God's presence; rather, it is training for clarity of vision and hence clarity of logic regarding the deep and devious connections between seeing double and oppression. The focus is not on the universality of the light, but on its biblical specificity and its call to action. By biblical specificity, Quakers refer to the self-emptying practice of Jesus on behalf of others, but what this meant in any contemporary situation was to be worked out with painful and often prolonged discernment. Woolman's journal is full of passages in which he agonizes over the process of subjecting himself to God's will, a process that he describes as going through a refiner's fire, purging the dross, carrying the cross, wrestling with his own weakness and illness, bearing the appearance of foolishness. At times, Woolman's life seems to be one long, arduous journey, plodding through muddy roads on foot while struggling inwardly with his own doubts and uneasiness about his vocation. He lived his life literally "one step at a time," as he walked between Quaker meeting houses trying to perceive what God would have him do next—not in general, but in particular: whether he should write a will for a sick man wanting to give a slave to one of his children, whether to offend a neighbor in refusing to use silver cutlery since it was mined under oppressive conditions. Here we see the focus on *experience* that is unique in Quaker thought: the focus on the experience of the changed life. Woolman did not seek mystical experience, but rather kenotic experience, on the pattern of Christ, to address particular, contemporary instances of injustice. The light of Christ within was for an outer, practical experience of committed action on the behalf of others' material sufferings. The experience of God in Christ is central, but it is experience *for action*. Thus Quakerism is interested in neither humanism nor mysticism, but in lives changed on the pattern of Christ's self-emptying love for others. As one commentator notes: the basic Quaker movement is from light to power, from insight to action. "The fundamental justification of the Quaker faith consists not in new doctrines, but in new lives. Quakerism rests its case on experience, rather than speculation, but the fundamental experience is not ecstatic union with God. It is the more practical experience of watching for light on the pathway, of being given power to follow it."[36]

Woolman's practice of consciously lowering his material needs and placing himself in situations where he physically experienced discomfort, ridicule, and oppression (all forms of voluntary poverty) opened his eyes to what he could not have seen otherwise: the clear logic connecting riches and injustice. Having his eyes opened meant he could now set about the task of discerning more precisely what next steps he should take to address these various issues of oppression. As a privileged, middle-class person, he had to consciously choose to get outside the womb of comfort that his status gave him in order to see clearly, to really pay attention to *others*. The primary metaphor guiding this long process is light and its constituents: seeing, insight, discernment, vision, dreams. In his final dream, mentioned above, he saw "a mass of matter of a dull gloomy color between the south and the east, and was informed that this mass was human beings in as great misery as they could be, and live, and that I was mixed with them, and that henceforth I might not consider myself as a distinct or separate being."[37] This amazing vision is one bookend to the other passage about the universal self with which his journal opens, where he describes "true religion" as exercising love not only toward God and all human beings but "also toward the brute creatures," including "the least creature moving by [God's] life."[38] He names the goal clearly as he ponders the meaning of "true religion": "My heart was tender and often contrite, and universal love to my fellow-creatures increased in me."[39] Woolman's story is a profound and clear illustration of the process we are following: the movement from the awakening of voluntary poverty to attention to other's needs to the becoming of a universal self. His assumption of poverty—both in selling his profitable grocery business and placing himself in various contexts so he would experience oppression (of native Americans, of steerage passengers on a transatlantic ship, of ridicule for wearing white clothing)—was certainly the wild space that allowed him to see differently.

By undercutting his own exceptionalism in a variety of ways, he opened up the possibility that he could actually pay attention to others. In so doing, he saw that the majority of human beings (and other creatures) lived lives of great misery and that he could no longer define himself as limited by his own body and its accidentally privileged position, but must empathize with their suffering. His tradition—the Quaker interpretation of Christian discipleship in which sharing in Christ's suffering is epitomized by his self-emptying love on the cross—demanded that he live differently day by day, step by step. A new paradigm emerged in which the individual exists only in radical interrelationship and interdependence with all other creatures. Woolman did not need contemporary cosmology to convince him of human beings' place in the scheme of things: his reflections on his killing of a mother robin leaving her young as his responsibility was an opening to this insight, and his lifelong practice of daily prayer and committed action brought his initial experience into a mature perception that this is indeed the way things are. We are, all of us, mixed up together, and the actions of one affect all.

Simone Weil

For both Woolman and Weil, attentiveness and prayer are closely linked. Woolman came to greatest insight, to clarity regarding what he should do next, through intense prayer. Weil actually declares identity between the two: attention *is* prayer. Interestingly, she does not say the reverse "prayer is attention," which would suggest she *knows* what prayer is; rather, she discovered slowly and painfully that by paying attention to something—anything—an attitude of prayer, of open listening for God's will, occurred. Both Woolman and Weil are suggesting a new epistemology, a new way of knowing, that is essential to the most important fruit of knowledge: what to do next on the path of discipleship. Knowledge that really counted for them was not information, but discernment of God's will; and this is only possible if one can get the self out of the center so one can see, and thus reflect in action what God desires. The classic Western model of knowing since Descartes, the subject-object model, in which I am the subject, the center of all things, and the world (as well as all other people) is the object of my wishes, is not only irrelevant for Woolman and Weil but also false. This Western, Cartesian model encourages insatiable, grasping, self-centered possession of the world—cannibalizing it, according to Weil. It authorizes the way of knowing and acting that characterizes our market-oriented economies with their objectification of the world for the fulfillment of the human individual's gratification.

The model of knowing and acting that emerges from paying attention to the material needs of the other is the opposite. It says, "Look, do not eat," and in this admonition are hidden two key differences from the reigning paradigm. First, and of central importance to its relevance for us twenty-first-century well-off human earth dwellers, is its focus on *food for others*. While our current model encourages unfettered acquisition of material goods for ourselves, the model Weil suggests, and that she lived, makes us pay attention to the most basic physical needs of others. Second, this new model, in turning attention to the *other*, implies a new relationship between the self and the world: the relinquishment of power *over* the world and the attainment of an attitude of waiting, listening, openness *to* the world. The new model encourages a "hands-off" stance toward others, a retreat from control and possession, to appreciation of, distance from others: it is a strangely "impersonal aestheticism," which lets things be, for themselves, in themselves. Whether in a math problem that demands its own ineluctable answer or the rain and sun that falls on the unjust and the just alike, the world, Weil believed, is not set up according to our wishes or our merits. Rather, we, not the world, must adjust to things are they are. This new epistemology—one that pays attention to the other's needs and reality—demands the decreation of the self, or as Woolman would say, the development of the single eye. Thus practicing "objectivity," even in as simple a matter as solving a math problem, is the beginning of a revolutionary way of knowing—and acting—one in which concern for others' needs is done within the context of an "impersonal personalism." Thus care for other bodies is not charity and is unrelated to their value to me or anyone else.

Let us look into two key differences from the dominant market model of knowing in more detail. Both of these are found in Weil's treatment of the iconic parable of the good Samaritan: the stress on alleviating real hunger (and others' material needs) and on treating the other as an equal, a being with intrinsic merit, whom one does not "eat" for one's own fulfillment. The first insight concerns the sharing of basic needs, and the second provides a critique of power as well as a new paradigm of relationality. Both demand attention to the other—paying attention not to my own hunger but to the hunger of the other, and doing so by refusing to "cannibalize" the world, to devour it egotistically.

Weil objected to the Roman Catholic Church's narrow view of the incarnation: she wondered how Christianity could call itself "catholic" if creation, the world, was left out.[40] Her understanding of incarnationalism included everything—all beauty, all suffering, all joy, all affliction—and it was, in fact, what she saw as the Catholic Church's exclusivism that kept her from joining the church. For Weil, food is a spiritual issue, as were workers' rights. A "truly incarnated Christianity" must concern itself with basic human needs. Hence, to see "food" as the central focus is to underscore the most basic and universal element of every living being's need; it is also to imagine fulfillment, as Augustine did, as the satiation of desire at every level. With such a materialistic understanding of fulfillment, the implication is that "food" must be shared. That is, the cannibalistic sensibility that hungers at all levels for self-satiation must be emptied so that others may share in physical and personal fulfillment. This is certainly a point of central relevance for us today. Just as the good Samaritan attended to the food, shelter, and medical needs of the stranger, so a radical incarnationalism today must do the same thing. Weil's theology is opposed to any spiritualizing of need: the Bread of Life is also and first simply ordinary bread.

Moreover, her reading of the good Samaritan story suggests a new view of power: radical attention to the honoring of the other as subject, not object. Her understanding of "affliction," the most serious despair and degradation that human beings can undergo, is symbolized by slavery. The "slave" loses "half his soul" to a sense of inevitability, of doom, of feeling that one has no intrinsic merit and is simply an object of use to another.[41] We see the opposite in the Samaritan's story: the Samaritan's care for the stranger's needs is the ultimate recognition of the other as other; in fact, of treating the other as an equal. In Weil's eyes, justice and the love of neighbor are the same thing: "The supernatural virtue of justice consists of behaving exactly as though there were equality when one is the stronger in an unequal relationship."[42] Just as important as filling the hunger for food is the hunger of every creature for recognition of its existence. "Creative attention means really giving our attention to what does not exist. Humanity does not exist in the anonymous flesh lying inert by the roadside. The Samaritan who stops and looks gives his attention all the same to this absent humanity, and the actions which follow prove that is a question of real attention."[43] Just as God denies the divine self to give existence to others both in creation and in the incarnation, so the Samaritan's attention to the other, while diminishing himself, gives existence to another, one who is lying naked and inert in a ditch. "The attention is creative. But at the moment when it is engaged it is a renunciation. . . . The man accepts to be diminished by concentrating on an expenditure of energy, which will not extend his own power but will only give existence to a being other than himself, who will exist independently of him."[44]

Weil's interpretation of the Samaritan story, based on God's action in creation and salvation, is both a radical critique of conventional views of power and a suggestion for a new paradigm of relationality. The new view is based on kenosis. What we see in the good Samaritan story is a reflection of God's self-emptying in Christ and even, Weil asserts, of the heart of God. For Weil, "God is . . . the perfect friend."[45] The Father, Son, and Holy Spirit is the epitome of friendship—both nearness and distance realized perfectly. Here the giving and receiving is both "infinite nearness or identity" and at the same time "infinite distance." "This love, this friendship of God, is the Trinity."[46] Such a total self-emptying in love with preservation of distance at the same time provides Weil's template for all love. In light of this, power that either cannibalizes and controls the other or ignores and dismisses the other is false. God in God's self is friendship of total intimacy and total respect for difference and distance; God is this within the divine self and in relation to the world.

Weil's critique of power as control over another and her new vision of relationship as self-emptying giving while at the same time preserving the dignity of the recipient is highly suggestive for us today. It means that "loving the neighbor" must be aimed not only at the neighbor's basic needs but also at their self-esteem. A model of compassion and justice based on friendship creates equality between the partners—even when there is no equality—for such love, like the friendship within the Trinity, preserves the existence of the other. In giving of himself to the inert matter in the ditch, the Samaritan gave him life: "In denying oneself, one becomes capable under God of establishing someone else by a creative affirmation. One gives oneself in ransom for the other. It is a redemptive act."[47] Rather than power over the afflicted, Weil recommends giving life to the afflicted as our standard relationship to the needy. It is hard to imagine a more complete shift in paradigm.

DOROTHY DAY

Dorothy Day's whole life was a living testimony to the dictum, "one who pays attention to the material needs of others." But in her case, her attentiveness did not arise from prayer, as with Woolman and Weil; rather, it began with a childhood fascination with observing other people, a tendency nurtured and deepened by her experience as both a novelist and a journalist. She was neither a theologian nor philosopher, but a lover of people with all their fascinating life stories. She loved the city, in part because of its human energy and diversity, the great mix of people in Chicago or New York that fired her imagination and captured her wish to help them in their ordinary, mundane struggles for food and shelter. She claims in the introduction to her autobiography that her life falls into two halves—the first half focused on her training to observe and accurately report the contemporary struggles for justice in the heady atmosphere of workers' strikes influenced by Communism and a youthful, Bohemian lifestyle. She entered into several love affairs; traveled widely; tried nursing for a while; was imprisoned for joining a suffragist protest; wrote an autobiographical novel (*The Eleventh Virgin*), of which she was subsequently ashamed; and in general was experiencing the cutting-edge social and political events of her time as a journalist. This was the "secular" phase of her life. The second half of her life began with her conversion to Catholicism (1927) and meeting Peter Maurin (1932). Everything would change, but her early experiences of paying close attention to the lives and miseries of others would not.

Like Woolman and Weil, she would join together prayer and work, attention and action, the personal and the public, but hers would be a different mix from theirs. Woolman sought the single eye through prayer, and Weil found paying attention (prayer) the way to insight: both sought "objectivity"— moving the self out of the center—as the way to really and truly serve others.

Woolman's attention-based prayer was structured on the Quaker discipline of probing dissection of motives and the relinquishment of egotistic desires in order to "take the next step," to discern among the many possibilities what one should do next. Woolman did his dissecting reflection not in his private study but in the midst of the physical hardships that visiting Indians and walking between Quaker meetings involved. It was insight that arose while actually experiencing deprivation, discomfort, and sometimes danger. Weil sought "objectivity" through the novel practice of "objective" fields of study— math problems, the implacable laws of nature, the "impersonalism" of fate and destiny. She did everything she could to force herself to "look and not eat," to move the ego so that her attention could be focused on the suffering of those without bread and board. Day sought the same goal as these two, but she came late to prayer, and it was her journalist/novelist eye for detail and compassion for the oppressed that was the opening in the self's defensive posture against sacrificing for others. Her night in prison and her assignments following workers' strikes for basic necessities were the experiences that cut through her middle-class cloak of exceptionalism.

The distinctive mark by which she united contemplation and action was Christ. For Day, prayer and action were both Christ centered—meeting Christ in the Eucharist and in works of mercy. She became a Benedictine oblate, practicing the order's linkage of prayer and work, with the primacy of prayer, but always a prayer oriented toward hospitality for the other, and the "other" was always Christ.[48] The two favorite saints of the Catholic Worker movement were Francis of Assisi and Benedict, one emphasizing the personal and the other the communitarian. Both were critical influences on Day's Christ-centered spirituality, which was never focused on the self nor merely on the alleviation of oppression. Rather, both in prayer and in action, the focus was Christ. As Day comments in one of her notes from the many retreats that she undertook, "Every action must receive [the] touch of Christ. . . . The only way is to do it *for Christ*. Not for self. The only thing which gives importance to actions is Christ."[49] Her spirituality was synonymous with neither personal mysticism nor secular justice movements; rather, it was a Christ-centered mysticism grounded in daily attendance at the Mass (where she met Christ in the Eucharist) and in work (where all the "guests" in her hospitality houses were reflections of Christ). And yet she never lost her "humanism," for to love God *is* to love Christ in all his many human masks: The child who needs socks is Christ; the man who needs a job is Christ; the woman who needs a hot meal is Christ. Day's love of God and her love of human beings came together in Christ—here she found the synthesis of prayer and work. "Christ, as God made human, was the Way, the link between past, present and future, the bridge between material and spiritual, and the model for human integration."[50]

In significant ways, Day's attention to the other's needs was the longest and the most "natural." While a strong whiff of prophetic duty haunts the reflections of Woolman and Weil, Day's early fascination with the mundane stories of other lives was strengthened by a love for the natural world. Her brand of Catholicism included the sacramental embrace of all worldly pleasures—the first shoots of spring in the country, the touch of a lover's hand, the exuberance of children playing, the delight of friends sharing food. Early in her autobiography she makes a telling comment: she says "I wanted life and I wanted the abundant life. I wanted it for others too."[51] This is not a sentence that one imagines falling off the lips of Woolman or Weil, but for Day, not only was heaven a "banquet," but "life is a banquet, too, even with a crust, where there is companionship."[52] We recall that another of her most influential saints was Teresa of Avila, who "loved to read novels when she was a young girl, and she wore a bright red dress when she entered the convent."[53] When the nuns became melancholy, Teresa "fed them steak," and danced with castanets "to make life more bearable."[54] Like Woolman and Weil, Day exposed herself to, lived with, the poor and the suffering, in part to keep her eye single (as Woolman would put it) and to remain "objective" (as Weil would say), but also because she *loved* the vitality of ordinary people with all their joys and sorrows, and found fulfillment not in solitary righteousness but in conviviality. Overcoming "the long loneliness" was achieved through community, especially the sharing of life's necessities with *all*.

As we reflect on the significance of paying attention to the others' needs as a second step in our process of kenotic, universal love for all, we see that, at least for our three saints, developing a certain kind of knowledge is critical. They insisted on experiencing what those whom they were attempting to love were also experiencing. If such love was to be realistic and helpful, one had to *know* what others needed. For them, it was necessary to *live with these others*. Only then could one hope to keep at bay the constant pull of one's own ego, one's sense of exceptionalism, that, as Iris Murdoch reminds us, keeps us from realizing "that something other than oneself is real." Loving the neighbor as oneself means *knowing the neighbor*, for we cannot love what we do not know— or, if we try, we will be loving "double," through the lens of our own eye, as Woolman claims. Knowledge that matters, knowledge that helps us live the good life (for ourselves and others), involves both inward and outward attention: reflection on the many ways we engage in denial of others' needs in order to protect our own special status, and action in which we place ourselves in situations where we can learn to see the world the way it is and not simply as we would like it to be. While it is highly controversial whether good thoughts lead to good actions (the Greeks claimed that to know the good is to do the good, and many religious traditions claim that "it ain't necessarily so"), can we not claim that there *is* some connection? What, then, is the connection? If the goal is to enlarge our capacity for compassion, so that we consider that "who we are" does not stop with the limits of our own bodies (or the bodies we produce), but to include all that is (universal compassion), is there a place for knowledge of the other, for paying attention to the others' needs? Can this do anything but make us feel more guilty, more shameful, more depressed, more despairing? It is doubtful if imitation of our saints would be very profitable: we do not practice the strong meditative traditions they did (Bible reading, daily prayer, mindfulness exercises, retreats, daily attendance at the Eucharist), nor can we learn about the poverty-stricken simply through "slum tourism," voluntary jaunts to deprived areas of the world, practicing simple living in the midst of our plenty, or limited exposure to poverty's discomfort, when we know that at the end of the day that we can look forward to a hot shower and a good meal.

No, we have to admit that at one level what is needed is a revolution of our whole way of living: the daily and continuing practice of prayer and action conducted in a situation of voluntary poverty in which we become "saints" ourselves. There is a reason why the folks we have been considering are called saints: "What is important about saints . . . is their complete and uncompromising devotion to promoting the welfare of others."[55] This is just not in the cards for most of us—and we had best admit it. But does it help to *see* clearly, to see who we are and who others are in the scheme of things (as the best science of our day tells us)? Does it make any difference whether we live our daily lives on the basis of one model of reality or another? How much credence should we put in insight, knowledge? Most studies today, as evidenced by the advertising industry, show that emotion is stronger than reason (or knowledge) in making decisions, but is it necessary to separate the two—insight and feeling—so dualistically? The *kind* of knowledge that we seek here is not facts, but how to live well, and this embodied knowledge is surely a combination of reason and emotion. When a new model of knowing becomes widespread—as the market-oriented model did for us and our contemporaries—it *does* influence our decisions, and has been shown to do so in such thoroughgoing ways that the deterioration of the planet is its witness. It is the combination of "knowing something that feels good" that probably lies behind most of our subconscious decisions for a particular direction. Even our saints are not hair-shirt decision makers, intentionally choosing life decisions that are alien, unfulfilling, or negative. While the joy of sharing the last crust of bread with others in community is more evident in Day than in Woolman or Weil, the latter two nonetheless also found the path they had chosen deeply fulfilling—a path in which the self disappears is a search as well for the ultimate self-fulfillment, for joy unbounded, for Augustine's restless heart finding its true home, the love of God. While we are not all going to be saints, the attention we pay to others can open up a new vision of the self—not the cramped, narrow, individualistic, greedy self, but the all-inclusive, magnanimous, limitless self whose "body" embraces the whole world—and is also an answer to the "long loneliness" that each of us experiences in our search for self-fulfillment. If one accepts that the human being is not a singular individual, bounded by the limits of its own body and concerned only with its basest, most self-centered desires, but that the human being *is* all the others that make up our cosmos, that the "self" has no borders and that its well-being rests on the health of others, then would this insight not move us to knock down those barriers we place around ourselves, recognizing others in their own reality and at the same time appreciating them as gifts to us? Would we not begin to *feel* compassion for them in continuity with the way we feel compassion for ourselves in the more narrow model? If in fact we are not singular individuals that find satisfaction in living by ourselves, for ourselves, but are open, porous organisms intrinsically and inexorably related to and dependent on all the others that make up our planet, how can we not care about, have concern for, work on behalf of, suffer with, and appreciate all these others?

It is, I think, no accident that the moments in our lives we describe as moments of illumination—perhaps the birth of a child, a fleeting connection with the eyes of another animal, a vision of a mountain that blows us away, a hand reaching out to us when we are sinking fast—are never isolating experiences. These "liminal" moments, when the mist seems to clear and we see what life is all about, are never about just "me," but always about these "others" that make up the world, be they human, creature, or mineral. "In the beginning was relationship," says Martin Buber (someone who called trees "thou"), and whether one is a cosmologist studying the beginnings of the universe, a naturalist listing the forty-two species of birds of paradise, or a theologian discussing the radical relationality of love within the Trinity, all would agree that the present dominant model of radical individualism that controls our economics, our family relations, our democracies, and most all of our advertising is *false*. To be sure, the connection between knowing and doing is fraught with all kinds of difficulties, but it is certainly the case that false knowledge, knowledge that supports a lie about who we are in the scheme of things, cannot serve action for a just and sustainable planet.

What our study of attention to the needs of others has shown us is that such knowledge is a necessity, and while we will not all be saints, we need not be the total slackers that we presently are, sinking into abysmal behavior under the weight of ignorance and denial. The powerful stories of our three saints, their paths of radical attention to others—one of the most difficult things for us to acknowledge—tells us in large letters what the scientific story is also telling us: we cannot live without these others—and deep down, we want them to thrive.

NOTES

1 Words: Lesbia Scott, 1929; Music: John H. Hopkins Jr., 1940.

2 See "Saint," Wikipedia, last modified Sept. 5, 2012, http://en.wikipedia.org/wiki/Saint.

3 Elizabeth A. Johnson, *Friends of God and Prophets: A Feminist Theological Reading of the Communion of Saints* (New York: Continuum, 1998), 219.

4 Lawrence Cunningham, The Meaning of Saints (New York: Harper and Row, 1980), 65.

5 Emmanuel Levinas, *Totality and Infinity: An Essay on Exteriority*, trans. Alphonso Lingis (Pittsburgh: Duquesne University Press, 1961), 247.

6 Ibid., 46.

7 Edith Wyschogrod, *Saints and Postmodernism: Revisioning Moral Philosophy* (Chicago: University of Chicago Press, 1990), xxii.

8 Ibid., 96.

9 Ibid., 183.

10 Andrew Michael Flescher, *Heroes, Saints, and Ordinary Morality* (Washington, DC: Georgetown University Press, 2003), 175.

11 Ibid., 179.

12 "Poverty," Wikipedia, last modified on Aug. 31, 2012, en.wikipedia.org/wiki/Poverty.

13 Ibid.

14 Dorothee Soelle, *The Silent Cry: Mysticism and Resistance* (Minneapolis: Fortress Press, 2001), 220.

15 Ibid., 209.

16 See Daniel Goleman, *Emotional Intelligence* (New York: Bantam Dell, 2006).

17 Wyschogrod, *Saints and Postmodernism*, 52.

18 Simone Weil, *Waiting for God*, trans. Emma Craufurd (New York: Harper and Row, 1951), 76.

19 *The Confessions of Saint Augustine, Books I–X*, trans. F. J. Sheed (New York: Sheed and Ward), 4.1; 7.10.

20 The Eastern Orthodox Christian tradition's understanding of salvation as deification (growing into the image of God), through death to the self and new life in God (self-emptying allowing for divine fulfillment) feels comfortable with this language, though it is less prevalent in the West. See, for instance, Norman Russell, *The Doctrine of Deification in the Greek Patristic Tradition* (Oxford: Oxford University Press, 2004); Michael J. Christensen and Jeffery A. Wittung, eds., *Partakers of the Divine Nature: The History and Development of Deification in the Christian Traditions* (Grand Rapids: Baker Academic, 2007).

21 Quoting Peter Maurin in Dorothy Day, *Loaves and Fishes* (San Francisco: Harper and Row, 1963), 82.

22 Dorothy Day, *By Little and By Little: The Selected Writings of Dorothy Day*, ed. Robert Ellsberg (New York: Alfred A. Knopf, 1983), 110.

23 Dorothy Day, *The Catholic Worker*, February 1945.

24 See Karen House Catholic Worker, "Our Writings," http://karenhousecw.org/RB-VoluntaryPoverty.html.

25 Quoted from *Loaves and Fishes* in ibid.

26 Paul Lachance, "Mysticism and Social Transformation According to the Franciscan Way," in *Mysticism and Social Transformation*, ed. Janet K. Ruffing (Syracuse: Syracuse University Press, 2001), 69.

27 Later Rule 12.4, quoted in ibid., 55.

28 Ibid., 71–72.

29 Ibid., 73–74.

30 See "Poverty," Wikipedia, http://www.en.wikipedia.org.wiki/Poverty.

31 Donald K. Swearer, "Buddhist Virtue, Voluntary Poverty, and Extensive Benevolence," *Journal of Religious Ethics*, 26, no. 1 (Spring 1998): 74.

32 See, for instance, Goleman, *Emotional Intelligence*; Daniel J. Siegel, *Mindsight: The New Science of Personal Transformation* (New York: Bantam, 2011); Sharon Begley, *Train Your Mind, Change*

Your Brain: How a New Science Reveals Our Extraordinary Potential to Transform Ourselves (New York: Ballantine, 2007); His Holiness the Dalai Lama, *Ethics for a New Millennium* (New York: Riverhead, 1999).

33 Quoted in Beverly J. Lanzetta, *The Other Side of Nothingness: Toward a Theology of Radical Openness* (Albany: State University of New York Press, 2001), 105.

34 The witnesses here are legion, needless to say, but for a theological anthropology the broad picture of the evolutionary, ecological story is what is needed, replacing the eighteenth story of human beings as totally different and apart from other forms of life and superior to them. See, for instance, my treatment in *The Body of God: An Ecological Theology* (Minneapolis: Fortress Press, 1993), chap. 3.

35 Dalai Lama, *Ethics for a New Millennium*, 41.

36 D. Elton Trueblood, *The People Called Quakers* (New York: Harper and Row, 1966), 84.

37 *The Journal of John Woolman and A Plea for the Poor* (New York: Corinth Books, 1961), 214.

38 Ibid., 8.

39 Ibid.

40 See Weil, *Waiting for God*, 95–97.

41 See "The Love of God and Affliction," in Weil, *Waiting for God*, 117ff.

42 Weil, *Waiting for God*, 143.

43 Ibid., 149.

44 Ibid., 147.

45 Ibid., 214.

46 "The love between God and God, which in itself is God, is the bond of double virtue: the bond that unites two beings so closely that they are no longer distinguishable and really form a single unity and the bond that stretches across distance and triumphs over infinite separation" (ibid., 126).

47 Ibid., 147–48.

48 See, for instance, the analysis by Brigid O'Shea Merriman, *Searching for Christ: The Spirituality of Dorothy Day* (Notre Dame: University of Notre Dame Press, 1994).

49 From the *Catholic Worker* 12 (May 1944), as quoted in ibid., 149.

50 Ibid., 224.

51 Dorothy Day, *The Long Loneliness* (New York: Harper and Row, 1952), 44.

52 Ibid., 317.

53 Ibid., 161.

54 Ibid.

55 Flescher, *Heroes, Saints, and Ordinary Morality*, 179.

5

The Practice of the Saints 2

The Development of the Universal Self at Local and Global Levels

THE UNIVERSAL SELF

The process by which our saints prepare themselves to act with love for others' most basic needs involves varying degrees of self-emptying—relinquishing material and emotional possessions (voluntary poverty) and diverting attention from the self to others. Weil called this process decreation; Woolman described it as attaining single vision; and Day experienced it in the sharing of the last crust of bread around a table. For them, this process gradually resulted in a view of the self different the dominant one in either their culture or ours. This new view could be called the "universal" self. Its signature characteristic is that it has no boundaries: the understanding of the self here does not stop with one's own body, or the bodies of one's loved ones, or the bodies of similar people, or the bodies of human beings, or even the bodies of other animals, or amazingly even all bodies, for it includes the systems that keep bodies flourishing (water, land, climate, air). For these folks, nothing less than the world was their body. When I first began to read about the saints decades ago, I soon became aware that the boundary of who they thought they were kept expanding. While it usually started with one's own group—African Americans (Martin Luther King Jr.), the dalits (Mohandas Gandhi), fellow Quakers (Woolman)—the line became fuzzy, refusing to exclude any group or individual that was needy or oppressed. The line expanded, not because of sentimental feelings that "we are all alike," but because placing themselves in a situation of identification with those who were suffering developed an empathy in them, a "feeling with" others, that caused them to imagine their own selves differently. Through voluntary poverty and attentiveness, both practices to redirect their focus to others, the saints gradually grew in their own sense of selfhood.

This passage from a narrow, individualistic view of the self, one that stopped with the limits of one's own flesh, expanded, not primarily through reason (though the understanding of reality as interdependent certainly helps), but through emotion—getting inside someone else's skin, so to speak. The little incident in which Woolman came to realize that he was responsible for the baby robins whose mother he killed says it all in a nutshell: he *felt* the vulnerability of the baby robins and by so feeling became aware of his responsibility for their well-being. I can recall a similar incident years ago when I heard about "habitat destruction" as a main cause of species deterioration. It sounded abstract, but when described in the mundane example of a bear losing its home, I found myself readily identifying across the species divide: every creature needs a home, and we can all *feel with* any creature—bear or spider or horseshoe crab—that loses it. This identification is the key to the strange command to "love others as yourself": it is not a call to selfishness, but to radical love for the other. When our bodies know no limits, the suffering and joy of others becomes our own. Duty, knowledge, guilt—none of these is a sufficient motivator for a life of self-emptying love for others. Only feeling with, radical relationality—in other words, love—works, and it works because it is, in fact, who we are. These "others" that we *should* love are in fact the ones we *do* love, for none of us *is* (exists) as a single, isolated, autonomous item in the world. Hence, our own fulfillment lies with these others. The strange, countercultural statement by most religions that in order to find your life you must lose it is not a paradox or a mystery: it is simply a description of what science is telling us as well—we *are* universal selves. The main difference between the saints and the rest of us is that they actually acknowledge this and live by it, while we do not.

As we approach this central aspect of our study—the nature of the self—several questions come to mind. First, what is the current conventional view of the relation of the self and the world? Second, what view of the self and the world do our three saints model? Third, how is the alternative view of the self and the world reflected in the sciences? Fourth, how can the religions help bring about this change?

THE CURRENT VIEW OF THE SELF AND THE WORLD

The hallmark of modernity—and of postmodernity—is encapsulated in the statement by the twentieth-century German philosopher Erich Heller: "Be careful how you interpret the world. It *is* like that."[1] Of course, things are never that simple, but this chilling and yet hopeful reminder opens the door to the realization that we do not have to live with the current models of reality that happen to be dominant. While we do not "construct" reality, we do live within the interpretations of reality that we accept as true or conventional or natural. There are no descriptions of reality, only approximations that we suggest by the metaphors and models we propose.[2] The dominant Western model of the self and the world owes its flourishing to the eighteenth-century Enlightenment confidence in the importance of the individual—a wonderful heritage that supported innumerable battles for the rights of many, ranging from women to the other animals. Its basis was in Greek culture and in Christianity, both of which stressed the importance of individual human rights and responsibilities. Dante's picture of the lonely wanderer making his way from purgatory to heaven, based on the person's decisions during his or her brief earthly life, epitomizes the heavy burden as well as the possible glory of individuality. The American mantra of "life, liberty, and the pursuit of happiness," interpreted increasingly in libertarian terms (the right to carry a gun, to refuse to sign up for medical coverage, etc.), is but the latest link in a long line of influences by the state, economics, and religion to move this model of the self from its metaphorical, interpretive base to a *description* of how things are. Aided by decades of heavily funded advertising that "you deserve the very best" (whether it is a BMW or a tropical vacation), the image of human fulfillment has become increasingly selfish, materialistic, and individualistic. This is so widely accepted now that it is as if we were fish living in a fishbowl: it is the sea in which we swim.

There are many things wrong with this model, but for our purposes, three stand out: its treatment of others as objects, its lack of differentiation between different kinds of individuals, and its emphasis on the personal rather than the public dimension. All of these faults are advantageous for a market-oriented economy since they underscore the centrality of individual human beings as the focus of life's goal and its accepted ethics. The first fault says that the basic epistemology or way of knowing is subject-object: the world is seen from the perspective of the one subject (myself), with all other human beings, creatures, and realities as objects that are either "for" or "against" me.[3] An opposing epistemology and the one that supports the model of the universal self, sees all entities as subjects (and at times objects), in a world where there is no *one* perspective from which we know and evaluate everything. The subject-object epistemology objectifies the world and everything in it, protecting the self as subject from having to "feel with" others. It is a utilitarian worldview based on whatever furthers the plans and projects of its dominant subjects. Needless to say, competition, fighting, and winning drive this position. Such a worldview clearly does not support the flourishing of other life-forms or the health of the planet itself, since from the human subject's point of view, these are either assets or obstacles to one's own goals.

The second fault with the dominant, market-oriented model of the self is that it fails to differentiate between and among human individuals. The upside of this characteristic is that "all are equal" before the law, God, or whatever form of judgment one proposes. This has been the backbone, again, for many structural changes supporting a level playing field in cultures where family ties, ancient hierarchies, and various kinds of discrimination have controlled ordinary people from getting ahead. The downside of the model is that it makes no distinctions between the rich and the poor, the powerful and the vulnerable, the fortunate and the unfortunate, the healthy and the sick, male and female, white and colored, and so forth. All are simply "human individuals"; therefore, such issues as responsibility for greenhouse emissions and economic disasters are not focused on the individuals (and countries) that are principally responsible; rather, the same ethic applies to all, and that ethic tends to be individualistic: each of us should practice saving energy in our own homes, avoiding systemic changes such as taxing the rich or taxing carbon emissions at the level of federal or international law. One of the popular features of this individualistic ethic is the celebration of the Bill Gateses of the world who give huge sums to alleviate disease but object to substantial changes in tax laws that put them in much higher brackets. Americans, particularly, love the individual who overcomes adversity, makes good, and gives back: lavish charity based on individual accomplishment is the height of "saintliness" in this model.

The third fault of the model is related to the other two: it is personal rather than public, with roots in Western Protestantism as well as the Enlightenment. Just as the Protestant view of salvation focused on individual righteousness, so also its ethics tended to avoid meddling in the public sphere. In fact, the separation of the worldly and the heavenly was a major feature of the Protestant worldview, whether in its mainline form of the Lutheran two tracks (the religious and the secular) or the sectarian avoidance of things of the flesh for things of the spirit. Protestant incarnationlism was radically unlike that of Simone Weil, who criticized the Catholic Church for leaving the world out. But Protestantism, certainly in its Puritan form but also in its wider practice, tended to focus, fortunately for business purposes, on individual righteousness, leaving the world out as well. One of the surprising things about our saints—Woolman (a Protestant), Weil (a nonconformist Catholic), and Day (an orthodox Catholic)—is that all three insist on the continuity between the personal and the public. For example, Day's ethic of "personalism" involved strikes for workers' rights every bit as much as it pertained to acts of charity at the most humble level. The universal model of the self does not allow for either "misplaced concreteness" or focusing on the personal and the immediate as a way of avoiding unpleasant revolutionary actions. What we need is a model that functions at both levels: for instance, my suggestion of three house rules for planet earth that have both a personal and a public application. These rules are: (1) take only your share; (2) clean up after yourself; and (3) leave the house in good condition for others.[4] While you can pin them on your refrigerator and follow them on an individual level, they are also pertinent at all public levels, though their application at these levels will involve imagination, great cooperation, and willingness to sacrifice for others.

Thus it is evident that in a number of ways, the current model of the self is hopelessly inadequate for the problems we face: momentous climate change and vast economic disparity. The model *is* certainly injurious to our planet and, as many studies have shown, to human happiness; the surprising thing, however, is that it is accepted with so little controversy. Since modernity and postmodernity have shown that we are not in fact imprisoned within our interpretations, and since an increasing number of people find the model unfulfilling if not dangerous, then why do we continue to inhabit it? The reasons are undoubtedly legion, and many have tried to unravel them, but what our saints at least have shown us is that *it is very difficult to live otherwise.* If voluntary poverty and radical attention to the needs of others are the necessary preparation for a different view of the self—the universal self—then we should not fool ourselves about the challenge before us. At several places in this essay, I have pointed to what I call "wild space," the chinks in the fortress of the enclosed self that occasionally open to lure us to a different way of being. We all have this possibility—it is what makes us human, the ability to think otherwise, to imagine another future, to realize that the current model is oppressive, wrong, or false. Saints seek a lot of wild space—they are "wild people," refusing to live within the confines of the world as interpreted by others. They say, something else is possible, something else is better.

THE MODEL OF THE UNIVERSAL SELF

As we turn now to this most central aspect of our study, we will be aided by two sources: In this section, we will look again at the lives and insights of our three saints, and in the following two sections, we will look at some current research supporting an alternative view of the self from science, and then at the contribution of Buddhism.[5] Throughout these comments, we will be guided by that strange phrase "love your neighbor as yourself," which appears in all three Synoptic Gospels (Matt. 22:39; Mark 12:31; Luke 10:27). This used to strike me as oddly self-centered, suggesting that you could not love others until you loved yourself. Does self-love come first? Some have suggested so; in fact, much New Age wisdom claims that being good to oneself, taking care of oneself, attaining self-esteem, is the first step toward eventually turning outward to love others. But I no longer believe in that interpretation of the phrase; rather, I believe a better interpretation is much more radical: *you* are the neighbor, the neighbors. The world is your body; you are a universal self, and hence to love others as yourself means the extension of the same feelings of empathy, attention to basic needs, and concern for recognition of intrinsic value that one "naturally" has for oneself. As each of us is inside our own skin, feeling the pain of hunger, the joy of a sense of value, so also, by extension, we are capable of feeling others' delights and suffering at physical and emotional levels.

Several times in these pages, I have referred to the parable of the good Samaritan as the iconic Christian story of self-emptying discipleship, and here, once again, it speaks to us (Luke 10:25-37). It is introduced by a lawyer's question of how to attain eternal life, to which Jesus replies, "love your neighbor as yourself." The characteristics of the universal self that emerge from that story, as illustrated by our three saints, are fourfold: the self is universally empathetic (the "stranger," I submit, could have been a dog); human action on behalf of the other is both anonymous and impersonal; the goal of the action toward the other is materialistic; the parable about the love of neighbor is illustrative of how one should love God. To rehearse briefly: Jesus replies to the lawyer's further questioning of "who is my neighbor?" by telling a story of a man who was robbed, beaten, and left for dead, while some "good" people (a priest and a Levite) "passed by on the other side." A Samaritan, a despised foreigner who had no civil duty to help the man, was, however, "moved with pity" (the empathetic identification with an anonymous, distant other). He then embarked on a series of extraordinary measures: treating the man's wounds with oil and wine, carrying him on his own animal, taking him to an inn where he not only paid the innkeeper to oversee the recovery of the injured man but also assured him that he would cover all further expenses (the act was, in other words, limitless). At the end of the story, Jesus asks, "Which of these three, do you think, was a neighbor to the man?" The answer is short, obvious, and without qualification: "The one who showed him mercy," and the implication is equally short, obvious, and without qualification: "Go and do likewise."

This is a chilling story because it brooks no halfway measures, no exceptions, no "qualifying circumstances." It fits perfectly with our three saints, whose actions invariably showed similar characteristics: a refusal to limit one's empathy to the familiar or close neighbor; love to another that is anonymous (one does not seek gratitude or recognition) and impersonal (the recipient need not be special in any way, except as another subject worthy of attention); the content to the gift is material—a basic physical need such as food or medical care; and the action is seen as an extension or manifestation of one's love of God. Woolman's typical mode of operation is a clear example of these notes in the parable of the good Samaritan, as is evident in his visit to the Indian villages. He opens the description of the trip with the following words: "Love was the first motion, and thence a concern arose to spend some time with the Indians, that I might feel and understand their life and the spirit they live in."[6] He was drawn to a hands-on experience of the suffering the Indians were undergoing, not from a sense of duty but from love, from empathy. He mentions elsewhere in his account of the trip that "people who have never been in such places have but an imperfect idea of them."[7] Indeed. This understatement illustrates a remarkable feature of Woolman's ministry: the necessity of a close encounter with the particular kind of oppression that he is seeking to address, which led him then to the outrageous behavior of actually living with Indians for a while, and later in his life, sleeping steerage with the sailors on a transatlantic voyage so he could experience the discomfort of such quarters. Woolman was driven to do his good works not out of a sense of guilt or duty, but because he *loved* these others like brothers. In an amazing comment on his feeling for the Indians, he writes: "A near sympathy with them was raised in me, and, my heart being enlarged in the love of Christ, I thought that the affectionate care of a good man for his only brother in affliction does not exceed what I then felt for that people."[8]

It would be impossible to find a better description of a universal self than this: by "sympathy" his heart was "enlarged" so that it included these anonymous human beings, quite apart from any personal relationship with them, yet, how he felt toward them was expressed by analogy with his "only brother in affliction." Had Woolman lived a different kind of life—one that did not in fact embody what he says here—such a remark could be dismissed as merely sentimental. However, his conduct mirrored his words perfectly and stunningly reflects the characteristics of the good Samaritan story: universal, anonymous, impersonal love to alleviate the suffering of others as a way of loving God. At the beginning of his journal, Woolman spells out this major insight of his life in a "credo," and at the end of the book he sums it up with the dream in which he hears a voice say, "John Woolman is dead." The credo is in the same language of empathy and love that we find elsewhere in his reflections on his motives for action: he says that true religion consists of a heart that "doth love and reverence God," and is thus taught to exercise "true justice and goodness" to all creatures, including nonhuman ones. He links love of God and of all other beings inextricably: "I looked upon the works of God in this visible creation, and an awfulness covered me. My heart was tender and often contrite, and universal love to my fellow-creatures increased in me."[9] The logic here is tight and irrefutable: one cannot love God without loving the world, including "the least creature moving by [God's] life." A better summation of the universal self would be hard to find. At the close of his life, Woolman makes the connection even clearer: in his dream he hears the phrase "John Woolman is dead," explaining that this means "the death of his own will." However, he is given a new life in the crucified Christ, a universal self, in whom all suffering human beings are joined, and hence he can no longer consider himself "as a distinct or separate being."[10] This is about as far from our conventional market-oriented view of the human self as it is possible to imagine—and, in its stark description, a novel and effective pedagogy for people like us who need an example as outrageous, clear, and honest as the humble, quiet reformer John Woolman. It is no accident that over the years my students have found Woolman's story to be one of the most powerful, as well as the most difficult to dismiss.

Simone Weil's use of the good Samaritan story is even more explicit than Woolman's. One could say it epitomizes both her theology and her own life story. Just as God in creation and salvation empties the divine self, giving life to all creatures, so the good Samaritan gives his own substance to what does not exist: "the anonymous flesh lying inert by the roadside."[11] This decreation of the self "diminishes" the giver, for it is an expenditure of energy to "give existence to a being other than himself, who will exist independently of him."[12] Weil understands this decreation whereby another is given life as both physical and emotional: the creative attention to what does not exist not only heals the man's wounds but also his self-esteem, recognizing him as an other who exists in his own right. Weil states clearly that such action reflects God's action on behalf of humanity: "In denying oneself, one becomes capable under God of establishing someone else by creative affirmation."[13]

Here, the story of the good Samaritan is indeed the iconic Christian act: becoming nothing so that God might be everything. Weil's concept of decreation, the one act of which we are capable—giving up our false, autonomous existence in recognition that all life, physical and spiritual, comes from God and that we, at most, can only be conduits of that love—is concretely illustrated in the story of one who imitates divine love by literally becoming *food for others*. Weil's radical incarnationalism—God as the "food" of creation—is reflected in the outrageous suggestion in her "paralytic prayer," where she prays that her very being (her body, mind, experiences) "be stripped away from me, devoured by God, transformed into Christ's substance, and given for food to afflicted men whose body and soul lack every kind of nourishment."[14] What this means practically is less to the point than the contribution it makes to the notion of a universal self: the pushing of the boundaries of the self so that one becomes identical with divine inclusivity—the expansion of the self to include all suffering beings. And for Weil, this identification with God comes not from a sense of duty, but of delight. "Attention animated by desire is the whole foundation of religious practices."[15] The desire for God is expressed in one's ability to "transport himself into [another] by sympathy," by the desire to feel what God feels for all creatures: unlimited, self-emptying love.[16] Weil speaks of "transporting" oneself into another, consenting to take on the other's affliction, which while it will mean the destruction of the self (the false self), it will be the beginnings of the growth of the true self, the one who serves as a conduit of divine love. Since only God is capable of love, we, like the good Samaritan, can at most imitate God through our mundane daily renunciation of self-serving acts, refusing more for oneself (food, reputation, comfort, honors), so that others might have the basics of physical and emotional existence.

Weil's focus on food—her analogies of giving the self as food to others or, its opposite, cannibalistic "love," devouring others to feed one's own body and soul—powerfully illustrates the extremity of her position: nothing less than a universal self can adequately express what we human beings are called to be and do. Human nature, far from being the narrow, insatiable, individualistic self of the market-oriented culture of the twenty-first century, is the opposite: feeling with others to the point of living their pain in the bowels of one's own being. The context of near starvation (and loss of dignity) that French citizens experienced during the Nazi occupation was the backdrop for Weil's anthropology: an incarnational theology says that human beings are created and re-created by the gift of God's love; hence, they are defined by their recognition of this reality in giving life-sustaining bread and attention to all others. No one gets credit for living this way: it is simply the way things are and hence what one is to do. There are no limits to this attention, and it is not based on merit or personal closeness: like the sun and the rain, God's love falls on all—and so, then, should ours. Here we see once again the notes of the good Samaritan story: universal, anonymous, impersonal, empathic action that addresses the suffering of other beings as a way of fulfilling one's desire for God. We love the neighbor as ourselves if we see who we are as including all other beings whose suffering one feels directly in imitation of divine creative and saving love.

While Dorothy Day did not explicitly refer to the story of the good Samaritan in the fashion of Weil, she *lived it* on a daily basis. Her dedication to Thérèse of Lisieux's "little by little," the saintliness of mundane, persevering, attention to producing unending kettles of soup and washing daily piles of dirty sheets, was testimony to her commitment to the most basic physical needs of other human beings regardless of their merit or status. She was not a conceptual theologian, she had no theology of the incarnation, but spending forty years following the radical teachings of Jesus day in and day out was her version of an embodied incarnational theology. Robert Coles refers to this commitment when he writes of her life: "As for Jesus Christ, who of any importance in the West's intellectual or political world now pays any real attention to his teachings?"[17] Dorothy Day did, and her incarnational inclusiveness was as broad and as deep as Weil's, for every needy person lying in a ditch, hungry and bleeding, was in her mind a reflection of Jesus. Her focus on Jesus' humanity meant that every person who wandered off the mean streets of Depression-filled New York City was a mirror image of Jesus himself. It is telling that the people whom she served were called "guests" and the run-down tenements that the Catholic Worker made into places for the guests to eat and sleep were called "hospitality houses." Like the Samaritan, Day's manner of attending to the needs of others focused first on their dignity as persons of intrinsic worth and only then on people in need of basic care.

It is difficult to be certain about the influences that caused her to embody the universal self, but a few do stand out, particularly her need for community. From her earliest experiences as a child, she expressed a deep desire for all others to know what gave her the deepest joy. In her autobiography, as we have noted, she writes: "I wanted life and I wanted the abundant life. I want it for others too."[18] Throughout her life, as she struggled in her own spiritual journey to unite physical with spiritual love—love that excludes no human joys, including the delights of the table and the pleasures of sex—she always brought others along with her. She cannot imagine an abundant life that would be hers alone. In another early passage in *The Long Loneliness*, she recalls: "I always felt the common unity of our humanity; the longing of the human heart is for communion."[19] Two key experiences that illustrate the breadth and depth of inclusive participation in the abundant life are her imprisonments in her early years and the birth of her daughter. Day was jailed twice—once with the suffragettes in 1917 and again a few years later, when she was unexpectedly swept up in a raid on prostitution. Both of these experiences were world-changing events for her, at both the physical and emotional levels of suffering. They encapsulated for her a quotation by Dostoevsky that she recited many times: "Love in action is a harsh and dreadful thing compared to love in dreams." She claimed she lost all sense of making a radical protest for women's right to vote, feeling only "darkness and desolation all around me," having no sense of her own identity: "I reflected on the desolation of poverty, of destitution, of sickness and sin. That I would be free after thirty days meant nothing to me. I would never be free again, never free when I knew that behind bars all over the world there were women and men, young girls and boys, suffering constraint, punishment, isolation and hardship for crimes of which all of us were guilty."[20] And later she makes the same point even more strongly: "Never would I recover from this wound, this ugly knowledge I had gained of what men were capable in their treatment of each other."[21] In a phrase very similar to Dostoevsky's, she gives the reason for the depth of her new knowledge: "It was one thing to be writing about these things . . . but it was quite another to experience it in one's own flesh."[22] Like Woolman and Weil, what kept her going in her "little by little" way of attending to others' needs was her identification with others in experiences of despair and desolation: "I was sharing, as I never had before, the life of the poorest of the poor, the guilty, the dispossessed."[23] After these imprisonments, she was never able to imagine the abundant life with any sense of exceptionalism, either for herself or for others like her. She had experienced mental and physical depravation, as well as disgust with herself as weak, guilty, and fearful, that would be permanent pieces of learning in diminishing her own ego, allowing the love of God to work through her for the alleviation of the suffering of others.

The rest of her life was a continuation, in small, daily steps, of the conversion experienced in her imprisonments. Life in the "hospitality" houses had eerie similarities to life in jail: it was noisy, smelly, crowded, with bad food, lumpy beds, and little privacy. The smell, one of the deepest and most primitive of our senses, captures the discomfort: "Above all the smell of the tenements, coming up from basements and areaways, from dank halls, horrified me. It is a smell like no other in the world and one never can become accustomed to it. . . . One's very clothes smell of it. It is not the smell of life, but the smell of the grave."[24] And yet, within these surroundings, Day found the abundant life, not only for herself but also for others.

Another experience, one of joy, was to be of equal importance to Day: the birth of her daughter, Tamar. The love of a mother for her child became Day's keystone in her journey toward fulfillment. Like Woolman, who in his sojourn with the Indians expressed his universal love for them with the analogy of a person's love for his only brother, Day's inclusive love for all began with the love of a mother for a child. "I found myself, a barren woman, the joyful mother of children."[25] This sentence, from the end of her autobiography, sums up what she claims is the most significant thing about life—community, a community identical with the sharing of food among all. As a mother loves her child, so, she claimed, should we love one another, which is surely not too radical an analogy for loving the neighbor *as yourself*. In a way similar to Weil, Day saw both suffering and joy as ways to God: imprisonment and motherhood are both openings, moving us beyond our own narrow selves toward a sense of human fulfillment that included all other beings. However it occurs, experiences that disorient us, wild spaces that open us up to alternative ways of imagining who we are in the scheme of things, are critical in acting in ways that counter accepted, conventional ways. Two examples illustrate the point. In Albert Camus's novel *The Plague*, in which Paris is mysteriously hit by a terrible infectious disease that is terrifying and decimating the population, one of the characters, a Dr. Rieux, fights it with all his expertise. He sees nothing exceptional in his behavior, exclaiming that he sees himself as "fundamentally connected with those around him."[26] As commentator Andrew Flescher notes of such people, Rieux's view of human nature is one of empathy toward others rather than of personal liberty.[27] Flescher compares Rieux's view of himself as similar to that of "Holocaust rescuers," those people who, during World War II, put their own lives in danger in order to hide Jews in their houses. It was, Flescher maintains, a choice between seeing human solidarity or one's own personal liberty as primary: "Rescuers are propelled by their distinctive way of looking at the world. They perceive vividly, while others perceive palely, or not at all, the responsibility to a common humanity."[28]

In sum, as we look at our three saints and the various ways they under-stood and lived out the universal self, we see how important is the basic assumption they acted on: the sense of the self as composed of, embodied in, dependent on, other beings, both human and nonhuman. This view is not "natural" to many (if any) of us; however, our goal is to accept or assume it to be "the way things are" and to practice it in daily, mundane, and lifelong ways. A version of it is endemic to Christianity (and different versions are found in most religious traditions); it is therefore, I believe, one of the central contributions that the religions can make to the current conversation on changing our minds so we can change the world.

The religions are by no means alone in their interest or contribution to this challenge. Research in brain science suggests compatible findings as well as support for religion's long and deep commitment to loving the neighbor as oneself.

CHANGING THE MIND TO CHANGE THE WORLD

We have been looking at the long, difficult process involved in thinking differently so that we might act differently. With the help of our three saints, I have traced the journey from the initial stage of the wild space of voluntary poverty through the opening it provides for attentiveness to the basic physical and emotional needs of others, toward the growth of a universal self, which is diametrically opposed to the narrow, selfish, parochial, limited view of human nature that our society promotes and that most of us live by. We have seen that alternative ways of living are possible, mainly through the lives of some outrageous people whom the world often writes off as crazy, infantile, or naive, but whom most of us, when we read about such people (and occasionally meet one), are convinced that they hold the key to both a more fulfilling personal life and a better alternative for our planet's flourishing. Are we wrong?

The religions of the world have been suggesting the alternative of the universal self for centuries, but now some scientific experiments in brain plasticity are supporting the significant idea that we may be hard-wired for altruism, an idea that used to be brushed aside as idealistic or merely sentimental.[29] While it is always unwise for religion to base its statements of faith on science, tempting though it may be, science and religion nonetheless ought not and need not present oppositional views of the world.[30] Unless one is willing to live in two worlds, a religious and a scientific one, one looks for "consonance," compatible or sympathetic connections, between the two. And fortunately, this is what contemporary science is offering to religion. For instance, the so-called creation story of the cosmos in which radical interrelationship and interdependence of all beings is now the scientific consensus, allowing for a fruitful conversation with the religions, which, as we have suggested, agree on the dictum of loving the neighbor as oneself. In other words, radical relationality at all levels, from the pull of gravity on the stars to the attraction of living creatures to one another, is an invitation for the religions to see what the sciences have to offer for the task of changing minds so as to change the world.

Studies in the plasticity of the brain—its ability to change under focused attention and to grow new neurons into the eighth decade of life—have opened up possibilities for developing altruistic behavior that the old positivist science, which claimed that brains are static, did not permit. "Science has shown that well-being and true happiness come from defining our 'selves' as part of an interconnected whole—connecting with others and with ourselves in authentic ways that break down the isolative boundaries of a separate self."[31] It is no surprise that brain science is moving in this direction, given the present consensus that the development of the cosmos is not a linear, simple, causal pattern of separate entities growing in isolation; rather, it is defined in macro and micro ways as thoroughly interrelated and interdependent, with all entities and processes interlocking in ways that boggle the imagination. While the separate self, the individualistic, static self fitted the eighteenth-century atomistic science of the Enlightenment, it is totally out of date today. Although brain-science research is still in its infancy, it is in line with the overall currents of other branches of the scientific community, in emphasizing the complexity, multidimensional causation, and fuzzy edges of all growth and development. "Our minds are created within relationship—including the one we have with ourselves."[32] Our very ability to think about thinking (what makes us human) means that we can become aware of awareness itself and thus pay attention to our own intentions. Moreover, such attention (as, for instance, in meditative practices) has been shown to actually change the neurons in the brain—thus we are not predetermined to be either solely at the mercy of our reptilian brain (the fight-or-flight response) or of our baser instincts of insatiable selfishness, but might be "naturally" open to altruism. "This would seem to mean that the brain is designed from the beginning to respond to specific emotional expressions—that is, empathy is a given of biology."[33] One must be careful at this juncture not to fall into the trap of a reverse biological determinism; namely, that we are innately loving, thus naively claiming that it is easy to be good. Just the opposite: our study of the saints has suggested that there is nothing more difficult than paying attention to the genuine needs of others; nonetheless, this chink in the former scientific wall of survival of the fittest, which supported a "dog-eat-dog" world, allows for other possibilities. All it need suggest is that alternatives are possible, that the so-called outrageous claims of the religions that one should love one's neighbor as oneself are not totally impossible for us, and that we might in fact be hard-wired for such self-development, given sufficient practice, training, and attention.

Two recent studies illustrate this conversation: *SuperCooperators: Altruism, Evolution, and Why We Need Each Other to Succeed*, by Martin A. Nowak, and *Braintrust: What Neuroscience Tells Us about Morality*, by Patricia S. Churchland. Nowak argues that mutation and natural selection are not sufficient to explain evolution: cooperation is the third component. "Cooperation was the principle architect of four billion years of evolution. Cooperation built the first bacterial cells, then higher cells, then complex multicellular life and insect superorganisms. Finally cooperation constructed humanity."[34] He believes that the conclusions of science and religion might meet, for he finds that "the teachings of world religions can be seen as recipes for cooperation," and comes up with a witty take on the dog-eat-dog view of evolution: "To succeed in life, you need to work together—pursuing the snuggle for existence, if you like— just as much as you strive to win the struggle for existence."[35] He suggests a number of mechanisms that promote cooperation at the human level, among them "indirect reciprocity," a somewhat cynical interpretation of the Golden Rule: if I am good to someone today, then someone might be good to me in the future, especially if one follows the advice, "Do good and talk about it."[36] Nonetheless, the crucial point for our purposes is that studies in the theory of mind have shown us that the human ability to infer motives and intentions from another's perspective promotes many possibilities for cooperation, not all them from sheer altruism, but nevertheless useful for the kind of collective action needed for the kind of problems he claims we face today, such as climate change.

Churchland's thesis sees the rapprochement of science and morality from a different base: not in cooperation as the third leg of evolution, but in the attachment of mammalian mothers and infants. "In brief, the idea is that attachment, underwritten by the painfulness of separation and the pleasure of company, and managed by intricate neural circuitry and neurochemicals, is the neural platform for morality."[37] She refutes the naturalistic fallacy— that an "ought" cannot be built on an "is"—and claims that morality *is* based on biology: "In the most basic sense . . . *caring* is a ground-floor function of nervous systems." By extension of the primordial urge to seek our own well-being, we move, with the help of neuropeptides such as oxytocin, from self-caring to other-caring. Just as the baby wails at its mother's absence, so also we respond to such issues as peace, resource distribution, and trade.[38] A path that begins with mammalian instinct to increase pleasure and reduce pain moves from the well-being of self to *caring* for offspring, mates, kin, and finally strangers and "others" (perhaps all flora and fauna?). Churchland writes, "Morality seems to me to be a natural phenomenon."[39] Does this make it less pertinent to religion? Must religion have a unique or total claim on morality? No, says Churchland, for she sees the world's religions as further extensions to her thesis: the Golden Rule is not universal; rather, it is the extension of her thesis to its epitome—loving all others as oneself is the goal of a morality that begins with caring for the nearest and dearest.

Both Nowak and Churchland open an important door for the possibility and promotion of a universal self. Rather than undermining the goal of the religions, they provide the most basic hope for it: we are programmed to be cooperative, to be caring. The universal self, it turns out, is not unnatural or alien to our most basic desires and needs. It is consonant with Augustine's famous line that our hearts are restless until they rest in God: *we are lovers from the beginning.* The "snuggle for existence" finds its ultimate fulfillment in the love of God. The work of such scientists gives us hope that the wild space of religion—radical relationality at all levels, togetherness rather than isolation—is indeed at the heart of human existence. Hence, policies that build on this base—even to deal with such enormous issues as climate change—are not as wild or crazy as they might seem. In other words, the saintly dream of a universal self is the very self that has been brewing in us from the time when the first cells joined together.

Churchland's attachment theory resonates with the compassion we have seen in our saints: it lies behind the kind of empathy between people that is the foundation of altruism. The attunement or affinity to her child's feelings that a good mother develops is the basis for her altruistic response to the deepest preverbal needs of the infant. Being empathetic, being able to "feel into" another's mental and emotional needs, lies at the base of our saints' response to the suffering of others. Woolman, Weil, and Day took every occasion to place themselves in physical contexts that would allow them to move out of their own narrow egotism into the sphere of feeling with others: living with the Indians, working in factories, eating and sleeping in New York slums. Thus another researcher into early relations between mothers and children extrapolates from his studies to argue "that the roots of morality are to be found in empathy, since it is empathizing with the potential victims—someone in pain, danger, or deprivation, say—and so sharing their distress that moves people to act to help them."[40] Such research suggests that attunement, feeling with others, provides a sense of "we-ness," clearly evident in infants and their sense of fuzzy edges between themselves and others, but available to human adults in a second naïveté; that is, the growth toward a universal self in saints. It is not surprising that the earliest and most basic human relationship—that of mother and infant—should be paradigmatic of our most fulfilling and mature relationship of which we are capable and that the saints illustrate for us. For such people, their ability to read emotions in other people, their extraordinary ability to *pay attention* to others, lies at the heart of their equally extraordinary action to alleviate another's needs.

THE RELIGIONS AND THE UNIVERSAL SELF

While we have seen a manifestation of attachment leading to compassion for others in Christian saints, we also see it in other religions: In Hinduism, we see the notion of *ahimsa* (refraining from doing harm); and in Islam, we see that mercy and compassion are foremost among God's attributes, and that the purpose of fasting during Ramadan is to help us sympathize with the hungry and destitute. It is especially prominent in Buddhism. As one commentator remarks, "Compassion is a key virtue in all major religions; but none more so than in Buddhism."[41] While the boundaries of the Western view of the self, as we have seen, are narrow, inward oriented, and individualistic, the same is not true of many forms of Eastern thinking, where the self has no intrinsic nature and where reality is seen not in terms of substance, but of process.

Since the self "is" not, having no predetermined, defined substance, it, like everything else in the universe, is the result of "dependent origination."[42] This is a complex and difficult notion to express, especially for Westerners, who are used to a simple, linear, cause-and-effect explanation of, say, the existence of a chair. Buddhist Thich Nhat Hanh, however, using the notion of "dependent origination," writes as follows.

> When we look at a chair, we see the wood, but we fail to observe the tree, the forest, the carpenter, or our own mind. When we meditate on it, we can see the entire universe in all its interwoven and interdependent relations in the chair. The presence of the wood reveals the presence of the tree. The presence of the leaf reveals the presence of the sun. The presence of the apple blossoms reveals the presence of the apple. Meditators can see the one in the many and the many in the one. . . . The chair is not separate. It exists only in its interdependent relations with everything in the universe. It *is* because all other things *are*.[43]

If even a chair can be described only by the most mind-boggling, complex, multidimensional set of networks of cause and effect, imagine attempting to understand the human self in a similar way. At the very least, we realize that the Western notion of the separate, individualistic self that determines its own direction, goal, and success is diametrically different. Science has increasingly shown us that the Buddhist notion of co-origination is much closer to reality as understood in postmodern cosmology than is the Western view. Moreover, the Buddhist view, like the scientific one, has interesting possibilities for our problem of moving from belief to action, from who we think we are to its embodiment in our daily lives. Because this alternative view includes others in its constitution—that is, the self *is* because all other things *are*—the basis for a "we" view of the self is built in. If I do not exist, grow, or prosper except in intricate patterns of radical relationality with all other beings, then I cannot see my well-being apart from that of others. The "self" is not, in this view, "naturally" altruistic in the sense that each of us *decides* to widen our circle of compassion; rather, each of us *is* because of everything else. Hence, my happiness or well-being cannot logically or actually be separate from that of the whole. Thus we once again return to the fundamental importance of the question of who we are in the scheme of things. If Westerners were to *internalize* this alternative view—one that is open, inclusive, fluid, and interdependent—in the same way that we have the individualistic view, so that it becomes the unacknowledged but effective basis for our decisions about how we live in the world, then it is obvious how differently we might evaluate things like carbon taxes on greenhouse emissions or taxes to support the health and education of all people, regardless of their ability to pay. In other words, the huge task of "changing our minds so we can change the world" must begin not only with different assumptions about who we are, but also with training, practice, and incentives to internalize the new view so it flows from our very beings.

For our saints and some Buddhists, the key to this transformation is described by our closest relationships: brothers, friendship, mother and child. As the Dalai Lama puts it: "Treat everyone as if they were a close friend."[44] Given the notion of "dependent origination" or "loving your neighbor as yourself," these analogies are not outrageous, for these dicta suggest that the distinction between self and others has been grossly exaggerated, especially in the West. The "undifferentiated self" lies at the base of empathy (feeling another's pain as one's own), which in turn is the emotion that is intrinsic to what Buddhists call the "great compassion" and Christians call the Golden Rule. Great compassion is the kind of love for others that not only wishes their suffering to be diminished but also involves the willingness to make it so oneself. "Great compassion is in fact an even deeper type of compassion, an undifferentiated type of compassion toward all beings. But it's not only that it's undifferentiated. There is a strong sense that 'I wish to protect.' It's engaged, it's taking on responsibility, taking on the burden."[45] Here we come to the heart of the matter: *empathy for others that includes the responsibility to act.* Just as a mother who hears her child's cry of pain responds immediately and totally to relieve it, or as friends lay down their lives for each other, so according to this alternative paradigm, we are called to respond from the heart, from the gut, from our very bodies. Thus, as Edith Wyschogrod concludes in her study of saints, altruism—compassion, renunciation, sacrifice, and generosity—is not "added on" to the saint; rather, the saint's corporate existence *is* these properties. The meaning of a saint's life in both its form and content is embodied: what these values mean and how they are expressed come together in the story of a life. Saintly lives do not communicate in propositional form, nor is their content what society might mean by "compassion" or "renunciation"; rather, form and content are both contained in the actual, lived particulars of the saint's mundane, embodied existence. "The saintly body acts as a signifier, as a carnal general that condenses and channels meaning, a signifier that expresses extremes of love, compassion, and generosity."[46] From the saints we learn the meaning of "altruism," and we see it performed in a way that is both more particular and more powerfully expressed than an essay on "ethics" could possibly convey. Like a mother's focused attention on the particular needs of her child, which provides the content and the impetus for her action—how to respond appropriately and the will to do it—so also the saint's response, based on attention to the other's real needs because of one's own self-emptying, flows from the saint's very being. It appears "natural" in that it comes from what the saint has become, and it is "physical" because it is not just a wish for someone's pain to be lessened but the willingness to lessen it oneself, with one's own body. The mother-child relationship is paradigmatic and primordial of the mature self, but now it is not based on the instinctual bond (evident in motherhood across the species), but on attention to the needs of others possible because of years of self-emptying practice that has allowed us to acknowledge the existence of something outside of our (narrow) selves. The mother-child bond is a metaphor for the universal self, the highest form of human behavior we can imagine.

In sum, from various sources, among them Christianity, Buddhism, and contemporary science, an alternative paradigm of the nature of the self is emerging. While it has particular characteristics in different religions—for Christianity, the life of Jesus is the model par excellence, for Buddhism, the notion of dependent origination is its basis, and for science, reality is at all levels interdependent—there are some overlapping similarities that converge so that the Dalai Lama, for instance, can speak of this alternative paradigm as not limited to religion: "Whether or not a person is a religious believer does not matter much. Far more important is that they be a good human being."[47] However, in the Dalai Lama's mind, this does not mean that living within the new paradigm will be easy, for the "spiritual revolution" involves "a radical reorientation away from our habitual preoccupation with self."[48] Indeed, it calls for "restraint," for "we cannot be loving and compassionate unless at the same time we curb our own harmful impulses and desires."[49] As we have seen with our saints (and as we know from our own spiritual journeys), this is probably the most difficult task that people and nations can undertake, for as the Dalai Lama insists, we do not merely increase our level of charitable giving or even spread around our excess wealth; "compassion" at the level we are discussing it is "the inability to bear the sight of another's suffering."[50] In line with our earlier discussion of the love between close friends, brothers, and mothers and infants, it is a level of empathy that intrinsically calls forth action to relieve another's pain. While this response may be "natural" in the sense that one sees glimmers of it in nature and in some of our most intimate relationships, nonetheless, "great compassion" or "loving the neighbor as yourself" takes enormous attention, effort, and practice.

The ideal of universal, unconditional, and undifferentiated (impersonal) love is surely, we say, far beyond most of us. So why bother? The Golden Rule and great compassion are certainly demanding at the personal level, and even more so at the public, but unless they can speak to issues of increasing human poverty and planetary destruction, they quickly become self-serving and merely another form of narcissism. Doing the minimum is acceptable in a society where the view of the self focuses on personal liberty (as the Western one does), but if our basic assumption about who we are is understood within the terms of the alternative paradigm of the compassionate, universal self, then the minimum is not acceptable. In fact, "doing the minimum" often results in mere band-aid methods of patching up disasters after they occur. The classic case of the Exxon oil spill in Alaska, which contributed to the

GDP by generating massive clean-up dollars, is a case in point, but so also are most forms of foreign aid, which attempt to feed starving populations after crop failures due to farming policies encouraging monocultures rather than sustainable practices. In other words, if the paradigm of our very selves should change so that the pain of "others" were not seen as merely a consequence of business as usual, but as a preventative responsibility—structuring society so that the planet's creatures are treated justly and its systems are sustainable— then minimum clean-up policies would be seen as anathema. Just as we take all precautionary measures to protect ourselves and our closest relatives from disaster as well as provide for their flourishing, so the same attitude should inform our public-policy decisions.

KENOTIC ACTION AT PERSONAL AND PUBLIC LEVELS

With these comments, we come to the last of our four-point process for moving from belief to action: the insistence that self-emptying attention to the needs of others not stop at the personal level of charity but include the public dimension as well. As we recall, Dorothy Day's whole action ideology was based on this premise: that the classic "works of mercy"—feeding the hungry, giving shelter to the homeless, and healing the sick—not stop with personal acts of generosity but include governmental policies, pacifism, and workers' unions. One of the oldest and most constant criticisms of religion by business and government institutions is that it "stick to religious matters," and not meddle in what should not be its concern. This convenient separation of the sacred and the secular has served the individualistic model of human life handsomely, and it continues to do so in our day when religious organizations are rebuked for supporting universal health care or the rights of workers to unionize.

One should not underestimate the difficulty of this last step, for as we have seen, not only is it challenging to change the mind when caring for even one needy individual, but when the focus moves to world justice and sustainability, its "foolishness" is all too evident. The few people who attempt to live this way—saints who do so only with the help of a deep prayer life or monks who meditate half the day—demonstrate adequate reasons why uniting the personal and the public is dismissed as unrealistic at best and fantastical at worst. But I would mention three reasons to the contrary: the personal and the public can both be included within this alternative paradigm of the universal self if (1) all planetary beings and systems are part of it; (2) distinctions are made among human beings so that matters of class, power, money, and "chance" are taken into account; (3) the paradigm is mundane and physical rather than merely vague, "spiritual," or future-oriented. Let us look in more detail at each of these.

Inclusion of All

This requirement raises two difficult issues. The first is the question of how inclusive it must be: can we love caterpillars as well as the climate in which they can flourish? We have noted that when it comes to ethical action—to whom are we responsible?—we have to ask how far the line must be moved. It used to be that one's obligations ended with concern for one's fellow human beings, with the closest ones getting the most attention, and the more distant ones, less. We recall that Woolman chastised his fellow Quakers for rationalizing large landholdings (and sometimes slaves to work the land) by their wish to provide legacies for their children. For Woolman, "universal love" demanded attention to the "least creature moving by [God's] love." Such concern for other species was rare in Woolman's day and still is for most people who, for instance, find a child's delight in patting a caterpillar strange and literally "infantile," observing that he or she will "grow out of it." Growing out of it—what E. O. Wilson calls our natural "biophilia," or love for other animals—is precisely what should *not* happen, for it is this experience of first naïveté regarding other species that we return to when in our second naïveté we acknowledge our kinship with all these others. But what about "loving" clean water, good land, and pure air—all the systems and forces that make our planet a viable environment for millions of different species? If the word *love* is not too strong for how we might feel about the land (ask any Native American what she or he feels about "the land"), then must it not also include those complex planetary systems that monitor the health and flourishing of the land we love? One of the most eye-opening pieces of information I have encountered during my study of the planet is the matter of nature's "free services," the trees that provide erosion control, suck up tons of greenhouse gases, give us new medicines from plants, provide us with air conditioning, as well as those hours spent hiking a forest trail. It is not only the number of board feet of lumber that trees provide, but countless other (and more basic) services without which we could not survive—or experience such exquisite levels of enjoyment. Surely our love, in the sense of respect for and conservation of these services, can know no bounds. It is not "silly" to love water and waste management if one "loves the earth" (as we all, rhetorically, frequently claim). Hence, the first requirement for universal love moving from the personal to the public is to widen the circle of concern so it knows no bounds. If we love the earth, then we must include policies and laws that protect it—and these cannot be merely personal acts of recycling, riding one's bicycle, or using china coffee cups (as worthy as all these things are). Rather, one must organize and fight for changes in the system that will protect the systems that protect us.

NECESSARY DISTINCTIONS AMONG HUMAN BEINGS

While the new ecological consciousness that we all need and celebrate underscores the oneness of all life—the vast network of interrelationships that bind us together in inextricable ways—it is also necessary to recognize that all human beings are *not* equal or the same. This issue involves two important questions: Who should we love most, our closest neighbors or more distant ones? And are all human beings equally at fault for our current ecological crisis? The first point asks, How "other" should the other be? Emmanuel Levinas puts the bar high: he calls the other "the 'orphan' or 'widow,' the color of whose eyes is not yet known."[51] Or, to summarize the point, "For saints, sympathy toward the Other is inversely proportional to how familiar the Other is."[52] Simone Weil agrees, and in some striking words she presses the point home that human love should be identical with God's "impersonal" love for all. "Our love should stretch as widely across all space, and should be as equally distributed in every portion of it, as is the very light of the sun. . . . Every existing thing is equally upheld in its existence by God's creative love. The friends of God should love him to the point of merging their love with his with regard to all things here below."[53] Weil extends this impersonal, anonymous criterion to loving the neighbor, for she claims that as in the good Samaritan, "the neighbor is a being of whom nothing is known, lying naked, bleeding, and unconscious on the road. It is a question of completely anonymous, and for that reason, completely universal love."[54] In other words, universal love for the world, patterned on God's impartial, inclusive love, must now become our daily, hourly practice, and we should ask God to increase this kind of love in us "as a famished child constantly asks for bread."[55] Weil's comments about this passionate, inclusive love for the world occur within the context of her criticism of the Catholic Church's leaving out the world—"those things that are outside visible Christianity"—but they are even more relevant to us today as we contemplate the limits of our love for a planet in dire need of our total, informed, and active love. Such a perspective—loving the world through God's eyes—is certainly a lofty goal. Its relevance, regardless of whether it is reachable, reminds us once again of the importance of what Woolman calls seeing with "single" vision; that is, getting the ego out of the center so that paying attention to something other than oneself (and one's nearest and dearest) is possible. The individualist paradigm does not suffer from a lack of love; rather, it suffers from the direction of its love, not simply to the needy person whose plight makes headlines in the news or goes viral on the Internet, but inclusive of the less attractive neighbor the color of whose eyes is not known, or who (which) does not even have eyes, such as a threatened river about to be dammed to provide water to keep lawns green. Some of the most difficult issues we face concern prioritizing love to close or distant neighbors, and considerable nuanced reflection will be necessary as we decide how to allocate scarce resources. For instance, should one send one's own child to an exclusive, expensive private school when the same amount of money could support four needy children in less spacious institutions? Or should foreign food aid focus on feeding programs for those presently starving or on seed distribution to encourage food sustainability over the long haul?

The second question that making necessary distinctions among human beings involves is responsibility for both past ecological destruction and future remedies. For example, do not the well-off, Western counties that are behind most of the current growth of greenhouse gases bear greater responsibility for remedial actions to stabilize and reduce such growth than do the poorer, developing countries that contributed far less? This is at present one of the paralyzing issues facing international negotiations. It is tempting for the wealthy nations to use the ecological mantra "we are all one" to avoid taking the lead in greenhouse reductions; moreover, it makes rational sense, since China and India, for instance, two countries with huge populations poised to dump massive amounts of gases into the atmosphere, "must" be part of the solution. Nonetheless, the rhetoric (and reality) of the oneness of all humanity should not be used as a cover to impede necessary and painful steps that Western countries must take to put the process of climate control in action. The "essentialism" of universal oneness has been used many times to block needed social change, as in the case of different kinds of oppression that different women undergo—there is a world of difference between the power and privileges of women like myself and one of my sisters shrouded under a burqa. Differences of class, gender, access to health care and education, sexual orientation, race—not to mention chance and luck—*make* a difference, such a huge difference, in fact, that one must be careful mouthing the comforting words of "oneness." In particular, on the issue of vast differences in wealth and in responsibility for climate change, people like myself should be the primary audience for books like this one: it is only right that those of us who venture "solutions" to planetary problems speak first to ourselves. There is certainly a place for underscoring the marvelous and world-changing information from the sciences of our radical interdependence with all life-forms—and in fact it forms the backbone of arguments, such as the one I have been putting forth in this book, for the necessity of a planetary ethic—but when one gets to the point of assigning roles in such an ethic, empirical, sociological, cultural, and biological differences should be front and center.

Hence, two insights should function under this rubric of distinctions among human beings—that our nearest and dearest are not our only or perhaps main responsibility, and that those of us who have caused the most damage must lead the way to repair it.

A MUNDANE, PHYSICAL PARADIGM

High-flying rhetoric about good intentions, future plans, and anecdotal evidence of charitable acts to "needy cases" are rampant when it comes to putting beliefs into action. Religions are especially adept at such maneuvers to avoid hard-headed, pragmatic, systemic changes in behavior that will actually change the direction of the wealth-poverty split or the deterioration of the planet's health. In fact, because religious rhetoric is so high, its abysmal performance is often both more painful for those who care and more susceptible to ridicule for those who wish to criticize. However, the best of the religious traditions make significant contributions to the putting ideals into action. Two come to mind—one from Buddhism and another from Christianity. The Buddhist notion of dependent origination, discussed above, is an invaluable insight in the effort to include all levels in any action plan: since all things *are* only because of all other things, nothing can be left out, and it certainly cannot stop at the personal, ignoring the public and planetary. Inclusion is not, therefore, simply a nice spiritual ideal of "loving" others; rather, it claims that all change of any sort occurs at the most mundane, physical, elementary, and basic levels. There can be no break between the spiritual (concerned with religion) and the secular (concerned with basic survival needs). Christianity offers yet another crucial insight: incarnationalism. While Christianity has often been interpreted in a dualistic, spirit-versus-flesh fashion, the saints we have been discussing certainly defy that view. The belief that "God became man" (however one might understand that) at the very least underscores the fact that the physical life and needs of human beings are a central issue for Christians. For those who accept the interpretation of the incarnation we have seen in our saints, this belief has been the foundation for their extraordinary attention to feeding the hungry, healing the sick, and providing shelter for the homeless. Taken together—dependent origination and the incarnation—they form a powerful impetus for action policies that are broad and deep, including the basic needs of all creatures as well as the systems that support the means to supply those needs. For instance, the iconic parable of the good Samaritan has implications not only for merciful actions to individuals in need but also for the establishment of a universal medical care system. "Love" as understood in most religions becomes, at the public level, "justice"; in fact, it is probably a better term to use at all levels, since "love" has been so sentimentalized and individualized that it often serves as a means for avoiding justice.

If we seek a "change of mind," then in order to change action, we must understand how thorough that change must be. Robert Egan claims that one cannot overestimate the depth of change that is necessary. To "change the mind" is literally to change the person: "This consciousness . . . is something that has to be *developed* socially. It is uncovered or constructed through tracts and novels, speeches and assemblies, family arguments and . . . through thousands of small acts of personal integrity, reflection, judgment, risk, and commitment, that then, somehow, become the basis for public acts. It requires, in other words, that people change their minds."[56] In other words, "changing the mind" is like getting a *new* one. We have seen this process in our saints: the lifelong, gradual process embodied in a million small actions and reflections that eventually made them the people they became. Dorothy Day summarizes this process in her mantra "little by little," her humble acknowledgment that she was not born a saint nor changed by showy acts, but accomplished what she did (which she always claimed was "little") by hard work and determination. "And . . . the older I get the more I see that life is made of many steps, and they are very small ones, not giant strides. I have 'kissed the leper' not once but twice—consciously—yet I cannot say I am much better for it."[57] Likewise, Woolman agonized daily over the "next step" he was to take, turning to the "inner light" to discern his next action. As one commentator on the moral life muses, "We stand a fair chance of becoming Eichmanns ourselves if we do *not* make the assumption that we are, from the start, accountable for our character."[58] This is certainly not to assume that we determine who we become, but it is a reminder of what the Dalai Lama calls *kun long*, the "disposition" that drives and inspires our action, or "the individual's overall state of heart and mind," which is commensurate with who one is.[59] Thus what we see in an Eichmann or a Dorothy Day is the personal dimension of what became the policies of the Third Reich (ending in the Holocaust) or the movement for pacifism during World War II. Personal dispositions become public policies and protests.

Hence, when a society wishes to "change its mind" concerning such issues as poverty and climate change, one thing that must happen is that "thousands of small acts of personal integrity, reflection, judgment, risk, and commitment" become the basis for public acts. This is certainly not the only thing that needs to be done, but it is, I think, one of the special tasks that the religions should undertake. Which is why, for instance, when a change is needed in the model of who we are in the scheme of things—a change from the individualistic to the universal model of the self—small actions count. Thus our three saints, who interpreted the main issue of their time to be injustice caused by differences in wealth, which limited basic services for all, undertook voluntary poverty as a means of clearing their minds so that change could happen. This was the wild space that, when practiced on a daily basis, kept their vision clear, making actions possible at both the personal and the public levels.

Finally, as I have stressed that changing the mind to change the world is a mundane, physical problem, I need to mention the importance of one feature of most religions—their vast power at both the local *and* global levels. For instance, "roughly 85 percent of people on the planet belong to one of 10,000 or so religions" and "adherents of the three largest traditions—Christianity, Islam, and Hinduism—account for about two-thirds of the global population today."[60] Many have noted that while religions do not command armies, their moral powers of persuasion can be immense, as the lives of people like Mohandas Gandhi, Martin Luther King Jr., and the Dalai Lama illustrate. In addition, not only do the religions of the world provide meaning to people's deepest desires and fears, but their sheer numerical presence, material assets such as property, and their ability to build social capital through building communities is immense. It is almost as if the religions of the world provide a spiritual Internet, with outlets in every corner of the world. Should these numbers and powers of influence be marshaled on the side of restraint in terms of energy use, the results could be huge. The "hardware" (religious buildings) and "software" (the message of restraint) are already in place. All that is lacking is the *will* to put these assets to work. When people say, as many do these days, that they are "spiritual" but not "religious," perhaps what they mean is that the platform (the buildings) is already in place and what is needed is new programs for running the vast, complex network that constitute "the religions." I am suggesting in these pages that one feature of the new program for the religions is the message of restraint in using the world's energy, so that the planet may flourish.

Summary: The Process of Sainthood

Having looked at the stories of three saints in chapter 3, I have attempted in the last two chapters to unravel the process by which they became who they were—three remarkable "universal selves" who through voluntary poverty and paying attention to the needs of others developed a form of both personal and public action that might serve as a model for us as we seek a way to move from the belief that something needs to be done about the world's crises to putting such belief into practice. However, these daunting stories of Woolman's impeccable integrity, Weil's sacrifice of her health, and Day's battle with the miseries of poverty can be off-putting, to say the least. My initial reaction fifty years ago, when I first read them, was to dismiss them as irrelevant and/or impossible. As we come to the close of our study, we must raise these responses for consideration: Are they irrelevant to us and/or impossible for us? There are at least two schools of thought about the influence of saints on the rest of us: an absolute one and a relative one. The absolute one is held by Emmanuel Levinas, who proposes that our response to the "Other" must be primary, total, and without qualification. Edith Wyschogrod describes this position as the saint's "ethics of excess," which is a recommendation not just for saints but also for society in general. "The subscriber to the 'ethics of excess' is morally required to respond to the imperative force of the Other's cry for help before attending to his or her own welfare. If this Other is truly 'Other'—naked, destitute, and vulnerable—then this is a cry that shall never cease, and the subscriber shall remain eternally bound."[61] In other words, an ethics of excess has no limits: our responsibility to the other is infinite. Needless to say, this position is a hard sell and one that is very difficult to imagine transformed into public policy.

The other view, described by John Hick, claims that our lives and the lives of saints are continuous but not the same: saints are not "a different sort of being, traveling a different road, but are simply persons who are farther ahead of us on the same road."[62] William James is the classic exponent of this view, describing saints as "impregnators of the world, vivifiers and animators of potentialities of goodness which but for them would lie forever dormant."[63] What starts with an experiment by one or a few outstanding people can, with time and familiarity, become accepted as commonplace. One thinks, for instance, of the "absurd" battle by the early suffragettes for women's right to vote or the equally "absurd" notion in our day that animals and even trees might have "rights." Who knows what policies can develop "little by little," as many begin to follow the lead of the few? It is also the experience of most who read the lives of the saints that their stories cause the reader to turn back to his or her own life and question what might be possible. A few wise people recommend the "relative" way: Confucius said "It does not matter how slow you go, as long as you don't stop," while T. S. Eliot suggests that "only those who will risk going too far can possibly find out how far one can go."[64] And the Dalai Lama says, "I do not believe everyone can or should be like Mahatma Gandhi and live the life of a poor peasant. Such dedication is wonderful and greatly to be admired. But the watchword is 'As much as we can'—without going to extremes."[65]

With either of these positions—the absolute or the relative one—the question of doing *something* presses us. As we have noted before, our time is characterized by paralysis: on the climate issue, for instance, we *know* that something must be done, but we simply do not take action (or much action) at either the personal or public level. We need to acknowledge, as one character in Camus's *The Plague* does concerning the crisis that the plague has made obvious, "This business is everyone's business." Similarly, the issue facing us today is that climate change is everyone's business, but we refuse to acknowledge it. We have come to the place where we need to take a stand, but we do not. In commenting on the Holocaust rescuers, those people who opened their doors to strangers in dire need of help, Philip Hallie writes, "There are only people who accept responsibly, and those who do not. . . . A person either opens the door or closes it in the face of a victim."[66] The sense of urgency is not misplaced either for those people during World War II who decided to hide Jews from the Nazis or for us today who dither "as the world burns" (quite literally). *Our time has come.* Wyschogrod claims that saintly time is "the time that is left": "The saintly future is the-time-that-is-left in which to alleviate suffering before it is too late."[67] Is it too late for us?

In conclusion, I have been claiming in these pages that the religions have a special role to play in the climatic and economic crises of our day. It is not the only task that needs to be done, but it is a crucial one: opening the window to another way of being in the world. The religions are about alternatives, alternatives to accepted and dangerous or oppressive models of how to live that are stifling both personal and planetary flourishing. The religions are about disorienting, surprising, and often countercultural models that at first may seem absurd or ridiculous or impossible, but upon reflection often turn out to be effective and fulfilling in unexpected ways. Thus the use of parables, the lives of saints, paradox, and extravagance in order to touch that wild space in all of us that says, "Things do not have to be this way. They could be different. They could be better." Sometimes it takes a painful experience with poverty or some other kind of suffering, or a stranger's point of view that is different from the conventional ones, or an experience of exquisite beauty or joy—whatever upsets the expected and the ordinary and raises our hope that life is not "just one damn thing after another" but that a different and better way of living, both at personal and public levels, is possible. It is as if the conventional models of how we live—and must live—create a blind spot, so we literally can't *see* any other way. I have noted how important the sight metaphor has been for our saints. Woolman insisted that being able to see with the single eye allowed him to recognize the needs of others and not just his selfish desires; and Weil said that paying attention to others was both rare and illuminating, putting aside our own egos so that we can really listen to someone else. One of the key contributions the religions make to our current crisis of denial and inaction in regard to climate change is the encouragement to think outside the box, to imagine a world in which we sought satisfaction not in narrow, selfish ways, but through the interdependence of all life-forms as they interact to supply the needs of all. We have seen research coming from the life sciences suggesting that mutual dependence, cooperation, attachment—and in human beings, altruism and compassion—are factors in the cosmic scheme every bit as much as are "the survival of the fittest" and the "selfish gene." The religions suggest we try the "other way"—the way of extravagant generosity, of willed sacrifice for the vulnerable, of recognizing radical interdependence, of self-emptying—since it is no more absurd (in fact, less so) than the selfish, individualistic model of human existence behind market capitalism. The philosopher Ernst Bloch said a map of the world without a "Utopia" on it is not worth much. Indeed. Utopias are not maps as real places, but as incentives to live *as if* they were possible—at least approximations of them are possible. Since we always live within models, is it better to live within one that moves us in the direction of narrow, mean individualism or one that encourages us to think and act in ways that promote individual human fulfillment within the context of the planet's flourishing?

In other words, let us endeavor to be "saints," responding to Dorothy Day's caution that we not let ourselves off the hook.

NOTES

[1] Erich Heller, *The Disinherited Mind: Essays in Modern German Literature and Thought* (Cleveland: World, 1961), 211.

[2] A major discussion of this important epistemological issue—the role of language in our interpretations of reality—is beyond the scope of our concerns here. However, I have in many other publications laid out my perspective on these matters. See, for instance, the following: *Metaphorical Theology* (Minneapolis: Fortress Press, 1982), chaps. 1–4; *Models of God* (Minneapolis: Fortress Press, 1987), chaps. 1–3; *Super, Natural Christians* (Minneapolis: Fortress Press, 1997), chaps. 4–5; *The Body of God* (Minneapolis: Fortress Press, 1993), chaps. 2–3; *Life Abundant* (Minneapolis: Fortress Press, 2001), chaps. 4–5; *A New Climate for Theology* (Minneapolis: Fortress Press, 2008), chap. 6.

[3] For a more thorough treatment of the subject-object and subject-subject epistemologies, see McFague, *Super, Natural Christians*, chaps. 4–5.

[4] For further elaboration, see McFague, *A New Climate for Theology*, chap. 3.

[5] The scientific research is wide-ranging, but here I will only mention a few books among the many mind and brain studies that show the mind can change the brain and change it in more altruistic directions: Sharon Begley, *Train Your Mind, Change Your Brain: How a New Science Reveals Our Extraordinary Potential to Transform Ourselves* (New York: Ballantine, 2007); Daniel J. Siegel, *Mindsight: A New Science of Personal Transformation* (New York: Bantam, 2010); Daniel Goleman, *Emotional Intelligence* (New York: Bantam, 2006); Jeremy Rifkin, *The Empathetic Civilization: The Race to Global Consciousness in a World in Crisis* (New York: Tarcher/Penguin, 2009); Frans de Waal, *The Age of Empathy: Nature's Lessons for a Kinder Society* (New York: Harmony, 2009); Paul Zak, *The Moral Molecule: The Source of Love and Prosperity* (New York: Three Rivers, 2009). The writings of His Holiness the Dalai Lama have made use of this research from a Buddhist perspective. See, for instance, *Ethics for a New Millennium* (New York: Riverhead, 1999).

[6] The Journal of John Woolman and a Plea for the Poor (New York: Corinth Books, 1961), 142.

[7] Ibid., 157.

[8] Ibid., 152.

[9] Ibid., 8–9.

[10] Ibid., 214.

[11] Simone Weil, *Waiting for God*, trans. Emma Craufurd (London: Routledge and Kegan Paul, 1951), 149.

[12] Ibid, 147.

[13] Ibid., 147–48.

[14] Simone Weil, *First and Last Notebooks*, trans. Richard Rees (London: Oxford University Press, 1970), 244.

[15] Weil, *Waiting for God*, 197.

[16] Ibid., 147.

[17] Robert Coles, "In This Pagan Land," *America*, November 11, 1972, 380.

[18] Dorothy Day, *The Long Loneliness* (New York: Harper and Row, 1952), 44.

[19] Ibid., 31.

[20] Ibid., 89.

[21] Ibid., 90.

[22] Ibid.

[23] Ibid., 120.

[24] Ibid., 58.

[25] Ibid., 317.

[26]Quoted in Andrew M. Flescher, *Heroes, Saints, and Ordinary Morality* (Washington, DC: Georgetown University Press), 124.

[27]Ibid.

[28]Ibid., 153.

[29]See n. 5.

[30]Much has been written on this issue, including my own contributions: see, for instance, *The Body of God*, chap. 3; and *Life Abundant*, chap. 3. For a somewhat dated, but still classic discussion of the issue, see Ian G. Barbour, *Religion in an Age of Science* (San Francisco: Harper and Row, 1990), chap. 1.

[31]Siegel, Mindsight, 259.

[32]Ibid., 86.

[33]Goleman, *Emotional Intelligence*, 103.

[34]Martin A. Novak with Roger Highfield, *SuperCooperators: Altruism, Evolution, and Why We Need Each Other to Succeed* (New York: Free Press, 2011), 280.

[35]Ibid., 273, xvii.

[36]Ibid., 56, 61.

[37]cia S. Churchland, *Braintrust: What Neuroscience Tells Us abut Morality* (Princeton: Princeton University Press, 2011), 16.

[38]Ibid., 191, 8.

[39]Ibid., 191.

[40]See Martin L. Hoffman, "Empathy, Social Cognition, and Moral Action," in *Moral Behavior and Development: Advances in Theory, Research, and Applications*, ed. W. Kurtines and J. Gerwitz (New York: John Wiley and Sons, 1984).

[41]Begley, *Train Your Mind, Change Your Brain*, 184.

[42]See the discussion of this concept from the Madhyamika ("middle way") school of Buddhist philosophy in the Dalai Lama, *Ethics for a New Millennium*, 36–40.

[43]Thich Nhat Hanh, *The Sun My Heart: From Mindfulness to Insight Meditation* (Berkeley: Parallax, 1988), 90.

[44]Dalai Lama, *Ethics for New Millennium*, 236

[45]Alan Wallace, as quoted by Siegel, *Mindsight*, 240–41.

[46]Edith Wyschogrod, *Saints and Postmodernism: Revisioning Moral Philosophy* (Chicago: University of Chicago Press), 52.

[47]Dalai Lama, *Ethics for a New Millennium*, 19.

[48]Ibid., 24.

[49]Ibid., 26.

[50]Ibid., 64.

[51]Quoted by Flescher, *Heroes, Saints, and Ordinary Morality*, 205.

[52]Ibid.

[53]Weil, *Waiting for God*, 97.

[54]Ibid., 98.

[55]Ibid., 99.

[56]Robert Egan, "Discernment, Cultural Analysis, and Social Transformation: On Letting Love Make History," (address to the Ignatian Spirituality Institute, Portland, Oregon, August 1987), 15.

[57]Dorothy Day, Loaves and Fishes (Maryknoll, NY: Orbis, 1997), 84

[58]Flescher, *Heroes, Saints, and Ordinary Morality*, 316.

[59]Dalai Lama, *Ethics for a New Millennium*, 30.

[60]Gary T. Gardner, *Inspiring Progress: Religions Contributions to Sustainable Development* (New York: W.W. Norton, 2006), 49.

[61]Flescher, *Heroes, Saints, and Ordinary Morality*, 206.

[62]John Hick, *An Interpretation of Religion: Human Responses to the Transcendent* (New Haven: Yale University Press, 1989), 307.

[63]William James, *The Varieties of Religious Experience* (New York: Penguin, 1982), 358.

[64]Quoted in Flescher, *Heroes, Saints, and Ordinary Morality*, 235.

65 Dalai Lama, *Ethics for a New Millennium*, 178.

66 Philip Hallie, *Lest Innocent Blood be Shed*, quoted by Flescher, *Heroes, Saints, and Ordinary Morality*, 138.

67 Wyschogrod, *Saints and Postmodernism*, 256.

6

"It's Not About You"

Kenosis as a Way to Live

Introduction

When we turn from the stories of some remarkable people—in fact, saintly people—to their relevance for our own life and times, we are in for a culture shock. The world that greets us scarcely appreciates or even understands the meaning of the words *restraint*, *self-sacrifice*, *give-and-take*, *limitation*, and so forth. From their understanding of the self as universal, we move to a view of human life as radically individualistic and even narcissistic.

"It's Not About You" is the title of an op-ed column written by David Brooks, a columnist for the *New York Times*. It returns us to our opening chapter, titled "But Enough About Me," as it outlines the contemporary American Dream, which "preaches the self as the center of a life."[1] In these pages so far, we have been considering two central paradigms for living the good life: One advises developing the self from the inside, with the goal of realizing the limitless possibilities that lie within us and of reaching our dream of self-fulfillment, while the other view, the universal self, is very different. The first view expresses, as Brooks suggests, the "whole baby-boomer theology," a gospel of radical individualism in which one should "follow *your passion*, chart *your* own course, march to the beat of *your* own drummer, follow *your* dreams and find *yourself*."[2] Unfortunately, the 2011 graduates did not enter a world devised to fulfill their lofty goals, and they, encouraged by "helicopter parents" who hovered over all their decisions and congratulated them merely for "trying," were scarcely prepared for the bitter realities of a world in financial recession and planetary decay. Moreover, as Brooks claims, genuine fulfillment seldom comes from the conscious pursuit of happiness. As he suggests, if you read the biography of someone you admire, the things that impress you are not what "they did to court happiness—[rather, it is] the things they did that were arduous and miserable, which sometimes cost them friends and aroused hatred."[3] How strange this seems! Here is a writer for the *New York Times* who claims that the narcissistic American dream

141

of self-fulfillment should be "outer" not "inner" directed. He notes that "most of us are egotistical and most are self-concerned most of the time, but it's nonetheless true that life comes to a point only in those moments when the self dissolves into some task." He ends his comments with a riff on Matthew 10:39: "The purpose in life is not to find yourself. It's to lose yourself."[4]

How odd that the seemingly esoteric, archaic notion of kenosis, of self-emptying, is infiltrating even the corridors of the *New York Times*! What is happening? Are the threads weaving the fabric of the American (and now worldwide) gospel of self-realization through the hoarding of material goods fraying at the edges? Are people beginning to realize that "Enough really is enough" and that more is not better? Are the signs coming to us from the financial meltdown and the warming of the Arctic beginning to question not only the possibility of the growth of the GDP as the barometer of well-being but also its satisfactions? Is the age-old question of how to live the good life sending us back to Aristotle, the poets, and the religious traditions for insight into the most fundamental questions of human existence: Why are we here? Who are we in the scheme of things? What should we be doing? Are we finally open to alternatives to the accepted, conventional, and presumably "natural" model of human life as centered on the individual self? Does "It's Not About You" begin to intrigue us, and are we, at last ready to consider an alternative?

In the last several chapters of this book, we have been looking at the lives of three extraordinary people—people we have called saints—who have written in large letters and shouted in our ears that such an alternative is a possibility: a life fulfilled by responding to a call from outside the self to give the self away. Their lives suggest that fulfillment does not come about through expressing a developed inner self; rather, it is a slow process of growth in response to a call, a need, a cry, from the world. In the process of this gradual development, we become who we are and, strangely, find it not only good for some tiny fragment of the world, but also good for ourselves. Woolman, Weil, and Day, through accepting the wild space of poverty, experienced sufficient disorientation from the bonds of self-centeredness, that they were able to pay attention to something other than themselves, gradually becoming "universal selves" who responded appropriately to "who they are" (creatures radically interdependent with all other life-forms) by helping these others flourish. In other words, they did not fulfill a paradigm that came down from heaven de novo but, through a complex process of responding to glimmers of a better way, created the alternative pattern, even as they discovered it. Woolman's experience of killing the robin, Weil's intimations that everyone should eat the same rations, and Day's bonding with the prostitutes in prison—these ordinary events became the tiny openings that allowed for a different response, not of indifference or rationalization, but of a willingness to offer *themselves*, their bodies and their material goods, so that others might live and flourish. As we shall see, this alternative paradigm, while it does not seem instinctual or "natural" to human beings (given all the evidence to the contrary in wars, genocide, rape, pillage, greed, and ordinary selfishness), is nonetheless found not only in these strange, countercultural saints we have been studying, but also in evolution and in most religious traditions. In other words, it is both a "fact" and a "fiction": It is a fact in that we see rudimentary forms of it in the evolution of the cosmos as well as in the kenotic tendencies in most wisdom traditions, but it is a "fiction" in that it must be created as well as discovered. It must be intuited, claimed, elaborated, and lived out in order to make a difference in the way the world functions. We now realize that our species has reached such a size and power that it has the possibility of steering this paradigm toward good or toward evil.

In this chapter, we will look at two major issues associated with this alternative way of living: First, at the glimmers, intimations, and signs of the model in the world, including evolution, and second, at its nature and characteristics in one religious tradition, Christianity. I will be building on the insights from previous chapters, attempting to paint a picture of this alternative with sufficient scope and detail to offer it as a response to the dominant, self-centered one.

KENOSIS IN THE WORLD

How different are the two paradigms for abundant living that we are considering, and does it matter whether we follow one or the other? I want to suggest that the difference between the two is huge, that in many ways they are polar opposites and that lives lived on the basis of the assumptions underlying the two patterns would be substantially dissimilar. They each rest on a set of basic assumptions that, while seldom clearly articulated by most of us, nonetheless rule our behavior in complex and subconscious ways. One of them assumes that reality is structured around self-centered individuals, while the other assumes a communal base. But this generalization does not get at the heart of the matter. The individualistic model is basically positive, upbeat, and hopeful, recommending, as Brooks suggests, "rapturous talk of limitless possibilities,"[5] beginning with the automobile of American dreams, which comes outfitted with every imaginable electronic gadget. Within this model, one sees the world as a playing field where each one wants to be the winner and the winner takes all. The communal model, however, is basically sober, recognizing the necessity not only of restraint but, more profoundly, of sacrifice, and—horrors of horrors—even of death. In fact, the communal model acknowledges that only through restraint, sacrifice, and death can the system function, and that the individual, all individuals, are willy-nilly part of the system. Life only comes through death, according to the most basic premise of evolution, with this reality operative at the most primitive level of organisms, all the way to the stark statements of a religion such as Christianity. This faith claims that death, the crucifixion, must precede new life, the resurrection, both for the pioneer of the tradition, Jesus of Nazareth, as well as for all his disciples. The following statement suggesting such continuity makes the point. "It is interesting to put side by side [Jürgen] Moltmann's statement that self-giving is 'God's trinitarian essence, and, is therefore the mark of all his works' with Fran de Waal's statement that 'aiding others at a cost or risk to oneself is widespread in the animal world.'"[6]

KENOSIS: A BROAD-BASED NOTION

Kenosis is a broad-based notion, seen in rudimentary (and mainly unconscious) forms in nature, but it is also evident in a wide range of human activities, including not only religion but also artistic endeavors, scholarship, peace movements, humanistic ethics of the common good, interfaith discussions, and so forth. Kenosis is the recognition that restraint, openness, humility, respect for otherness, and even sacrifice (diminishment and death) are part of life *if* one assumes that individual well-being takes place within political and cosmic well-being. Thus an artist "listening" to the material with which she is working, a scholar open to alternative interpretations of an idea, a parent paying attention to the budding independence of a child, a panel attempting to find justice in reconciliation rather than punishment, and a peace movement disciplining its members to overcome violence with restraint are all instances of kenosis, broadly interpreted. It is an attitude that respects and pays attention to "otherness," whether it be found in a sculptor studying a piece of wood in order to intuit its own potential, or in an NGO dedicated to finding a peaceful way between violence and defeat. It is an interfaith discussion in which the participants are interested not in proselytizing but in learning the unique insights from another religious tradition. It is a father pulling back from punishing a wayward son to hear his side of the story. It is a First Nations person sacrificing overfishing a salmon stream so that fish will be available for "seven generations."

None of this is strange or novel: it is what people do all the time when they see themselves as responsible to and fulfilled by a community (from a family to the planet), rather than as responsible only to the individual self. Kenosis manifests itself in attitudes of curiosity, delight, interest, and openness about the world in which we have mysteriously been "set down" and left to figure out what to do. It is an attitude significantly different from the model of radical individualism, which promotes certainty, absolutism, imperialism, and violence. Kenosis does not know but asks questions, beginning from a stance of appreciation and awe for the wonder of being a wide-awake human being, conscious that we did not create ourselves, and that we must discover who we are. It claims that "another way is possible," from either passive acceptance or violent aggression; it claims that at various levels and by various forms of self-emptying (limiting the ego's selfish desires), space is given for others to flourish, flourishing that not only is good for them but, in a strange way, is good for oneself as well. Kenosis is not sackcloth and ashes, depriving the self of all worldly goods and pleasures for personal purification or salvation; rather, it is a hardheaded, sober analysis of the way things are; that is, the recognition that "something other than oneself is real" and not only deserves space but requires and demands it as well. But what is recognized as reality—and hence the way things must be—also becomes the basis for one's own fulfillment, for, as we heard David Brooks suggest earlier, "The purpose of life is not to find yourself. It is to lose yourself."

If, as evolution insists, every individual, from the atom to the human being, is composed entirely from "others," if neither an atom nor a human being is an individual in the sense of being the cause of their own existence, but has been gradually constituted and composed over eons to become what it is—a process so complex, interdependent, and intricate that no words can even begin to express—then it is self-evident that no individual at any level can flourish or even exist apart from the whole. This recognition, let alone internalization, is a profoundly difficult task for us human beings to come to, in part because the other paradigm, the individualistic one, is the warp and woof of our daily lives at every level, including family life, business practice, advertising, sports, and often religion itself, which preaches a gospel of individual salvation in another world. *Hence, what I am suggesting is that "kenosis," far from being an esoteric, ancient religions practice of self-negation is, in fact, deep within the very processes that created the "individuals" we now think exist by and for themselves.* Many religions, as well as evolutionary science, suggest this continuity, which I will now attempt to sketch—following its intimations in the natural world and its flowering in religious traditions, especially Christianity.

A question as we begin: Why is it important to note the continuity of this sequence of death and new life throughout all our experience of living on planet earth? It is important so that we might have a holistic interpretation of how to live well. If it were the case that the major religious traditions held a totally different interpretation of right living from all the rest of our experience—scientific, psychological, personal, sociological, artistic, and economic—one would wonder about their assumptions and be forced, if a believer, to embrace two conflicting ideologies. But we are discovering that this is not the case. We do not have to park our heads at the chapel door as we enter our religious sanctuaries; rather, we are invited to take our whole being, mind and heart, into the way of life recommended and practiced by those we call "saints."

Kenosis and the Natural World

While it is not necessary to embrace Richard Dawkins's positivistic assertion that "the selfish gene" is the only force in evolution, neither is it appropriate to suggest that kenosis is a "natural" process. Ecologist Holmes Rolston helpfully sets the ground rules for a discussion of intimations of altruism in evolution. "There is a sense in which there can no more be self-emptying in nature than there can be selfishness. Both are equally category mistakes, projecting human possibilities onto a nature incapable of either. Nature, including botanical and zoological nature, just *is*. There is neither good nor bad about such an amoral nature."[7] I wish to explicitly and firmly divorce my argument for the "continuity" of kenotic tendencies from any suggestion that nature is "naturally" moral, but I would likewise object to the assertion that nature is "naturally" selfish. The terms are not appropriate. However, Rolston's further remark suggests another possibility. "But there are other senses in which organismatic selves both can be and regularly are limited in nature, checked by and poured out ('emptied') into processes transcending such selves, discharging themselves into the resulting genesis of biodiversity on Earth."[8] In fact, the process of evolution is nothing but this complex and continuous process of competition and interdependence: "Any particular self, with its integrated genes from the skin-in, distributed genes round about, and its web-worked connections from the skin-out, is a kind of holon, a genuine whole but one in which also its environment, its niche, is fully reflected."[9] There is nothing mysterious about this process: all that is being claimed is that the upper levels of evolution depend on the lower levels in order for the complex, diverse world we actually have to exist. "If the higher forms had to synthesize all the life materials from abiotic materials (also degrading their own wastes), they could never have advanced very far. The upper levels are freed for more advanced synthesis because they depend on syntheses (and decompositions) carried out by lesser organisms below."[10] And this process is precisely the one of death for purpose of new (and more complex, diverse) life that we see everywhere about us. It is the process of life preying on life, since advanced life requires food pyramids, eating and being eaten. Thus, while there is no kenosis in nature, there is limitation, struggle, sacrifice, and death everywhere: it is the heart and soul of the process. Take plants, for example. "Seen in this more comprehensive scheme of things, plants function for the survival of myriads of others. We could even say, provocatively, for our 'kenosis' inquiry, that they are 'emptied into,' given over to, 'devoted' to, or 'sacrificed' for these others in their community."[11] But it is of course not just a one-way scheme: the plants also "benefit." "Plants become insects, which become chicks, which become foxes, which die to fertilize plants."[12] We must keep in mind, however, that none of this is conscious, but is simply the way the system works: it works in a self-interested fashion but within a system of interdependencies that demands "sharing." The self-units are structured into ecological communities, with these networks constituting the identity of the genetic "selves" as much as anything internal to them.

While it is not necessary for our purposes that we understand all the intricacies of the evolutionary process, it is essential that its major outlines, stressing radical individuality and radical unity, both be given full expression and credit. Thus, while "individualism" in the sense of existence by and for oneself is anathema in evolution, it is also the case that it only works by "individuality"; that is, each part, no matter how small or large, makes its contribution to the creation of more and more complex and diverse forms of life. Hence, were we to make a leap to the human scene, we could at least say that if reality is put together in this fashion, then it is impossible to imagine fulfillment for any individual apart from the whole. It is not as if individuality is added to the process when it reaches the human level; rather, we become the individuals we are only through the unimaginably old, complex, intricate, gradual process that has created all the other individuals (of whatever species) in the world. At the very least, this new way of looking at individuality should make us open to contemplating the possibilities for the abundant life, for human flourishing, not with terms such as *me and mine*, but *us and ours*.

KENOSIS: THE WHEEL OF LIFE VERSUS THE MACHINE

Throughout this book, I have been attempting to identify the assumptions and weigh the pluses and minuses of two major ways of being in the world: one organic and the other mechanical. The organic model insists that we see ourselves within the evolutionary, biological, cosmic community of living beings and the systems that support them, while the machine model separates human beings, claiming that the forces that control and support other life-forms do not pertain to us. This latter model claims that we are the masters of our fate, the captains of our destiny, and apparently no evidence to the contrary—including massive financial failures or planetary degradation—can shake this belief. In the few years since the 2007 UN Intergovernmental Panel on Climate Change issued its dire warnings of irreversible global warming with catastrophic results unless immediate actions are taken by the world's nations, indifference and denial have only increased. There is little talk now of "mitigation"—that is, setting stringent goals for world emissions controls. Rather, the talk is increasingly of "adjustment," changing to drought-resistant grains and building higher sea walls. As the situation worsens, the response does as well, until there is little doubt that we are ignoring not only the apocalyptic warnings but also the interdependent picture of reality—the Wheel of Life—that science is increasingly insisting is the sine qua non. Once again, we are retreating to the machine model, where hope is placed in the master hands of the technocrats, either through biological wonders of new strains of genetically modified plants that will feed the world or even stranger wonders that remind one of the "rainmakers" who work with magical techniques of creating and managing the climate so as to produce water and control heat according to our desires.

But one does not have to be a scientist to know that this is madness. Poets and farmers, like Wendell Berry, have expressed our two paradigms—the communal and the individualistic—in basic metaphors that all can understand. At one level, it is as simple as exchanging the metaphor of a road for a wheel, acknowledging that life on planet earth is not linear, but circular, that we do not have a store of energy that is given to each user until it runs out, but an exchange of energy that must circulate and recirculate in all its myriad forms that sustain all the users. Energy is not a "store" extractable by machinery with no limit: "Let loose from any moral standard or limit, the machine was also let loose in another way: it replaced the Wheel of Life as the governing cultural metaphor. Life came to be seen as a road, to be traveled as fast as possible, never to return."[13] The moral order of biological energy consists of production, consumption, and *return*, but the linear pattern disregards this third and critical step. Hence, creating stores of energy, hoarding at the expense of others, is contrary to the complex, indissoluble patterns of exchange that actually govern energy use on our planet. The users "die into each other's life, and live into each other's death," and "this exchange goes on and on, round and round, the Wheel of Life rising out of the soil, descending into it, through the bodies of creatures."[14] What evolutionary scientists are telling us—that the American dream of unlimited growth at both personal and public levels—is a lie, modest farmers (and even more humble poets!) are telling us as well. The machine model encourages infinite, unrestrained growth, clouding our vision from accepting the very different reality of restraint, a moral dictum that has none of the flash and dazzle of limitless consumption. "In any biological system the first principle is restraint—that is, the natural or moral checks that maintain a balance between use and continuity. The life of one year must not be allowed to diminish the life of the next; nothing must live at the expense of the source."[15] Berry finds "restraint" inescapable. "It is more likely that we will have either to live within our limits . . . or not live at all."[16] We do not want to hear these sobering words; in fact, we are determined not to hear them, as the current response to climate change is illustrating. The sciences and simple farmers are telling us the same things the religions have been saying for centuries: one cannot have life except by losing it. To receive energy, to use it, one must first destroy it—lives that feed us must be killed before they enter our mouths—"to receive energy is at once to live and to die."[17] Why is it that science and religion, as well as life lived close to the earth, come up with the same paradox (and now platitude): to have life you must lose it? If this insight is close to being universal—not only in the advanced sciences and the most ancient of wisdom traditions, but also in artistic endeavor, wise parental discipline, peace movements, alternative economics, and so many other dimensions of life—why do we not acknowledge it and practice it? It is not only mavericks like Thoreau who exclaim, "Superfluous wealth can buy superfluities only. Money is not required to buy one necessary of the soul," but also an establishment theologian such as Augustine who advised, "It is better to have fewer wants than to have larger resources."[18] Kenosis and its derivatives appear to have a long and deep, if somewhat countercultural tradition.

These reflections from the sciences and other cultural endeavors reveal that there is a platform, a basis, in the real world for the kenotic behavior. While it is necessary to stress that kenosis is not a natural phenomenon, nonetheless, there is a thread joining evolution to such an unlikely event as the sacrificial death of Jesus of Nazareth, as understood by Christians. As Holmes Rolston notes, "The theme of dying to contribute to life beyond one's own is . . . willingly or unwillingly, everywhere in the plot. . . . All creatures are forever being sacrificed to contribute to lives beyond their own."[19] Only at the human level is this conscious; only with us can the pattern that we and all others necessarily participate in *also* become one that we embrace. Thus, while all must suffer for others—suffering is an evolutionary process not as end in itself but as contributing to the ongoing of life (for others)—it is also in humans the basis for *empathy*. That is, we can decide to extend our moral vision beyond our own well-being to include not only other human beings but also nonhuman others—other species, and even ecosystems. Thus kenosis is at the center of a truly moral human life, one that is willing to practice restraint, sharing, limits, and even sacrifice and death for the good of others, even all others. This expresses well what I have meant in these pages by a "universal self," the paradigm that is inclusive of well-being for all other life-forms. What appears to be "saintly" behavior turns out to be simply "human" behavior—accepting and deepening the natural pattern of give and take, restraint and limits, the Wheel of Life, dying in order to live—that is the best truth we presently have about the way our planet works. We are, then, basing human ethical behavior on "what is," rather than, as is true in the current reigning individualistic paradigm, on "what is not," a proposal for human behavior that is contrary to the way the world works. As "tragic" as this might seem to the rosy-colored glasses with which we well-off North Americans view the world, it is liberating for those who desire to live in the real world, even if it will involve some deep changes in our minds and actions. Thoreau puts it succinctly: "I went to the woods because I wished to live deliberately, to front only the essential facts of life, and see if I could not learn what it had to teach, and not, when I came to die, discover that I had not lived. I did not wish to live what was not life, living is so dear."[20]

Kenosis in Christianity

Before looking at the idea of kenosis in Christianity, we will reflect on its broader place in the religions and its transformative potential to confront the current paradigm.

Some Preliminary Reflections

As we reflect on what the religions might offer a new paradigm for living in the twenty-first-century world, we see a countercultural but biologically based model coming into view. While it has many aspects that lie outside of the religions and some aspects that are peculiar to only one religion, there is a feature—I have called it the "universal self"—that seems to be widely current in most of the world's religions. Its central concept is nondualism accompanied by self-emptying. For instance, we see features of the universal self in both Buddhism and in Christianity. The concept of nondualism, the belief that there is no self separate from the social world, is typical of much Eastern thought (dependent origination), while the distinctively Christian notion of incarnation underscores self-emptying action for the good of others. These overlapping insights, one underscoring the radical interdependence of all with all, and the other emphasizing losing one's life for others, are the linchpins in the new paradigm. Donald Swearer suggests the continuity between the Buddhist and Christian traditions on this question with the following comments.

> [One] might argue that the keystone for understanding Christian virtues is love and that the validation of love is Christology. Biblically this claim couples Johannine *logos* theory ('In the beginning was the *logos* . . .') with *agape* ('God so loved the world . . .'). I propose . . . that for Theravada Buddhists, moral virtue is grounded ontologically in the concept of interdependent co-arising . . . and Buddhalogically in the paradigmatic legend of the Buddha, in particular in the moral values associated with renunciation, restraint, and voluntary poverty, on the other hand, and generosity, loving kindness, and benevolence, on the other.[21]

While scholars of each tradition will find as many differences as there are similarities, for our purposes—suggesting a distinctive contribution that the religions might make to the current problem of moving from belief to action—it is sufficient if we can paint in broad outlines the features of a paradigm different from the present individualistic one and powerful enough to challenge it. The model of the universal self fulfills these criteria: it is significantly different and it is literally world-shaking, able to disrupt our basic, conventional assumptions about the world. Its difference and power lie in part in its assertion that living as a universal self is not just a different moral ethic for acting in the world; rather, it presents a different ontological picture of who we are. That is, it claims that our "being" (who we are) is not as assumed by our society, for if in fact we *are* only in relationship to and in dependence on all other beings, then in order to act differently we must accept a different picture of *who* we are. We cannot be asked to act in ways contrary to who, or what, at the most basic level constitutes us. If we honestly come to believe that "salvation is social" (or nonexistent) and that the only way for such salvation to occur is if those of us who have an unfair share of the world's limited resources are willing to severely limit ourselves ("sacrifice for others"), then it becomes plausible to suggest that not only should we live as universal selves, but we must do so.

Hence, deep within the new paradigm of the universal self is the belief in and acceptance of a different view of power than that which currently operates within the individualistic model. In a word, it claims that *power is love*—the power that fuels the cosmos and potentially lives within each one of us—not the force of unilateral control of some by others, but a far more nuanced and complex kind of power that works by all the characteristics I have identified in the continuity between the joining of the simplest units in nature (dying to self for newness in generations to come) to the sacrificial death of Jesus. "Put one way, the organism is 'sacrificed' to its species line; put still another way, the organism is 'empowered' for such contribution."[22] *In other words, what we have seen in the lives of our saints—voluntary poverty, restraint, sharing, limiting desires, appreciation of otherness, attention to the physical needs of others—and discovered as well in both science and the insights of those who live close to the land (farmers, First Nations people, naturalists, and even humble bird-watchers), these characteristics become the footprints of a new paradigm that understands power as empowerment for life and its flourishing.* Once this understanding of power becomes "normal," it is difficult to deny; as they say, "You can't go home again." We may not like this view, and those of us who have profited unfairly from the individualistic paradigm may wish to deny it, but if one accepts that it is deep within the natural world as well as at the base of most religious traditions, then it becomes increasingly difficult to "live a lie."

An illustration on this point is instructive: in the sixteenth century, when Copernicus first suggested that the earth went around the sun rather than vice versa, no one believed him; in fact, they thought he was mad. But gradually, as more and more anomalies had to be explained to defend the old view, people began to realize that something was wrong with the old model and eventually came to accept Copernicus's view, even though it demoted the heavens to ordinary earthly realities, as they were no longer divine "celestial spheres" but mundane bodies governed by the same laws that governed the Earth. Similarly, as people realize that the individualistic, capitalistic, hoarding paradigm is destroying our planet and undercutting the just distribution of resources to all life-forms, perhaps we too are finally ready to desert a model for living that is, in fact, encouraging decay and death. Initially, of course, there is bound to be resistance, since those who exercise the kind of power operative in the old model—power through control, hierarchy, absolutism, dualism, and denial—will not give up our privileged position easily. But it can be done—and stories of "conversion" illustrate the possibility and the process.

As we begin our reflections on kenosis in Christianity, I pause to suggest how deep and widespread the notion of "conversion" is. While it is often identified with evangelical and "conservative" branches of the Christian faith, it is, in fact, an almost universal phenomenon in religion, characterized by giving up control through self-surrender, self-denial, and emptiness. Since conversion is the opposite of what our society recommends and practices, it is at the very least a rude awakening, often occasioned by disorientation. As Franciscan Richard Rohr comments, "In the west we have called this transformation process salvation, the Jews might have called it passing over, Buddhists perhaps enlightenment, we Franciscans call it poverty, but the Eastern church has most daringly . . . called it divinization."[23] Rohr further characterizes this transformation as the "spirituality of subtraction" in contrast to the "spirituality of addition." The latter is the capitalist version, leaving the ego in the center and adding to it in consumer fashion.[24] In contrast, a spirituality of subtraction is "about letting go; how to let go of our security, our good reputation, our identity and our self-image."[25] This spirituality can be compared to Jesus' experience in the wilderness, a place of emptiness: "We all have to start from the assumption that our path too leads into the wilderness and that we have to look exactly the same three demons in the eye: the need to be successful, the need to be righteous or religious, and the need to have power and get everything under control."[26] Again, we hear the note of property as power versus letting go as power, a strange kind of power that is summed up in a pithy phrase by Thomas Merton: "The most wonderful thing about the world is that it is nobody's property, not even God's."[27] In commenting on this baffling assertion, Merton writes: "God, who owns all things, leaves them to themselves. . . . His love is not like ours. His love is unpossessive."[28]

Needless to say, this interpretation of conversion is not attractive to our society, and as Merton notes, "The real job is to lay the groundwork for a deep change of heart on the part of the whole nation so that one day it can really go through the *metanoia* we need for a peaceful world."[29] Is this the role of the religions in our time of financial and planetary crisis due to the overpossessiveness of its human population, especially those who are well-off? Is our desire for the power of control over the resources needed for all to prosper—our spirituality by addition—so rampant that only a reversal of the values of our now planetary culture of consumerism is adequate to address the situation? And is it the peculiar role of the religions, those wisdom traditions that claim there is another and better way to live, to proclaim the necessity for such a reversal? Is conversion necessary? Theologian Dorothee Soelle thinks so: "Religion's role is to remind people of limits, to give them practice with limits of natural existence, not to deny these limits. Religion counters our culture's technology—crazed delusions with reminders of the true limits of life and life experience."[30] Is this religion's unpopular role, what Merton calls "a kind of arduous and unthanked pioneering"?[31] I believe it is, and I think the religions should assume the responsibility to tell it like it is.

THE HEART OF THE MATTER

I shall now attempt, in a few paragraphs, to suggest the crucial features of a Christian understanding of kenosis, which I will flesh out and analyze throughout rest of this chapter. Kenosis is a particular understanding of the self, or more accurately, of the self in the world. The Enlightenment view of the self rampant in our culture sees the self as constituted by its inner, individual experience—a substantial subject that fulfills itself by expressing its internal desires and goals. It prospers by taking more and more of the world's goods into itself and sees other selves as either contributing to or limiting its own fulfillment. The Christian (and postmodern) view of the self is not "something" in itself, but is constituted by its response to an external call—a call from the other, the neighbor, and/or God.[32] This self is totally dependent on others, both for its biological and its spiritual reality, finding its sustenance only through the gift from others as well as its response to the need of others. Its journey is not one of self-discovery, but of attention to others, both as source of its own existence and as call to respond to their hungers. This radical exteriority is summed up as follows: "The saintly desire for the Other is excessive and wild."[33] Just as the Enlightenment model relies on atomism and internalization, so the postmodern model is based on interdependence and externalization: the one says we are fulfilled by pulling the world into ourselves, whereas the other claims that we are constituted and fulfilled by pouring ourselves out to the other. In Christian terms, one says that we are fulfilled by spiritual experiences of God, while the other says we are fulfilled by loving God as we respond to the needs of the neighbor.

Both postmodern and Christian models rely on the evolutionary story of radical interdependence and various forms of giving, sharing, sacrifice, and death, while the Christian story adds to this cosmic story faith in God understood as radical relationality. What Christians see in their interpretation of salvation—total self-giving of Jesus the Christ for the flourishing of the world—becomes for them also the story of God. Hence, "God" is not a superindividual who expresses the divine self by controlling the world; on the contrary, God is the epitome and the foundation of total openness and self-giving. The Trinity *is* God: the total openness of self-giving of the "persons" of the trinity to one another—and to the world. The "Trinity" is an attempt to express selfhood as nothing but the self-emptying of one into the other (Creator, Savior, Spirit). It constitutes what Christians understand creation to be (God's self-emptying to create a world other than the divine self), salvation (God's self-emptying in and for this world in the life and death of Jesus as the model for the abundant life), and discipleship (human self-emptying for the neighbor by participating in God's love). Hence, kenosis is central throughout the Christian narrative: it is the story of creation, salvation, anthropology, as well as constituting the divine self—God is love, radical self-emptying for others. Here, as with postmodernism, the self is not a substantial subject constituted in isolation as an "individual"; rather, the self is a reflection of God's own life (and way of being in the world) in continuity with the pattern of interdependence and reciprocity that we see in the natural world. We become who we were meant to be by participating in the life of God by serving the neighbor. Thus kenosis appears to be central not only to the natural world but also to a wisdom tradition such as Christianity (and I believe to other wisdom traditions, but I am not equipped to substantiate that claim).

Interestingly, "food" is an excellent point of contact between science, postmodernism and Christianity as we attempt to define the heart of the matter on the issue of the self. Food is the sine qua non in nature; responding to the "hunger" of the destitute is the sign of genuine human living in postmodernism; and in Christianity, God's incarnation in the flesh of the world is its central symbol. In all cases, what is being called for is "feeding the other," giving goods, money, food, clothing. The focus, once again, is not on inner spirituality as the sign of genuine human action, but on external support at the most fundamental level for the well-being of others. Emmanuel Levinas sums it up well with these words. "To recognize the Other is to recognize a hunger. To recognize the Other is to give. . . . I can recognize the gaze of the stranger, the widow, and the orphan only in giving or in refusing; I am free to give or to refuse, but my recognition passes necessarily through the imposition of things."[34] Ah, yes, the "imposition of things," or in Christian terms, embodiment in the flesh of the world—at the most basic level, ethics or the good life, is all about "food." How fitting—and ironic—that the legacy of the modern, capitalist, individualistic self is precisely the problem of "food," whether there will be enough (climate change) and who will have enough (poverty versus riches).

In summary, genuine humanity in Christian faith is not the cultivation of inner experience of ecstasy or fulfillment, but it is participation in the astonishing self-giving of God's own self. What is fulfilling as well as demanded is not the soul's resting in the divine being, but the daily embodiment of the imitation of God in self-emptying love for others.

Self in the World; Self in God in the World

Continuity and difference are emerging as common features from our study of kenosis as an aspect not only of the evolutionary process but also of many religious traditions, including Christianity. That is, we have seen how features of kenoticism—limitation, sacrifice, sharing, dying—are essential to biological growth as well as human spiritual fulfillment, but while the meanings are analogous, they are not the same. What some religions add or, more accurately, assume as the basis of the process is usually (but not always) an understanding of divinity. In the case of Christianity, which is a monotheistic religion, the crucial difference is "God." But what understanding of God? Too often, discussions about religion and science or religion and humanism assume that "everyone knows what 'God' means," and therefore while the participants in such discussions are advised to become informed about one partner in the conversation—whether science or one of the social sciences—it is assumed that there is a common and often uninformed interpretation of "God." Even at levels such as the work of Stephen Hawking, the view of God functioning is that of a supernatural, deistic, unmoved "mechanic," who starts the big bang and then leaves the universe alone. I have attended conferences on science and religion in which the religionists were expected to be knowledgeable on the latest scientific findings, but the scientists were not encouraged to read the most current and informed theology. Such conversations make for one-sided, simplistic findings, with the goal of the religionists often to "prove" the existence of a God that few genuine practitioners of religion even care about! It is doubtful, for example, if Woolman or Day would have dedicated their lives to Hawking's interpretation of God. Hence, the "doctrine of God," the interpretation of what we mean when we use the term *God*, is critical to such discussions.

While not all interpretations of Christianity rest on kenotic views of God—in fact, in many respects, the establishment view does not—the understanding of God emerging from the stories of our saints certainly does. The establishment view—the view that often functions in our society as well as in conversations between scientists and religion—is one of *power*. God is the almighty Lord and Master of the world (universe), who created it out of nothing, rules it unilaterally, and saves it when it falls. The grand narrative is linear, historical, and awesome, picturing humanity as both woefully sinful but also immensely grateful for the atoning sacrifice of Jesus Christ, which turns history around as well as saves believers for eternal life.[35] It is a dramatic tale of fall and redemption, with a distant, transcendent God in complete control of creation and salvation, with his (this God is male) love manifest in the undeserved mercy that he offers to those who believe in the sacrificial death and glorious resurrection of his Son. It is a powerful story about a powerful God—the one and only power in the universe—whom Christians love to praise in such iconic songs as Handel's "Hallelujah" chorus." This God is the very opposite of the one emerging from the lives of Woolman, Weil, and Day. How can this be? How can one religious tradition—Christianity—contain such oppositional interpretations? The answer to this question would need several volumes to even suggest the numerous reasons for such an anomaly, but sufficient for our purposes is recalling the lives of the saints we have studied: Who among us chooses to live the life of a "universal self," the life that a kenotic God calls followers to lead? Contrary to most assumptions in a culture dominated by the American dream of the interior, expressive, goal-oriented self that realizes its dream through hoarding more and more goods, the saintly view of self-fulfillment must respond to the call of a dying, nonpossessive, vulnerable, self-giving God. This suggests that the chief role that religion, and I am focusing particularly on Christianity, has to play in our critical time of climate and financial crisis is *to underscore the "wild," countercultural (but not counternatural) view of the universal self*. In other words, what Christianity brings to the conversation of our time is not a different view of authentic human life from the one in nature as well as in our deepest understandings of human life in the arts and nontheistic ethics, but rather the *intensification* of it. It claims that the glimmers of self-emptying that we see in the arts and sciences be brought to the fore and become central in all aspects of our lives. The Christian view of living for God by loving the world is not a new view but one that has emerged in the best of our literature, politics, economics, philosophy, and religious traditions throughout the ages. What the religions offer—and I am centering on the contribution of the kenotic God in Christianity—is the insistence that living the life of a universal self is not simply one option (for the saints!), but is called for by all human beings because it is not only the way the world is but also the way God is. In other words, "reality," at all levels—natural, human, and spiritual—is governed by this strange notion of kenosis. In fact, what this interpretation of the Christian view of God is trying to say is that not only "to be good" but even to survive, we must live in a radically different way than we are presently doing. Hence, rather than the contribution of the religions to climate change and financial chaos involving a move away from the world and its most critical problems, it intensifies the necessity for radical, deep, and broad responses that demand substantial changes in the lifestyle of those of us who have an unfair share of the world's resources.

THE STRANGE NOTION OF KENOSIS

Going more deeply now into the Christian view of kenosis, we begin with a range of meanings within the tradition. Theologian Sarah Coakley iden-tifies "the 'family resemblance' sliding-scale of meanings, from 'risk,' to 'self-limitation' to 'sacrifice,' to 'self-giving,' to 'self-emptying'—and even to 'annihilation.'"[36] Thus the term has been used throughout Christian history, all the way from the early discussions on the issue of how an unmoved God could suffer (and thus "change") to the contemporary literature on "the death of God." It covers medieval theologies of the "negative way" (God is "beyond" all human attempts at connection) and theologies of atonement (the sacrifice of God for our sins). But, for our purposes, the most pressing issue is the early and ongoing question of how a powerful, unchanging, distant God could "connect" with a sinful, changing world. In other words, the view of God that dominated the early church, especially in the West, was heavily influenced by the Greek notion of an unmoved mover. This view contradicted the central assertion of the incarnation, that in Jesus God became human, "the Word became flesh and lived among us" (John 1:14). This dilemma illustrates once again the centrality of the view of God that is functioning—we cannot start with the assumption that God is a static, unmoved mover and then tack on the notion of the immanental presence of God in and with the world through the life and death of Jesus. Unfortunately, that is the way the "Christian story" is often told—beginning the narrative with an all-powerful, distant God who creates the world and when it "falls" devises a rescue strategy in which this God enters the world (presumably from "heaven" where he abides) to save the errant humans. This tale is neither credible nor consistent—it is entirely alien to a postmodern cosmology, and it paints a picture of God as a remote, imperialistic superbeing. It is doubtful if any religious person (and certainly not our three saints) would embrace such a sterile, outlandish view of God.

Rather, what we find in Woolman, Weil, and Day is a more empirical, modest basis for their understanding of God: faith in the picture of God emerging from the life and death of Jesus of Nazareth. This is not the old faith-versus-reason debate, for genuinely religious people never try to argue for the existence (or nature) of God. It is not a conclusion to any sort of argument; rather, on the basis of all the complexity, ambivalence, illumination, work, experience, and reflection of their lives, they moved gradually to an understanding of God that arose from the attempt to be disciples of Jesus. The text for such people is 2 Corinthians 4:6: "For it is the God who said, 'Let light shine out of darkness,' who has shone in our hearts to give the light of the knowledge of the glory of God in the face of Jesus Christ." In his "face," we see God. We do not know—no one knows—who, what, God is. Christians are those people who base their lives (have faith in) the story of Jesus as their source of the knowledge of God. (This does not mean the only source or the source for all people, but my source, our source as Christians.) It is betting one's life— becoming disciples of—this interpretation of who we are and who God is. Hence, the focus for talking about God is the story of Jesus, but here once again, all that a Christian theologian can do is to venture an interpretation of that story that is hopefully both faithful to the tradition and relevant to one's time.[37]

Hence, in order to speak of kenosis in Christianity, it is necessary to start with a brief sketch of the story of Jesus as the "face" of God. And here, what we discover from even a cursory reading of prime Christian texts is not an all-powerful, distant, imperialistic God, but a vulnerable, self-emptying, totally loving God. The classic biblical texts supporting this interpretation of the Jesus story help to fill out this picture. In Philippians 2, Paul exhorts the followers of Jesus to have "the same mind" that was in Christ Jesus, who "emptied himself, taking the form of a slave," who humbled himself and "became obedient to the point of death—even death on a cross." This admonition comes as advice to followers to reflect such self-emptying, so that one can "look not to your own interests, but to the interests of others." This strange advice fits with the Beatitudes, in which the hungry, poor in spirit, peacemakers, the meek, and the merciful are "blessed." It also fits with the temptations of Jesus, in which he turns away from the enticements to power and prestige.[38] The many passages in the New Testament extolling this manner of living are summed up in Luke 9:23-24: "If any want to become my followers, let them deny themselves and take up their cross daily and follow me. For those who want to save their life will lose it, and those who lose their life for my sake will save it." Likewise, the parables Jesus tells disorient the conventional rules of merit, worth, and power, as do the stories of Jesus' own life: he mixed and sided with the poor and dispossessed. And finally, of course, his death on a cross—the most shameful way to die imaginable at the time— underscores the interpretation that if Jesus is the face of God, then the kenotic view is at least a plausible candidate as the God of Christians. No attempt is being made here to claim that this is the only view of God supported by the New Testament, but only that it is plausible and credible.

Moreover, kenoticism assumes that the continuity between Jesus of Nazareth and God is not a mythological tale of a God descending from another world to rescue errant sinners, but that the "incarnation" of God in Jesus is similar to the union of wills with God's will that we have seen in our saints. Thus the incarnation not only exemplifies the fourfold process that we outlined in this book but is also its model and source. In this process, human beings, answering to the wild space of poverty and oppression, open themselves—pay attention—to the needs of others to such a degree that their own egos are emptied, allowing the love of God to determine "who they are." To say that Jesus is the face of God means that here in this person we have not only the prime example, but more centrally, the model par excellence of the process whereby human beings become "deified." Made in the image of God, so says the tradition, we become who we were meant to be by allowing God to take over our lives, so that as Paul (and Woolman, too) says, "I have been crucified with Christ; and it is no longer I who live, but it is Christ who lives in me" (Gal. 2:19-20). Thus Jesus is not a supernatural being (nor is God!); rather, the power that moves the universe also loves it so exorbitantly that it (he/she) gives of itself, dies, that life many flourish. The complex process of death and rebirth that we see in nature is also the faith of Christians who embrace a dying God, that new life might be possible. In the life and death of Jesus, we see the intimate union of the divine and the human in such a way that the finite can be the true image of God (what the tradition has called "fully God and fully man"). We see the same process in our saints, who relinquished their egos and offered themselves to God. This is not a power struggle between two alien beings—one supernatural and the other natural—but a "coming home" of creatures who were made by God for God, so that the will of God and the will of Jesus (and his followers) become united. Here the true self is not denied, but fulfilled. What is "denied" or emptied is the selfish ego that believes it lives in itself for itself, so that the true self, which, like God, can shine forth, defined by radical relationality, by radical love.

Everything else in Christian faith—its understanding of creation, salvation, and human life—emerges from this union of God and the human in Jesus Christ, and hence displays the same note of self-emptying. This model of God and the world claims that we read in the face of Jesus a mode of being very different from an imperialistic, absolutistic, exclusionary one. Rather, power as empowerment, power as love, power as self-sacrifice for others, becomes the model of authentic living at all levels. Thus creation is seen as the self-emptying of God, the self-limitation of the divine in order that creatures might be, might have freedom and space, to live and grow—and in the case of human beings, to respond to God's love. The world is given room within the divine reality to be itself, and God "retreats" in order that creation can be. (Even God, as we see in Genesis, appreciates others in and for themselves—"It is good," God says, seven times!) Thus we have a doctrine of creation based not on power as control but on power as the empowerment of others, the power of love to let others "be." Salvation is not the atonement of an angry, all-powerful God who takes upon himself what is rightfully ours—punishment for our sins—in order to allow us a fresh start. Rather, salvation is the fourfold process of responding to the call of God to empty the self of its false, egoistic attempt to ground one's life in oneself so that we may, like Jesus, become the face of God for others. Salvation is not an individual escape to live forever in another world, or personal fulfillment of one's inner desires and goals; rather, it is becoming who we were meant to be as made in God's image. Thus the pattern of dying for new life that we see in nature and in the face of Jesus (and thus, we extrapolate, to the very being of God, the dance of radical relationality signified by the Trinity) becomes the very model of all life, from its unconscious beginnings in the most primitive forms to the life of Jesus—and thus of God. This process of giving up and giving over, of sacrificing and dying, of allowing space and resources to others, is not a fluke, an anomaly, an aberration in the nature of things, but as close as we human beings are likely to get to the "mystery" of both human life and the workings of the universe. Thus discipleship or the implications for followers of this way of being in the world is similar: it is realizing our beginnings in creation as creatures made for abundant life in, through, and for others (for God and neighbor), who in salvation are invited into a deepening of the self-emptying model by responding to the call to relinquish the old (egotistic) self for the new (loving) self through the gift of God's own self-emptying love. We are now equipped to attempt reflecting this pattern in our own lives.

At the heart of this model is a different understanding of power from that which operates in our society and especially in the individualistic, market-oriented model of the abundant life. Rather than understanding the nature of things to be a power struggle between and among creatures, human beings, and God and the world, it is imagined to be a dance, albeit one in which participants are required to follow as well as to lead. The pattern of the dance is not determined in advance, but dancers must realize (or accept) that they are part of something larger than themselves, something that demands self-emptying in order to allow space for others to "make their moves." One must pull back, open up, and occasionally step up, bowing to others gracefully and with hospitality. Is this madness? Are human beings capable of giving others time and space to flourish? Must one be a saint in order to say yes to such a model of human living? I don't think so.

Two conditions lie at the heart of accepting this model: first, an acknowl-edgment that we did not create ourselves, and gratitude for the forces that did; second, the belief that these forces are not demonic, indifferent, or all-controlling. This model, while filled with all the complexity, ambivalence, destruction, waste, and uncertainty of the evolutionary process, at its core not only allows for but also "encourages" altruism, self-sacrifice, and compassion. This second condition is indeed a matter of faith: one cannot "read" self-sacrifice from or into the evolutionary story, but as we have seen, there are intimations of self-sacrifice in nature, and more importantly, it is not contrary to this story to claim that self-sacrifice is a plausible interpretation of how nature works. Faith in a God who *is* the epitome of intimations of altruism and self-sacrifice is not absurd; on the contrary, it acknowledges that in living this story of how things are—and should be—we can help make them be so. Our best interpretations at this level—the level of who we are in the scheme of things and what we should be doing—are a combination of discovery and creativity. We move from the glimmers, the intimations, that our life experience gives us—as Woolman, Weil, and Day did with their insistence that self-emptying is not only personally fulfilling but is also good for the polis (and the cosmos)—and create partial fulfillments of self-sacrifice by living it more fully in our daily lives and public policies. By so doing, we help to "make it real." What we believe we have discovered, we also create by emphasizing what we see *might* be the case by testing it out in our personal and public lives. "Truth" at this level is not, as idealism supposes, conformity with a perfect "form," but neither is it fabricated solely from dreams and desires; rather, as Aristotle insisted, truth is what is good for the polis (and I would add for the cosmos) but also the direction we "read" from reality as lived and, to the best of our knowledge at any time, understand. Thus, taking the evolutionary story of a complex network of give-and-take, dying and rebirth, sacrifice and limits, seriously, we attempt to create our own stories within that story, underscoring its features most beneficial for human and planetary flourishing. This is, of course, a *model*, an interpretation of who we are in the scheme of things and what we should be doing. Like any model, it sets up the possibility of fulfillment: "Be careful how you interpret the world. It *is* like that."

What if this understanding of God, one that emphasized self-emptying love, were to become widespread? What if, instead of assuming the stereotype of divinity in our culture of an all-powerful, imperialistic, absolutist, distant superbeing who starts up the world, we embraced the model of God as epitomizing the process of dying for new life that we see all around us? It appears that this may not be impossible, as the following quotation, from theologian John Haught, on the nature of God suggests.

> The point of Christian theology, Pope John Paul II wrote in is encyclical *Fides et Ratio*, is to explore the mystery of God's self-emptying love. "The prime commitment of theology is the understanding of God's *kenosis* [self-emptying], a grand and mysterious truth for the human mind, which finds it inconceivable that suffering and death can express a love which gives itself and seeks nothing in return." No theological radical himself, John Paul expressed here what countless other Christian thinkers now agree is the radical message of Christian faith. The God who for Christians became manifest in Jesus of Nazareth is vulnerable, defenseless love, the same love that Christians confess to be the ultimate environment, ground, and destiny of all being.[39]

If Pope John Paul II, scarcely an antiestablishment source, can claim, as I have been doing in these pages, that the central understanding of God is one of self-emptying love, not only for Christians but also as the ground of all being, as Haught points out (including of course the natural world), then there is hope that the interpretation of God that might function in the twenty-first century is one not of an all-powerful supernatural being, but the strangely countercultural God of Woolman, Weil, and Day. We return, then, to our central claim that the view of God and the world that one holds is central to any conversation about which model for human living we should accept. If such a view as that expressed in the papal statement Haught cites were to serve as Christianity's contribution to the current conversation of how religion might respond to our present economic and ecological crises, then I believe we would have made significant strides in my central thesis, as stated in the preface, that the religions of the world should suggest a different model of living in the world, one grounded in "their special gift—the millennia-old paradoxical insight that happiness is found in self-emptying."[40]

The Impossible Possibility: Living the Kenotic Life

The Problem of Moral Paralysis

When my longtime editor at Fortress Press read an early draft of this book, he commented on "the centrality of what we've discussed before, the problem of moral paralysis—as a personal disjunction and now at the center of a global jeopardy."[41] How true this is—and how chilling! What we have all felt at some time, summed up in Paul's lament that he knows the good but does not do it (see Rom. 7), has now morphed from a personal failing to a planetary crisis. The nagging question that haunts me—and perhaps also the reader of this book—is that we are not saints, so why bother? Reading folks like Woolman, Weil, and Day makes one feel bad at all levels—at the most intimate level of personal failure in the light of increasingly clear evidence that we personally need to change our daily lifestyle, to the most global level, where moral paralysis reigns supreme in national governments and international conferences. The worse the evidence becomes (the arctic is melting much faster than the UN 2007 climate report predicted), the stronger our denial grows. "Greenwash" is everywhere: auto manufactures, chemical companies, and oil retraction firms inundate the media with their "hopeful" reductions in greenhouse emissions from "terrible" levels to merely "awful" ones, trying to convince themselves and us that such minor efforts will stem the tide. What needs to be done—approximately an 80 percent reduction in emissions by 2020—is nowhere in the picture, but due to the economic recession, no one is sounding the alarm, and those few who do are vilified or ignored.

Certainly the religions are not going to turn this cultural mindset around. It may well be that nothing will. Nonetheless, that is not a reason to do nothing; success is not the necessary goal of religion's assignment to criticize the current worldview that is helping to fuel the catastrophic assumptions behind it; rather, the religions are called to both critique this worldview and to suggest a different one, one that would foster attitudes on the side of mitigation rather than mere adjustment. But we return to the seemingly impossible barrier of moral paralysis. If we cannot even will to change the kind of paper towels we use (to biodegradable ones) or give up our car for a bicycle, how can we expect mining companies and the air-travel industry to take stringent measures to significantly lower emissions? How can we expect business and governments to "limit" themselves, to sacrifice profits, to share with developing countries, to restrain their expansionist desires, when we can't do it ourselves at the most mundane levels? Is this whole project of kenosis merely a pipe dream, perhaps possible for a few saints such as the folks we have studied, but scarcely a program for either widespread personal morality or global ethics?

Let us attempt to unravel the issue of moral paralysis by turning once again to the parable of the good Samaritan, which has been an iconic text throughout our study of the Christian saints. Since we are discussing the issue of moral paralysis at its most basic and intimate level—the inability to change our minds and our behavior at the level closest to us—I suggest we see if that story has more lessons to teach us. Faced with the good Samaritan parable, our first reaction is often negative: "But I am not a good Samaritan." If the story is calling for moral perfection, for attending to another's needs, while ignoring one's own—we recall that the Samaritan gave his mode of transportation (his donkey), his material goods (his money), and his time (his detour to the inn to benefit the injured man) and presumably got nothing out of it. But let us look at another interpretation of the story, an interpretation in which the reader is not the good Samaritan but God is.[42] The story does not assume that any human being, even a superbly "good" one, can be the source of unconditional love to others. Like all the parables of Jesus, the point is not a morality tale about how we should act; rather, it is the announcement of the "good news" that God *loves us*, and hence, we too can love. We are the wounded man, the one in the gutter. As Arthur McGill comments: "As I see it, the common reading of the parable of the Good Samaritan simply imposes on the text the absurd illusion of selfless love, a one-way love—the . . . illusion that some people can give without receiving, can nourish others without becoming impoverished themselves—in short, the illusion of perpetual affluence. I find no trace in Jesus of that illusion."[43] This inversion of the usual interpretation certainly fits with the recorded experiences of our three saints: they never suppose that the love they show others—Woolman's relentless opposition to slavery, Weil's identification with factory workers, or Day's forty years living in poverty— was of their doing, that they somehow "willed" themselves to give all for others. Rather, they saw themselves as the most needy of all creatures, only able to be channels of divine love, not their own, and only able to do even that to the extent that they emptied themselves and allowed God to take over their lives. We are not commanded to deny our own need; on the contrary, to serve the needy neighbor we must admit that *"we too stand in essential poverty just as much as any victim we try to help."*[44] Hence, in spite of the tradition of interpreting the parable of the good Samaritan as a call to a strenuous display of will power—giving all one's time and worldly goods to another— the understanding of the parable from our saints is entirely opposite. For all three, the paradoxical Pauline statement as recited by Woolman is central: "I am crucified with Christ, nevertheless I live; yet not I, but Christ liveth in me." Here we see the paradigmatic exchange of the human will ("'John Woolman is dead,' meant no more than the death of my own will") for divine love, which now can flow through a human being.[45] In order for Woolman to *see* this, he had to develop the "single eye," the eye that can see God's love at work rather than his own interests. Weil took this paradox to another level with her notion of decreation: the death of oneself in order that God might re-create the self totally open to being a channel of God's love to the neighbor. Likewise, Day's "little way," the practice of personalism, from finding socks for the sockless to staging union protests, were not, she believed, due to her own will or brilliance, for, as she says, "I have done nothing well, but I have done what I could."[46] In a sense, all three of our saints saw their role as simply getting out of the way (their egos, that is) so that God's power and love might work through them.

Here we come to the heart of the matter, for *poverty*, both physical and emotional, is the wild space that opened the possibility in our saints for their long journey to the universal self, the self totally open to the needs of others. The fourfold process that we have been sketching begins and ends with a reversal of typical understandings of the good life. We move from the view that our own possessions (of whatever sort) are the criteria for life abundant to another picture of fulfillment, one in which by emptying ourselves of desire for such abundance we become the passageway for a love that gives itself away. When we identify ourselves with the needy man in the gutter in the good Samaritan story rather than with the Samaritan, we open up a new possibility for dealing with the issue of moral paralysis. *We* are not being called to be perfect givers; rather, we are being told that we must be total receivers. Instead of being the powerful ones, the ones who can give and give and give, first we must dispossess ourselves of everything that constitutes control over our lives. As Weil puts it, we must "decreate" the false ego that supposes it is the source of our autonomous lives. Her seemingly absurd notion that by being totally decreated, as passive as a pencil in the hand of a writer, now seems less so. We must enter into a lifelong journey of becoming radically open ("dead" to ourselves, so to speak), so that we can serve as a channel for *God's* love, not our own. To be "created" by God means to be "decreated" to ourselves as the source of life and love. This process, which must undo our belief that life comes from the interior, superior, separate, powerful self, begins with the simple realization that we depend on others for food, and even for the next breath.

The secret of voluntary poverty is that it starts this process of redefining power as control (possessions, prestige, and even life itself) to understanding power as love. The process moves toward its denouement with the realization of one's own death, the final decreation. Power as powerlessness to the point of death is scarcely the current view of power in our society, where we live within an entire world based on dominative power and self-enclosed security. As we have noted in the narcissistic memoirs currently being published and in David Brooks's analysis of the self as the center of American life, power as letting go, as self-expenditure, is not power at all. In a culture where power as self-expression and control is primary, one would be insane to consider self-expenditure, selfless action, as power. Thus death becomes the final insult, the final refusal to accept our own profound poverty and total powerlessness. For Christians, the cross of Jesus epitomizes this letting go of the control over one's self-identity, as well as openness to a new definition of the very character of life, one based on accepting life from God. Hence, we see why voluntary poverty is indeed wild space, for it assumes the first step is self-emptying in order that the power of radical love might begin to function in our lives. This is not "our" love but the love that comes to us when we give up control to the point of accepting our own death. Hence, it is God's love that helps the man in the gutter, who is, first of all, ourselves, before we can become channels for this power, the power of love that rules the universe.

But does this mean that the answer to moral paralysis is only available to practitioners of religion and specifically of Christianity? What if one is a nonbeliever? If the process depends on dealing with nonpossessiveness at the deepest level of accepting one's own death—at least the understanding of death as the relinquishment of the self-sufficient, individual self—is it possible for nonreligious people? Here Buddhism, a nontheistic religion, gives us a clue, for in this religion the old, individualistic, substantial self must be given up for the new self, which arises in codependency with everything else that lives. What needs to die is the autonomous, unrelated, separate self so that the rebirth of the codependent self of radical interrelationship and interdependence can arise. Christian faith would agree with this analysis, and given this interpretation, Christianity would also reject the deistic, supernatural lord and savior of the world that Buddhism finds anathema. In its place, Buddhism supports a radical view of the self-emptying "God," and so does Christianity, albeit a somewhat different one.[47] When one accepts the death of the old self, with all its desires for possessions, one is also in a position to accept death as commonly understood—the end of one's personal, individual life. Thus, even apart from "belief in God," surrender of "life as a possession" becomes a possibility. For instance, near the end of her life, Dorothee Soelle, a Christian theologian, contemplated such a possibility. She writes: "Is not my wish for this creation to remain alive much greater than my wish that I myself remain alive?"[48] To grasp the power of such an affirmation, imagine its opposite: that I (the narrow, substantial, individual self) should "live" and everything else should die? Imagine the loneliness (not to mention the impossibility) of living when nothing else is. What we love, I venture to suggest, is not individual eternal life for ourselves so much as the continuation of the entire awesome, beautiful, abundance of creatures, great and small, that causes us to gasp in wonder and thanksgiving that we have, at least for a short time, been a part of this glorious creation. We wish it to continue, not only in our nearest and dearest (our children, our tribe, our country, and our species) but also in all the forms, from slugs to stars, that lie outside our daily appreciation but are necessary to the health of the whole.

Hence, as we look at death as the final relinquishment of the possessive self, we see that a sense of the universal self—of valuing the whole, living creation rather than just one's own tiny scrap of it—is possible for nonreligious as well as religious people. Is it belief in God that is so critical or the acceptance of personal limits (*I* will die), along with the celebration that life will go on? Does a sense of the universal self—that I am part of life itself—save us from despair over our own deaths?

Much depends, as we have noted, on the view of God one holds. The all-powerful, imperialistic, absolute, superbeing who is merely a reflection of the separate, individualistic, autonomous individual—is not needed; in fact, it is counterproductive. What we need is a different view both of "God" and ourselves. This view, which in both cases—God's and ours—depends on radical self-emptying, embraces all who can see others as part of themselves and themselves as part of all others, whether or not one is a believer in a God.

SOME CHARACTERISTICS OF KENOTIC LIVING

"The love of God sanctifies our neediness for God and for one another, because neediness belongs properly and naturally to God."[49] This claim stands in sharp contrast to the conventional view of a supernatural, all-powerful God (and the human being "made in God's image"). Rather, it sums up the view of God that has emerged from the study of our three saints, a view in which the expenditure of self for others is the best description. Woolman, Weil, and Day held that the crucifixion is the clearest manifestation of Jesus' life and message, "for there no trace of identity by possession remains."[50] Self-possession is at the very heart of our fear of our individual deaths and is the central meaning of the autonomous self; thus, if the love that empowers the universe operates not by control but by total self-expenditure, what do we have to fear? This is the same pattern we have traced in cosmic evolution—a pattern in which death (self-expenditure) results in the communication of life to others. To be sure, such self-expenditure involves a dying on the part of the giver, whether it be grain of wheat dying to produce more fruit (John 12:24), or someone laying down his life for his friends (John 15:13), or relations of "*total and mutual self-giving*" within the divine self (the Father, Son, and Spirit)."[51] Even God, in this understanding, does not "stand alone," a single, autonomous being, but at the heart of the divine is relationship: God is radical relationality. In all cases, "neediness" rather than self-possession characterizes the love that is sought and given—the love of total self-expenditure for others. "Love is what Jesus does, and what Jesus does is communicate life to others, by laying down his life. Love, then, is not primarily a feeling or an attitude. . . . Love is primarily an activity, any activity by which life is passed from one person to another, from one community to another. Love is the communication of life."[52]

The inversion of the good Samaritan parable, from us as givers to receivers, from a position of control to one of self-expenditure, from holding onto to life to passing it on: this is countercultural contribution that the religions and the wisdom traditions have to offer the present climate and monetary crises. The inverted interpretation claims that in numerous and often mysterious ways, "death is the final communication of life."[53] What our false, autonomous self fears the most—the final dispossession that death signifies—becomes the basis for the insight into and the energy for new life. This new life is not the narrow continuation of eternal existence for a few individuals in an afterlife, but the passing on of divine energy, planetary energy, to others. What the Trinity epitomizes for Christians—the assurance that life has a direction, that it is not just "one damn thing after another," or worse still, evil or malevolent, is intimated in the very processes of biological life as well as the highest reaches of human sharing and sacrifice.

This inversion of the expectations of the narrow, autonomous self is not easy. It involves at least two difficult steps: really letting go of all possessions and living daily without assurance of control. As our saints have shown us, living a life of voluntary poverty involves dispossession at every level, from the peace and quiet of a "room of one's own," which Day desperately wanted, to the sacrifice of one's "reputation" for prestige and power, which Woolman's ridiculous practice of wearing white clothing signified. Middle-class living in the twenty-first century is practically defined by possessions and control. Being able to ensure that oneself (and one's nearest and dearest) have not only the basics for existence but also a comfortable cushion, and to have these things both now and in the foreseeable future, is a mark of living in this desired class of human beings. The inverted good Samaritan parable tells us is that this is not possible—not only is it undesirable from a religious perspective (it deprives others of the basics), but also our planet cannot support middle-class life for all human beings. "Neediness" is the center of both religious and biological life: we not only live from day to day dependent on God for our creation and salvation, but from day to day dependent on other life-forms and biological systems for clean air, arable land, and pure drinking water. To the extent that we recognize this model at all levels of existence—from the spiritual to the biological—we may have the possibility of fruitful life at both the personal and the planetary dimensions. We are constituted every moment not by control, as the American Dream supposes, but by need. Even Jesus loses his possession of religious assurance at the last moment—"My God, my God—why have your forsaken me?" but by losing everything (death on the cross), he inaugurates a new life (the resurrection), in which total possessionlessness, utter poverty, becomes the basis for another kind of existence, one characterized by the freedom to give oneself away. "Poverty" becomes the good news rather than the most feared conclusion. The new life cannot be possessed (it is given to us day by day, hour by hour, minute by minute, as we breathe and eat), and it is characterized by continuous dispossession—the giving of the self to others. As our saints illustrate with great detail and passion, the good news of poverty is that it gives life to others, even as we receive it new every morning: "We do not possess ourselves; we constantly *receive* ourselves and *expend* ourselves."[54] "I am when I generate in another. My giving is my being."[55]

Can we live this way? Is our moral paralysis so great that the thought of giving up the illusion of the model of the narrow, individual self is too painful, even for religious types, let alone for others? Is inverting the good Samaritan parable so that we become the receivers *before* we give (whether it is the giving of God's love or the gift of the grain of wheat) sufficient to accomplish the dying to self necessary so that others can live? Is it enough to imagine another model for abundant living, one in which by identifying ourselves with all others (the universal self), we can accept our own biological death, knowing, as Dorothee Soelle puts it, that "this creation . . . remains alive"? It may not be, in which case our prospects and the prospects of a just, sustainable planet are in serious jeopardy.

NOTES

[1] David Brooks, "It's Not About You," *New York Times*, May 30, 2011, http://www.nytimes.com/2011/05/31/opinion/31brooks.html.

[2] Ibid.

[3] Ibid.

[4] Ibid.

[5] Ibid.

[6] Malcolm Jeeves, "The Nature of Persons and the Emergence of Kenotic Behavior," in *The Work of Love: Creation as Kenosis*, ed. John Polkinghorne (Grand Rapids: Eerdmans, 2001), 78.

[7] Holmes Rolston III, "Kenosis and Nature," in Polkinghorne, *The Work of Love*, 61.

[8] Ibid.

[9] Ibid., 53.

[10] Ibid., 52.

[11] Ibid., 54.

[12] Ibid., 52.

[13] Wendell Berry, *The Unsettling of America: Culture and Agriculture* (San Francisco: Sierra Club Books, 1977), 89.

[14] Ibid., 86.

[15] Ibid., 93.

[16] Ibid., 94.

[17] Ibid., 81.

[18] Goldian VandenBroeck, ed., *Less Is More: The Art of Voluntary Poverty* (Rochester, VT: Inner Traditions, 1978), 67.

[19] Rolston, "Kenosis and Nature," 60.

[20] VandenBroeck, *Less Is More*, 227.

[21] Donald K. Swearer, "Buddhist Virtue, Voluntary Poverty, and Extensive Benevolence," *Journal of Religious Ethics* (1998): 73–74.

[22] Rolston, "Kenosis and Nature," 48.

[23] Richard Rohr, "Giving Up Control in Life's Second Half," *National Catholic Reporter*, February 8, 2002.

[24] Richard Rohr, *Simplicity: The Freedom of Letting Go*, trans. Peter Heinneg (New York: Crossroad, 1991), 40–41.

[25] Ibid., 107.

[26] Ibid., 174.

[27] Thomas Merton, *A Book of Hours*, ed. Kathleen Deignan (Notre Dame: Sorin, 2007), 119.

[28] Ibid., 118.

[29] Ibid., 121.

[30] Dorothee Soelle, *The Mystery of Death*, trans. Nancy Lukens-Rumscheidt and Martin Lukens-Rumscheidt (Minneapolis: Fortress Press, 2007), 61–62.

[31] Merton, *A Book of Hours*, 121.

[32] By suggesting a similarity between the Christian and the postmodern view of the self, I am referring to the work of such scholars as Emmanuel Levinas, Edith Wyschogrod, and John Caputo, who understand the self as constituted not internally but externally, by its response to a call to serve the other. While the Christian and the postmodern view of these scholars is by no means identical, they both fall, I believe, within the new paradigm as distinctive from the Enlightenment, modern, and capitalist views.

[33] Edith Wyschogrod, *Saints and Postmodernism: Revisioning Moral Philosophy* (Chicago: University of Chicago Press, 1990), 255.

[34] Emmanuel Levinas, *Totality and Infinity: An Essay on Exteriority*, trans. Alphonso Lingis (Pittsburgh: Duquesne University Press, 1961), 75, 77.

[35] For a fuller descriptions of this narrative of the Christian story of fall and redemption, see, for instance, Sallie McFague, "Who Is God," chap. 4 in *A New Climate for Theology: God, the World, and Global Warming* (Minneapolis: Fortress Press, 2008).

[36] Sarah Coakley, "Kenosis: Theological Meanings and Gender Connotations," in Polkinghorne, *The Work of Love*, 203.

[37] For further discussion of these issues of method in theology, see Sallie McFague, *Life Abundant: Rethinking Theology and Economy for a Planet in Peril* (Minneapolis: Fortress Press, 2001), chaps. 2–3.

[38] See Gospel versions of the temptations to power: Matt. 4:1-11; Mark 1:12-13; Luke 4:1-13.

[39] John Haught, *God and the New Atheism: A Critical Response to Dawkins, Harris, and Hitchens* (Louisville: Westminster John Knox, 2008), 92.

[40] Gary Gardner, "Engaging World Religions to Shape Worldviews," in *State of the World 2010: Transforming Cultures from Consumerism to Sustainability* (Washington, DC: Worldwatch Institute, 2010), 29.

[41] Michael West from an email dated June 16, 2011.

[42] I am indebted to Arthur C. McGill for the following interpretation of the parable of the good Samaritan, as it appears in several of his works: *Death and Life: An American Theology* (Eugene, OR: Wipf and Stock, 1987); *Suffering: A Test of Theological Method* (Eugene, OR: Wipf and Stock, 2006); *Sermons of Arthur C. McGill: Theological Fascinations*, ed. Daniel Cain (Eugene, OR: Cascade, 2007), vol. 1.

[43] McGill, *Death and Life*, 89.

[44] Ibid.

[45] John Woolman, *The Journal of John Woolman and a Plea for the Poor* (New York: Corinth, 1961), 215.

[46] Dorothy Day, *The Long Loneliness* (New York: Curtis Books, 1952).

[47] For a discussion of similarities and differences on this issue, see John B. Cobb Jr. and Christopher Ives, eds., *The Emptying God: A Buddhist-Jewish-Christian Conversation* (Maryknoll, NY: Orbis, 1998).

[48] Dorothee Soelle, *The Mystery of Death*, trans. Nancy Lukens-Rumscheidt and Martin Lukens-Rumscheidt (Minneapolis: Fortress Press, 2007), 94.

49 McGill, *Sermons*, 51.
50 McGill, *Suffering*, 96.
51 Ibid., 76.
52 McGill, *Sermons*, 79–80.
53 Ibid., 78.
54 McGill, *Death*, 61.
55 McGill, *Sermons*, 119.

7

Kenotic Theology

INTRODUCTION

Having looked at the uses of kenosis in fields ranging from biology to the arts and parenting, as well as its widespread importance in religion, we turn now to an in-depth study of kenosis in one tradition, the Christian. This is meant to be illustrative—spelling out the implications of kenosis in one religion in order to highlight some characteristics of its depth and breadth. The resources for this chapter are a combination of insights from our saints as well as my own interpretation of theology, while focusing on its relevance for our twin crises in ecology and economics. While the perspective will be Christian, the discussion here is not limited to Christian readers, for a similar analysis of kenosis in other religions would, I believe, bring similar though different insights.

A kenotic theology is necessarily a body theology, for kenosis is about the sharing of scarce resources among the needy. We are all needy at the most basic level of food in order to survive from one day to the next. This is certainly what the lives of our three saints tell us—the primary symbol of need at all levels of our existence is "food," whether it be Woolman's economics based on universal love, Weil's notion of "cannibalism" of others as the most basic sin, or Day's endless soup kitchens feeding hungry bodies. Our saints are not pie-in-the-sky spiritualists who see religious practice as focused on people's souls. Rather, the "pie" is concrete and physical. It is the grocery business that Woolman sold in order to keep his eye "single," in order to see his own body, as he says interpreting a dream, as mixed up with the mass of "human beings in as great misery as they could be," no longer considering himself "as a distinct or separate being."[1] Or the pie is Weil's "paralytic" prayer, in which she asks that her body "be stripped away from me, devoured by God, transformed into Christ's substance, and given for food to afflicted men whose body and soul lack every kind of nourishment."[2] Or the pie is the bread crust that Day shared with others. ("If there were six small loaves and a few fishes, we had to divide them. There was always bread.")[3]

A kenotic theology is therefore an incarnational theology, a theology that focuses unapologetically on "food," the lowliest, most basic need shared by all living beings. A kenotic theology is not a lofty theology, not a theology glorifying "God or man"; rather, it is a theology that begins with need, both God's need and ours, a need that runs all the way from the most elemental biological processes of the energy transformation to understanding the Trinity (the being of God) as one of continuous and total exchange of love. Kenosis is the process that begins and continues life, all the way from the splitting of cells to the sacrifice (and death) of some human beings for the nourishment of others, and of God's quintessential act of self-emptying both within the divine being and for the creation and salvation of the world. Thus Christianity's manner of making contact with the most basic physical, biological processes is through an inclusive, radical interpretation of its doctrine of the incarnation of God, not now merely in one human being, Jesus of Nazareth, but in the world as God's body.[4] This model attempts to express the most basic relationship of God and the world as one of shocking totality and intimacy, one that goes to the core of what it means to live and flourish. Moreover, it implies that we human beings, made "in the image of God," likewise might model our relationship with the world in a similar fashion: the world as *our* body. A thumbnail sketch of this model suggests that all flesh, all matter, is included within God (as God's "body") but that God is not limited to this body, to matter. Here, God is understood to be "more than" the body, more than the world, but intimately, radically, and inclusively identified with it. We human beings are likewise thoroughly linked with the world; in fact, to see the world as our body is one metaphor expressing what we have called the "universal self," the awareness that the self has no limits. Moreover, by focusing our understanding of the divine-world relationship at the most basic, physical, bodily level, we avoid tendencies by many religions, including Christianity, to "spiritualize" the relationship, insisting now that God is the creator par excellence and that creation is composed of bodies that must be fed.

This primary belief that God and the world are bound together in a network of physicality, vulnerability, and need sets the framework for a kenotic theology of power as love, not as control. It suggests that seeing the world as God's beloved rather than as his kingdom is the appropriate metaphor since, in this theological paradigm, God is *always* incarnate, always bound to the world as its lover, as close to it as we are to our own bodies, and concerned before all else to see that the body, God's world, flourishes. Thus a kenotic theology begins not with the doctrine of creation but with the incarnation, not with the picture of God fashioning the world like an artist from alien materials but from God's own body, as God's body. "The Word was made flesh" is first of all an empirical assertion on the basis of the life and death of Jesus of Nazareth, the judgment that Christians make about the meaning of the story of this man. Like the stories of our saints, which speak by embodiment, so also what Christians say about the basic God-world relationship is not a speculative assertion about creation but a tentative judgment that here in this story we have our best clue not only to the nature of God but to our own nature as well. Thus, as Paul puts it, we read in the "face" of Jesus the most basic relationship between God and the world. What we see in the face of Jesus Christ is knowledge of the glory of God, and this glory includes the creative light that shone out of darkness (2 Cor. 4:6). We "read back" into the creational relationship between God and the world what we see in the life and death of Jesus of Nazareth. This message is, first of all, about the God who empties the divine self into a human being both in his life of radical service to others and in his death on a cross, thus telling us that all God's relations with the world are of a kenotic character.

It is necessary to pause for a moment before continuing with the details of a kenotic theology to acknowledge how different it is from the traditional, establishment theology.[5] While there are many variations of this theology, its broad picture is of a powerful God who creates a world "from nothing," where the distinctive relationship is one of control by God and submission by human beings who are, in the most basic respects, different from God. The story starts with creation, includes a "fall" on the part of human beings, and hopefully a return to the pristine conditions of creation through the sacrifice of God's son, Jesus Christ. It is an "external" story, told "about" us rather than arising from anyone's lived experience with the divine. It is both individualistic and anthropocentric, taking as its primary focus the creation, fall, and salvation of particular human beings who are only marginally related to the rest of the world.

A kenotic theology, however, begins with the stories of people who claim to experience God as both the source of their own lives, as well as of everything else, with this experience, while mystical in the sense that it is a profound sense of personal engagement with the divine, is also prophetic, since it carries a call to love others in the same manner that God loves. It is deeply intimate (God, says Augustine, is closer to us than we are to ourselves) and yet at the same time universal in scope and focused above all on assuring the flourishing of all life at the most basic level of food. Since its primary source is personal stories that read the glory of God in the face of Jesus Christ, its central content is self-emptying for others, ranging from sharing food and healing bodies to the sacrifice of one's own body on a cross, the ultimate gift of the self so that others might have new, abundant life. No story could be more personal, intimate, bodily, or basic; no story could also be more universal, radical, or total. It has everything to do with us human beings (but it is not anthropocentric) and everything to do with power (but it is not about control). It is a countercultural story, calling on our "wild space" to imagine a different way to live in the world, one at odds with our economic, governmental, and often religious interpretations of the good life. This interpretation is best expressed in the lives of those who have attempted to live it, for it is not a set of concepts, but a journey of gradual self-emptying of the ego so that the new self, the universal self, may begin to develop at both personal and public levels. It claims that embodiment, lives as lived, is a more powerful statement than words about this way of life, since it involves a constant translation of the paradigm (the bare bones of disorientation, self-emptying, and a new direction for flourishing) from the lives and times of others to one's own life and times. What we see in the stories of Woolman, Weil, and Day—not to mention Jesus—is paradigmatic but not programmatic. A kenotic theology must be reconstructed for each new age and set of circumstances. Here, in these pages, I am attempting to see what it might mean for the twenty-first-century twin crises of increasing poverty and increasing temperatures, creating a situation that calls for a radically different lifestyle, one of restraint, sharing, limits, sacrifice, and death.

We turn now to some of the particulars of a kenotic theology—the understanding of God, Christ, human being, creation, sin and salvation, and related issues. We will be attempting to paint an overall picture of the beliefs and practices of kenotic theology, depending heavily on the stories of our three saints in order to keep theology grounded in the tentative, qualified, ambiguous, and lowly place from which it arises and to which it should speak. In these pages, I am interested in how belief is related to action, how the deepest and best insights that one religion, Christianity, might contribute to addressing the crucial issues of our time (which is always, I think, what theology should be doing). Because theology is necessarily and always metaphorical; it is also kenotic or self-emptying, more apophatic than cataphatic, more aware of the "is not" shadowing its statements, rather than the "is." Hence, both in content and in style, theology for the twenty-first century should, I believe, be kenotic—vulnerable, lowly, limited, self-emptying. I am less concerned here to be total, covering all issues, or systematic, doing so in an orderly fashion, than I am in being suggestive, invitational, and probing. I am asking what a kenotic theology for our time would "look like" rather than asking what answers it would give.

Jesus as the Face of God

The problem is always, where do we begin? How can we start talking about God and about ourselves when no one has ever seen God and, as Annie Dillard reminds us, "we're just set down here . . . and don't nobody know why."[6] This is hardly a propitious situation for gaining insight into the "big questions," the questions that in many ways dictate how we behave, the decisions we make using the considerable power that human beings have come to have in the world. Many of the most destructive behaviors against other human beings and our planet are the result of presumed "descriptions" of God and/or ourselves, the assumption that there *are* descriptions of these entities. When we take our interpretations for descriptions, they are likely to be rigid, self-serving, and overly confident. For instance, those who think that God is a static, all-determining, controlling, powerful superbeing also believe that God will clean up the mess we have made of the earth or at least save his "favorites" from its consequences. Likewise, those who think we human beings, made in God's image, have the right to control all other forms of life contribute to human refusal to take responsibility for our destruction. Thus what passes for "descriptions" of God and/or ourselves serve as "cover" for our most selfish and irresponsible behaviors. Admitting that there are no "descriptions" of either God or ourselves is the first step toward a sane, modest, and relative judgment on which "interpretation" (for we only have interpretations) is the best for the planet and ourselves—as well as having at least a passing acquaintance with the "truth," or the "way things are." I have suggested in these pages that an understanding of God and of ourselves that is in continuity with what else we know about our world is our best bet—and for us this means the cosmic, evolutionary, ecological network that operates at every level of biological existence, including the human. Since all of our decisions assume some worldview (whether we want them to or not and whether we are aware of it or not), it makes sense to become conscious of the view of God and ourselves that is actually operating in our behavior and, to the best of our ability, to ensure it is one that we can bet our lives on. For this is, essentially, what being a living, acting human being involves: a leap of faith—not an absurd leap, based merely on what we have received from others (though that should play a part) or on what we would like to be the case, but faith in the "best picture" we can imagine for the world's well-being and that also has grounding in empirical reality. Our tendency is to trust in worldviews from other times—for instance, in our case, the modernist worldview stemming from the eighteenth century, which assumed a static, powerful God and an individualistic, atomistic view of both natural and human life. This worldview no longer has the support of most fields of study in the twenty-first century. Rather, what is emerging is a very different picture of the "big questions." The world in which we live is a highly interdependent, fluid, open network of reciprocal actions and reactions, in which nothing stands alone and everything is both receiver and giver. One of the greatest challenges of our time is understanding and internalizing this new picture: it is far deeper, more complex, and nuanced than the much simpler eighteenth-century picture, where cause and effect had more of a one-to-one relationship. Here, in our new picture, where we are giver and receiver at every level, the internalization of such influence is much more difficult to imagine, let alone to assume, in our daily decisions. For example, the poet Gary Snyder suggests how the planet has given us the very shape that we human beings have: "Two conditions—gravity and livable temperature range between freezing and boiling—have given us fluids and flesh. The trees we climb and the ground we walk on have given us five fingers and toes. The *place* (from the root *plat* broad, spreading, flat) gave us far-seeing eyes; the streams and breezes gave us versatile tongues and whorly ears. The land gave us a stride and the lake a dive. The amazement gave us our kind of mind."[7]

In a world such as this, where "who we are" has evolved over billions of years of mutual give-and-take, chance and law, sacrifice and death—a form of influence so complex, deep, and old that our minds cannot comprehend it—the poet's attempts are probably the best we can do. At any rate, it is certain that talk of simple cause and effect in autonomous, individualistic decisions makes little sense.

Any attempt at answering the big questions of who God is and who we are must, I suggest, take this picture into account. To put forth interpretations of God and human being that are patently contradictory to this picture, as, unfortunately, many traditional Christian doctrines do, is not only incredible to the postmodern mind but also, as we increasingly see, harmful to our planet and to the poorer members of our own species. We *are* interrelated and interdependent more deeply, thoroughly, and inexorably with all other biological systems on the planet than we can ever imagine or express. The better part of wisdom, therefore, is to err on the side of assuming our radical dependence on each other and on our planet rather than the opposite, of supposing that we can "manage" the planet and solve poverty with band-aid charity efforts. So what should we do? Where do we start to talk about God and about ourselves? There will, I believe, be many starting points for big-question interpretations; in fact, that is in part what the various religions are about. As a Christian theologian, I take my starting place with Jesus of Nazareth—to be a Christian is to be called by that name, the belief that "Jesus is the Christ," a way to God, a way to know and talk about God. It is certainly not the only way (and it may not be the "best" way), but it is an ancient way that has served many people for a long time, a credible way that has made sense to many people, and I would assert, a way that is good for the planet and its life-forms.[8] I will try to make a case for it as one way that can help move people today from belief to action on the issues of climate change and increasing poverty. As we recall, the focus of this book is the question of how the religions can make a distinctive and important contribution to these twin crises of our time.

THE WITNESS OF THREE SAINTS

The following remark by biblical scholar J. M. R. Robinson is sobering as we begin our reflections on how our saints experience Jesus as the Christ: "The problem the historical Jesus poses is really not that we do not know what he had to say, but rather that, when we get wind of it, we do not know how to handle it."[9] To the extent that Woolman, Weil, and Day "get wind" of Jesus as the way to God, they would agree that it is tough to handle. Unlike the comforting story of divine power (and reflective human power) of the traditional Christian narrative, their experience is unsettling in the extreme. For Woolman, it is nothing short of his own death summed up in Galatians 2:19-20 ("I have been crucified with Christ, and it is no longer I who live, but it is Christ who lives in me"). The will of God that Woolman seeks to know (the inner light) is known by imitating the path of Jesus, the path of kenotic self-emptying on behalf of others in every nook and cranny of one's daily life, beginning with an experience so close to the death of his own body that he forgets his name, arising to a new life only for it to be mixed up with "a mass of matter of a dull gloomy color," which he learns is the mass of the most despised and oppressed humanity. It is hard to imagine a more thoroughly "body" theology—an incarnational theology—than this. One could, with justification, use the body metaphor as typifying answers to the two big questions of who God is and who we are: here not only is the world God's body, but it is also ours. God is known through reflecting in one's own ordinary life the life of the self-emptying Christ, and we are known to the extent that we embody that image. Knowledge of God and of ourselves is here not conceptual, but by the embodied story of one's own life. Woolman does not come to know God merely by studying or even by meditating, but only by undergoing the death of his own will, and hence of participating in God's life. And this life, as the crucified Christ illustrates, is one of radical self-sacrifice at the most basic level of economic equality. Woolman's own life testifies to knowing God's will by concrete actions of sharing and sacrifice— selling his profitable grocery business, experiencing the deprivations of native Americans, sharing the uncomfortable conditions of sailors' accommodations in transatlantic voyages, walking hundreds of miles rather than using post horses. What is critical to keep in mind, for our purposes—the translation of belief into action—is that the process is profoundly physical, immediate, concrete, and insistent. By waking up through voluntary poverty to the pressing and painful oppression of others, Woolman now "sees" the world differently—through, as it were, the eyes of the crucified Christ—and acts to embody that new reality in every aspect of his life. It is a journey that demands constant practice of emptying the ego in order to embrace the true self, the self that is one with the Jesus of the Sermon on the Mount, the parable of the rich young man, the commandments to love God and the neighbor as the self, the good Samaritan, and the admonitions to love enemies. This countercultural tradition of the New Testament is summed up in Matthew 16:24-25: "Then Jesus told his disciples, 'If any want to become my followers, let them deny themselves and take up their cross and follow me. For those who want to save their life will lose it, and those who lose their life for my sake will find it.'"

For Woolman, and for Weil and Day, as we shall see, the reason to focus on one's experience of the story of Jesus is not to learn more about Jesus, but about God and ourselves. If Jesus is the face of God (2 Cor. 4:6: "For it is the God who said, 'Let light shine out of darkness,' who has shone in our hearts to give the light of the knowledge of the glory of God in the face of Jesus Christ"), then what is important about Jesus is not what he tells us about himself but what he tells us about God. Jesus is the Christ of God for Christians not because he is a third big question besides the ones about God and ourselves, but because he tells us about both of the two big questions—who God is and who we are. Woolman learned about the will of God—and hence, about what his own life should be about—by following that will, through reflecting on and embodying the story of Jesus, to the extent that he experienced and understood it. That is the nature of Christian discipleship and the key matter to focus on for those of us who believe Christianity has something to offer our twin crises of climate change and increasing poverty.

Weil's experience of the story of Jesus deepens the direction that Woolman took. Her notion of "decreation" is not a negative statement decrying the importance of creation (as I and many others have at times supposed); rather, it is an intensification of Galatians 2:20: authentic human life is not formed by satisfying our own egos—standing on our own, by our own power—but rather it is the life that comes to us only as we allow God to "devour" the self-centered life so that we might be re-created in the image of God, Jesus the Christ. Weil's extreme language expresses both the death of our egos and the re-creation of the authentic self by God, and it only makes sense when seen in a context that few use: as the lens for seeing God in the face of Jesus. The food imagery of cannibalism, devouring, giving one's body as bread for others, decreating the ego to provide space for the new self to grow, and so on, is reminiscent of a comment made by Robert Coles regarding another of our saints, Dorothy Day. He wrote, "As for Jesus Christ, who of any importance in the West's intellectual or political world now pays any real attention to his teachings?"[10] Indeed, who does? Our three saints did; in fact, it is one of the distinguishing marks of their theologies—a focused, almost literal, reading of the most countercultural parables, acts, and sayings of Jesus of Nazareth is their primary source for knowing both who God is and who we are. Along with their own experiences of self-emptying love, and especially their attempts to embody it in their own times, our saints relied on the deepest, most total metaphors they could imagine for expressing the contrast between what God would have us do and what our own egos encourage.

And of the three saints, Weil is the most extreme in this matter, which is why she is so "difficult" to read, why she has been called crazy, why her anorexia has been used to dismiss her. Her reading of God's way in the face of Jesus Christ is simply too outrageous for middle-class, capitalistic culture to imagine. In Weil, we find that the notions of the world as God's body— and of the world as our bodies—are the most appropriate, because most radical, metaphors. Just as Jesus gave his body as the necessary food for the re-creation of new selves in God, so Weil desires to give her body for others in total obedience. Her astounding paralytic prayer says it all: "May all this [her mind, powers of sensation, and experiences] be stripped away from me, devoured by God, transformed into Christ's substance, and given for food to afflicted men whose body and soul lack every kind of nourishment."[11] Here Weil understands the incarnation of God in Jesus Christ literally, and she combines it with a reflection of divine incarnationalism in a follower. Weil sees continuity between the many stories of Jesus the healer, the sharer of food, the fellow sufferer who identifies with the poor, the teller of tales focused on upsetting the usual hierarchy of the haves and the have-nots—all of this occurs in the final act of his crucifixion, in which he gives his body in total self-emptying for others. This kind of love—impersonal in that it includes everything and everyone and materialistic in that it focuses on the basics for a good life at both the physical and emotional levels—is contrary to even the best of capitalism's acts of charity for the needy. It is based on suffering-with, compassion for others, all others, which is most fully expressed in the metaphor of the world as one's body, both God's and ours. Here incarnationalism does not mean the coming down of a superior God to earth, putting aside his power so as to identify with lowly human beings as a gesture of imperial condescension (as the tradition often suggests, even in its interpretation of the famous passage on divine self-emptying in Phil. 2:5-8). Rather, it is more like the compassion that one feels for what is part of oneself or someone so close that only body language, for instance, seeing the world as a "womb" within God, can suggest. For Weil, incarnationalism is not the remote concern that a king might have for his subjects; rather, it is more like a mother might have for her child, for what is from one's own being. Seen in this light, Weil's shocking images of divine and human self-emptying for others become less absurd; in fact, they are appropriate for the kind of relationship with the world that she has herself experienced, both in her reading of the scriptural texts and in her attempts at identifying with those who suffer in body and spirit. One of the important insights that the metaphor of the world as one's body gives to us is its ability to range from the most personal to the most public: from sharing a crust of bread with a stranger to attention to increasing climate-change-induced famines in sub-Saharan Africa. The metaphor, of course, also includes the daily needs of all other individual life-forms on the planet as well as the continuation of their species. Hence, what sounds like an esoteric, abstract notion—decreation—in fact hides a rich reservoir for imagining the journey of physical and mental self-emptying that twenty-first-century well-to-do human beings must undertake if others—and the planet itself—are to prosper.

David Tracy claims that Weil's theology describes well "why Christianity must be a mystical-political religion of and for the oppressed."[12] If this is a valid comment, and not only do I think it is but I also believe it sums up the theology of our three saints, then what dimension of it does Dorothy Day emphasize? Recall our attempt earlier to describe the contributions of our three saints: Woolman as the prophet of economics based on universal love, Weil as the philosopher of paying attention to the other, and Day as the practitioner of public personalism: each contributes a bodily-based, empirical, distinctive focus on some aspect of concrete oppression. Moreover, each combines the mystical (the personal) with the political (the public), but it is on this particular facet that Day's theology shines. One of the criticisms often made of environmental ethics is that it fails to do this, either stopping with individual efforts at simplified living or trying to engage people on systemic, public issues that have little connection with their daily lives (such as carbon taxes on greenhouse emissions). The genius of Day's contribution is that it is at the same time radically personal and radically political. Her theology of the "little way," learned from Thérèse of Lisieux, is captured in Dostoevsky's "onion" story Day narrates, illustrating in the beggar woman's cry when others attempt to climb up to heaven with her—"Only for me!"—that there is, in fact, no individual, but only a communal, salvation. As William D. Miller notes in his biography of Day, no division was possible in Day's theology: "Mass political and social pressures that ignored the poor at one's doorstep were false. The action of love came before the action of the world."[13] Many have questioned this sequence, claiming that waiting until hearts have changed in order to change the world is an exercise in both futility and denial of the urgency of the public issues facing us. However, the power of Day's form of finding God in the face of Jesus requires continuity (and therefore personal integrity) at all stages. Recall that Day tells us that we should indeed "dread" Thérèse's little way, for it does not let us off the hook; rather, it demands that we live what we preach and adhere to Woolman's similar advice that conduct is more convincing than words. For Day, God's incarnation is found not only in the face of Jesus but also in the face of every oppressed person: "What a simplification of life it would be if we forced ourselves to see that everywhere we go is Christ, wearing our socks we have to darn, eating the food we have to cook, laughing with us, walking with us, silent with us, sleeping with us. . . . He [Christ] made heaven hinge on the way we act towards Him in his disguises of commonplace, frail and ordinary human beings."[14] Summing up this powerful insight, Day remarks, "As St. Paul says, it is by little and by little that we are saved—or that we fail."[15]

If one of the central issues twenty-first-century middle-class Westerners face is denial of the seriousness of our ecological and financial crises, an increasingly ostrich-like pose in which we bury our despair with a refusal to face what in fact *we can do*, then Day's call for action on our doorstep is relevant, whether or not, it is successful. One of the key assets of religious belief in all traditions is the assumption that success does not lie totally with our efforts, that we are called to do what we can, having the faith that forces beyond the individual are on the side of the planet's flourishing. At times, this belief will take the form of darning socks and at other times of organizing protest movements, peace marches, boycotts, and other forms of mass political efforts. At all times, our intention, as Miller reminds us, is that "personalism was first a disposition to grow in 'active' love toward all creation."[16] "All creation" covers the map from the personal to the public but always with the same criterion of undertaking the action with the integrity required as if one were doing it "in the face of Christ."

In summary, as we consider how our three saints see God and human beings in the face of Jesus, several characteristic notes surface. First, they did not assume that they knew what they would find: ignorance and error was their common stance. The surprising twists and turns of actual, laborious, daily experience of attempting to live in the image of Jesus—his way of responding to the least of the needy—gradually bring insight to an otherwise inscrutable question: What *does* God require of us? Second, the only way our saints learned the answer to this question was by getting the ego out of the way (through voluntary poverty) and hence, making it possible to pay attention to the real needs of others. This process eventually "universalizes" the self, expanding the perimeters of self-concern to include everyone and everything. Woolman did this through imagining his own death and subsequent rebirth mixed in with all others who suffer; Weil expanded the limits of her own body so that in her paralytic prayer she asks that her body might be given as nourishment to all sufferers who need it; and Day found Christ everywhere, in all the many bodies who needed soup and socks as well as in nonviolent protests for fair wages. They saw with God's impersonal, inclusive eyes, which embrace all forms of suffering. The surprising result of these strategies of radical, inclusive love is a new definition of power, one that turns it upside down, one characterized not by control by one of the many but by self-emptying sacrifice of the many for all. The movement here is from a narrow, egotistic understanding of fulfillment of the subject—myself—to an expanded inclusiveness of mutual flourishing that is only possible through the self-emptying of each subject in the dance of give-and-take that characterizes life at all stages—biological, human, cosmic, and divine.

We now ask, What do we learn of God and ourselves from the process of reading the answer from the face of Jesus? The first thing we learn is that we do not know, and the little we do know is clothed in ambiguity. What we have both in Scripture and in the lives of those who have attempted to "live in Christ" are intimations of the divine (and the human) rather than clear statements or commandments. If one gathers together some of the most characteristic passages from the New Testament on the topic of self-emptying love, at most they paint a picture in broad strokes of disorientation and reorientation on the matter of how we should live, emphasizing depth but not giving clear instructions. For example, the advice that Jesus gives to the rich young man who asks how he might gain eternal life is daunting but not detailed: "If you wish to be perfect, go, sell your possessions, and give to the poor" (Matt. 19:21). In the Sermon on the Mount, the poor, the hungry, those who weep, and the persecuted will be rewarded, whereas the rich and powerful will meet a sad demise. In Galatians 2:19-20, we learn that the life demanded of us is one of crucifixion with Christ, even to the point of giving up our own existence. We should add as well the Golden Rule ("Do to others as you would have them do to you"); the two great commandments to love God with one's entire being and the neighbor as oneself; as well as the admonition to love our enemies and those who persecute us. Finally, the parable of the good Samaritan complicates matters still further, as some interpretations do not allow us even to *be* the good neighbor, finding it a well-nigh impossible for human beings. From this survey, we see how starting one's theology from the face of Jesus does not give us a program of moral action in regard to how to live before God and on behalf of others. What the face of Jesus tells us is that we can't do it; we can't live the way God would have us live. Hence, the single most important insight from the message, the life and death, of Jesus is that we will fail. This is, in fact, good news, for it is news that the salvation of the world (in our case, global warming and extreme poverty) is not entirely up to us to bring about. If the news were that God is the all-powerful potentate who can unilaterally decide whether or not to clean up the mess we have made and set the creation back on the right track, then we might feel called to take up this task in like manner, seeking to control nature. But that is not the case; rather, reading who God is and who we are from the face of Jesus brings us very different news: the power that fuels the universe is one of self-emptying giving and receiving; hence, this is the life to which we are being called. It is a life of participation in the life of God, and this turns our attention now to that big question: Who is God? The following comment says it well. "If the Incarnation is indeed our best window into the nature of God, then it makes sense that a kenotic Christology should lead to a kenotic theism, in which the self-giving love shown in Christ is seen as central to God's very nature."[17] Here we see the critical importance of beginning our reflections on who God is not with our preconceived notion that God is timeless and immutable, but with Jesus as the incarnation of God, for "the Incarnation seems to shout at us that God is intimately involved in the temporal world."[18] Yet this is seldom done. All too often, theologians as well as ordinary folks assume that they already know who God is. If that were so, then the entire project of this book (and of the insights of the saints) becomes superfluous. It is essential that we do not take that route, for Christology—the life and message of Jesus of Nazareth—is important only because of what it tells us of God. "Christ" is not a third big question in addition to who God is and who we are; rather, it is the way into answering these other two questions that identifies Christians as Christians. And, as we have seen, the insights from this way are not only radical and shocking but also contrary to most common assumptions concerning the nature of God and of ourselves.

MY OWN WITNESS

Why should I add my own witness? Certainly not because it is especially profound or in any way comparable to the witness of our three saints, but because in the face of such honesty and integrity as we meet in these folks, one is called to confess where one stands, even if this place is not particularly flattering to the observer! During the half century that I have been reading the three people's lives we have focused on, I have felt like a hypocrite. I do not "walk the talk"; I cannot say that studying their lives has brought me much closer to the kind of radical action for others that characterizes them. At most, I do what the Dalai Lama suggests—"As much as we can."[19] Some days that turns out to be very little. One way to deny guilt when faced with the saints is to avoid contact with them; surely, it must be some form of masochism to keep reading them for fifty years, always feeling, as Day puts it, that we are letting ourselves off the hook. But I find I cannot stop reading them; they fascinate me because I believe that they have in fact found, if not *the* secret to the abundant life, then at least one important avenue. Hence, at least I feel like a grateful hypocrite when I read them, grateful that their lives constantly and continuously call mine into question. Does it matter that I may have come closer to *understanding* them after all these years, even if I don't follow them? Is asking for forgiveness for not doing more the one step that the grateful hypocrite takes, realizing that forgiveness is the acceptance that it is okay to be me, as long as one does not defend one's paltry offering? Hence, all I can say at this point is that trying to understand the process of moving toward being a universal self is my vocation, my calling—it is very little, but as another wise person (Confucius) put it, "It doesn't matter how slow you go, as long as you don't stop."[20]

With all these qualifications, regrets, and confessions, I will add my witness on the matter of how we start talking about who God is and who we are. First, a brief list of assumptions, some of which I share with the saints, and some I do not. I accept the picture of the cosmos coming to us from the sciences as the worldview that should accompany all theology. Also, like the saints we looked at, I accept the story of the historical Jesus as a disorienting-reorienting portrait of how we should live in the world. One evening, when I was a sophomore in college, I read the Gospel narrative of Mark from beginning to end, and it blew my mind. I had no idea Christianity was such an upsetting, countercultural story—and that realization has only increased over the years. Like the saints, I have found that Jesus is important not in and of himself but because he, like a finger pointing to the moon, tells us who God is and who we are. This is by no means the only (or maybe the best) source of such knowledge, but it is the story I have bet my life on, and I believe it is a persuasive and healthy paradigm for the planet and its creatures. The longer I consider the sources for talking about God and ourselves, the more I realize how minimal they are—we do not know much, and it is wise to admit it. Thus religious language has always been metaphorical for me, with all our assertions of "is" and "is not," with more of the latter than the former. In particular, I have found that the model of the world as God's body is richer, deeper, and more powerful the longer I myself attempt to live within that model and think about the big questions in terms of it. It is similar in many ways to the various forms of incarnational language that we have found in Woolman, Weil, and Day and has the merit of keeping our eyes focused on the earth and its well-being, including the nonhuman dimensions of the planet. If one thinks within this model, food becomes a central way to interpret both our sins of greed and our responsibilities toward others. To see the world as God's body (and ours) is a powerful contemporary model for delving into the layers of what self-emptying or kenosis means for the twenty-first-century crises of economic and ecological destruction. It is, I believe, one of the contributions that one religion—Christianity—can make in particular to understanding better how we should live.

I will now try to express a few insights that contribute to the conversation of talking about God and ourselves. The first and one of the most important points is that we have to wake up and stay awake. Annie Dillard says, "We teach our children one thing only . . . to wake up."[21] "Children ten years old wake up and find themselves here, discover themselves to have been here all along. . . . They wake like sleepwalkers, in full stride; they wake like people brought back from cardiac arrest or from drowning."[22] It happened to me when I was seven years old. One day, coming home from school, I suddenly realized that I would not be here forever; I would not be "here" for Christmas, and even more amazing, the day would come when I would not be here for my birthday, May 25. I could not wrap my mind around this insight—it was like a canker sore in my mouth: I couldn't stop touching it; it both fascinated and hurt. Eventually, I realized, however, that I *am* here right now, and that, Dillard asserts, is what we have to keep reminding ourselves: we have to keep staying awake: "My God what a world. There is no accounting for one second of it."[23] Staying awake is one of the hardest things we have to do. At almost eighty years old, I find the best way to stay awake is to walk daily on a small trail in a park near my house. Each time I do this, I wake up again to the most basic faith that I have: that life is a gift. Like that day, at seven years old, when I realized that I did not have to be, that my life was contingent, an accident perhaps, but also surely a mystery and a gift, setting out on that little trail each day renews my sense of wonder and appreciation for my time on the earth. The closer I come to leaving the world, the more I love it. The poet Robinson Jeffers advises us to fall "in love outward" with the world around us. Many days when I stand still in little Jericho Park, listening to the wind in the trees, I feel a thrill go through me. The world, the wonderful, wild (and tame) world, the pocket park in the city is the place where I know my first love is the world, the gift of simply being here. Like Teilhard de Chardin, I have come to realize that I cannot love God *or* the world, but must love both at once. As I age, my eyes and ears have been opened, and I drink in the world and find God there as well. I feel more certain of that all the time: it is why the body metaphor makes sense to me—whether in beauty or suffering (as Weil reminds us), it is the flesh of the world that sustains us physically and spiritually. This is, I believe, radical incarnationalism at the heart of the Christian witness: the world as God's body and ours. God is found *here*, not somewhere else. It is a partial experience and witness, but a Christian one as well as a useful and thoughtful one. Just as Weil, Woolman, and Day experienced God physically, through the body of the world, so do I. My focus is more on the natural world, whereas theirs was more on the human, but these emphases are complementary, not contradictory. So, my first prayer is one of thanksgiving: "Thanks be to God that I do not have to love God *or* the world, but can (and should) love both together."

If life is a gift, and waking up is acknowledging this fact, then the depth of religion is gratitude, appreciation, a big, long yes! Each day now, I am grateful that I have this day, another day to live, a day that I did not expect and do not deserve (as Woolman remarks, a "day lent to me"). Life is a gift: we have been given everything, from our first breath of air to our last. There does not have to be any *purpose* to life other than recognizing this gift: the gift of experiencing it, of being awake, of listening and seeing the wonders of our planet. "To be" is a blessing. Human life is the glorious opportunity to be conscious of the gift of life on earth for a few years and to appreciate this gift. It is a chance to say yes to life and to contribute to its well-being.

However, it is not all yes. *Yes*, as Julian of Norwich reminds us, is the first and last word ("all things shall be well," although, as she adds, "we cannot begin to tell" *how*). Nonetheless, the beauty of the world does not negate its suffering, and here is where the mystery of the cross emerges in Christianity. Christianity is neither a tragic nor a sentimental religion; it is, I believe, a realistic, hard-headed one. While the dominant understanding of the cross in Christian theology has been some form of atonement theory— God takes the sins of the world upon the divine self in Jesus Christ as ransom, substitution, or sacrifice, relieving us of the consequences of our evil ways—it is not the only understanding and is increasingly, I believe, a questionable one. Christianity is not magic: it does not support a deistic, mechanistic salvation by divine fiat or action. Rather, as I have suggested, it is in line with the cosmic reading of evolution, that life is only possible through the shared sacrifice of all for others. If one is to live *in* God and *on* the earth—in other words, if the incarnation, the embodiment of God—is to be the context for abundant human life, then there is no escaping the harsh realities of biological existence. If, as Augustine says, we are satisfied by nothing less than living *in* God, and if we are satisfied by nothing less than living *on* the earth (and not in heaven!), then we must *feel* that we live in both places at once—in God and the earth.

This is, I believe, what the incarnation means: that we can (and must) so live. There is, then, no separation between heaven and earth, no dualism, no nature versus supernature, but one reality, which is not a being, even the highest being. Rather, reality is radical relationality, all life joined in a network of interlocking dimensions, with "God" as the source of life and love that holds it all together, and that gives it its direction, its goal, its trajectory: Julian's yes. God is not a being, but "love," and love is the warp and woof of the tapestry we call the universe. God is the Yes of the entire universe, the Yes that is life and the Yes that is love. This the cosmic story does not tell us: it does not tell us that the last (and the first) word is *yes*, a yes to life. The cosmic story does not tell us that reality is love.

But if this is the case, then we have to ask, Where do we fit into this scheme of things? As the one creature who has woken up, who is aware that life is a gift, we have the responsibility to help this direction toward life and love along its way. The mystery of the cross is not, then, atonement for our sins, but an invitation to participate in the life of God, since according to the Christian tradition we were made in the image of God, and therefore our goal is to grow fully into that image. We participate in God's life through the kenotic message, life, and death of the face of God, Jesus of Nazareth. Hence, our whole life—who we human beings are—is moving from belief to action, from acknowledging the gift of life to its fulfillment. The direction is always one way—from God to us, from gift to receipt of life, as we attempt to bring our wills into one with God's will. The present book has been about this movement: what the tradition has called "deification," growing into the image of God. As we have seen in the parable of the good Samaritan, this is not a moral duty that we can accomplish on our own. We cannot be the "good" neighbor; at most we can accept God's grace, power, and forgiveness as we struggle to become one with God's kenotic love for the world. In other words, the yes of Christianity is first of all a no, the no to the selfish, individualistic, narrow ego of our market-capitalistic consumer society that has been shown to destroy God's yes to all life.

And finally, I believe, that at each of our deaths we are received back into the great sea of life and love which is God. As Dorothee Soelle asks us, Can we care more about the beauty of creation and its continuing to flourish than we do about our own individual continuation in some future, heavenly existence? The tough love of Christianity demands this death, as does the natural world. If we have undergone some measure of displacement, or as Weil puts it, a decreation of the ego and the re-creation of God's life in oneself, then we ought to be able to say thank you to God like good guests as we exit. As Annie Dillard reminds us, we ought not to grasp at "more, more, more," but be grateful for the gift of having a few years to be wide awake in this world, so wonderful that "there is no accounting for one second of it."

"The Cross . . . Is the Center of all Christian Theology"

These challenging words by theologian Jürgen Moltmann cry out for interpretation. What the story of Jesus, culminating in the cross, tells us about God is shocking "good news."[24] The classic and still-critical text for kenosis in the New Testament is Philippians 2:5-11. It is preceded by Paul's admonition that the disciples should "look not to your own interests, but to the interests of others." Paul then illustrates this point by referring to the "mind" of Christ Jesus, who though he was "in the form of God" undercut his own equality with the divine, emptying himself into "the form of a slave," and humbling himself to the most extreme degree, "to the point of death—even death on a cross." These sentences have fascinated countless interpreters, with some focusing on the issue of God's "nature" changing its ontological status, holding back the divine attributes of power and prestige in order to appear as a convincing human being, while others see the text mainly as a moral injunction for disciples to behave without "selfish ambition or conceit." [25] The important issue at stake is, How central is this text for Christian theology? Is it mainly a matter of limiting divine power so that the human life of Jesus can appear credible, or is it instructions on humility for the church—or is it something much larger? Is it not only a critique of the Christian message as unilateral power and prestige, but also a new understanding of power—the power of the cross? If the cross is the summation of Jesus' life, and if this is where we learn both who God is and who we are, then self-giving love becomes the focus for all aspects of a Christian theology. Hence, a kenotic theism and a kenotic anthropology emerge as the central categories of theology, and the order of consideration is also given: first, the movement from the life, message, and death of Jesus of Nazareth as the face of God, to a discussion of who God is in God's self (the so-called Trinity), and then to a reflection on creation, human life, and salvation. In other words, a kenotic theology, one that sees the total self-emptying for others in the cross and moves from there to a consideration of all other theological issues, must begin in a comparable kenotic manner, with the clues given us in the story of Jesus. Our saints certainly traveled this humble, ambiguous, relative route, and I believe it is incumbent on all Christian theologies to do likewise.

A kenotic, metaphorical theology has no privilege, no exceptionalism, no assurance that it is the best or only theology; rather, like its central figure—the historical Jesus—it has at most only a shaky, minimal foundation. It is, however, a foundation in a manner that embraces reality in all its many phases and dimensions, from the interdependent universality of the evolutionary process, which is often cruel, bloody, and unfair (from our perspective) in its forms of give-and-take, sacrifice and gift, to the equally awesome and incredible self-emptying love of God in God's self for the world and all its creatures. What I am suggesting here of course is not only a criticism of common notions of power and privilege but also a new paradigm for understanding power—power now as the source of all flourishing life—though that route to flourishing often goes through the deepest, most tragic, most despairing, seemingly most fruitless paths to arrive at its goal. What we see in the Trinity, in God's very self, is on this reading in line with the cosmic story of evolution: here we do not have two stories, a secular and a religious one, but a single interpretation of reality, with the difference that the religious story claims that this is not just the story of life, but of "flourishing" life. Irenaeus's sentence sums it up well for me: "The glory of God is every creature fully alive." The trajectory of the universe's story is not, then, for Christians a tale of woe, indifference, or malevolence, but one of love, albeit self-emptying love, which for all creatures has a negative and often tragic dimension and, for us human beings, demands not only our acknowledgment that reality *is* this way (interdependent, universal, often "negative") but also our willingness to participate with God for the flourishing of life.

These reflections on a kenotic theology have been helpfully summarized over the ages in the Eastern Orthodox tradition of Christian theology with three terms: *kenosis*, *enosis*, and *theosis*, which is understood, in contrast to the Western theology of the atonement, as what "salvation" means.[26] It is usually called the process of "deification," whereby the four steps that we outlined with our saints—experiences of voluntary poverty, focus on attention to the needs of others, leading to the growth of a universal self that operates at all levels, both personal and public—take on flesh and blood. While this tradition has often started with the kenosis of God in creation (divine self-limitation in order to give "space" for the creation of independent creatures), I begin my reflections with enosis, the union of divine and human wills in Jesus of Nazareth. Or, in terms of the process of salvation in our saints, knowledge of deification for us begins with Jesus as the exemplification par excellence of the universal self. In other words, a Christology "from below," which one sees in our saints and in my own witness, is a kenotic theology that understands the doctrine of the "hypostatic union," the unity of the divine and human, not as the traditional view does in terms of substance or essence, but rather in terms of intentionality and action. Seeing this union of wills in Jesus of Nazareth causes people like our saints (and me) to locate "revelation," knowledge about the divine and the human, in this figure. Such a Christology claims that we see the revelation of God in the face of Jesus (as well as the revelation of humanity) because here we can read the actions of Jesus as the actions of God.[27] The life of Jesus is completely informed and freely directed by the Spirit of God; here, in an act of kenosis, Jesus is emptied of pride and egotism so that he may be entirely filled with the Spirit of God. Here a finite, human life becomes the true image of God. The process that we have analyzed in depth with the stories of our saints so that with Paul they can say, "Not I live, but Christ lives in me" (Gal. 2:20), begins with the prior story of Jesus as the process of enosis. "In the moment of enosis, exemplified supremely in the person of Jesus, God enters into the being of those who freely consent to such mediating action, and acts in and through them to make them living sacraments of the divine presence."[28] Thus, in spite of the hypostatic union seeming to be an abstract if not irrelevant doctrine, it is the central assertion that in the humble stories of people like our saints and quintessentially in Jesus of Nazareth we have a place to say something about God. The significance of this starting point, as I have insisted, is that it makes it possible for us to talk about God, and this is where we will begin.

What does the message, life, and death of Jesus of Nazareth tell us about God? Most essentially, it tells us that God does not "exist" in another world; rather, "God" is what/who makes this world go round. "God" is knowing that I owe my life to Something, Someone other than myself. What we learn from the lives and witness of Woolman, Weil, and Day (and I add my own) is that the questions the atheist or agnostic asks, Where is God? How great is God? Is God with us here on earth? are not abstract, useless questions but are at the heart of what Jesus tells us of God. God is not, on this reading, a distant, minimal, supernatural being, but rather, God is another name for reality, for the reality that actually creates, fuels, sustains, and saves all life. The lives of our saints witness to this God at both the macrocosmic and the microcosmic levels: God is both the Yes that the scientific story does not give us—that God is not only the source of life but that life has a directionality toward its *flourishing*, and that God is also the Yes that helps each of us get out of bed in the morning and keep going. For Woolman, Weil, and Day (and me), God is the plus in life, the "extra" that makes life worth living. God is why the earth is not flat and sterile, why it shines with glory. God is that specific Something/Someone that keeps us from sinking every day, who lifts us out of the pit of despair. God is everything and anything that is good, true, and beautiful. Does this mean that God is everything and therefore the world is nothing? No, but God is the Yes (however small) to all the big nos—the no of slavery to Woolman, of starvation to Weil, of market capitalism and war to Day (and of climate change to me). Is God, then, merely human hopefulness? No, because these folks do not believe that hope comes from themselves, no matter how dedicated their efforts. Rather, hope comes *to* us. It is a gesture of respect offered via human actions to the most degraded human being (Weil), a word of truth spoken to slaveholders in denial about their oppression of others (Woolman), an invitation to a country vacation among fields of flowers for children living in slums (Day), a march protesting the Canadian oil sands pipeline being built. We are not the source or strength of any of this; at most, we can try to move our narrow egos out of the way so that we can become channels of God's loving power for no to all that diminishes life and yes to all that promotes it. We are the receivers, the listeners, the admirers, the grateful ones. We live within a world cupped within the hands of God, who is all things good, true, and beautiful. We did not create any of this, and we cannot live apart from what/who did.

Starting with the most immediate, personal, and daily experiences of that Something/Someone beyond us but within whom we live from breath to breath—what I read as the experience of our saints and know from my own spiritual journey—embraces both the beauty and the suffering of the world. Neither is sufficient alone: Weil claims that these two—beauty and suffering— are routes to God, the beauty of the world that causes us to exclaim with wonder and gratitude just for another day in this glorious place and the suffering of millions of individuals and species, human and nonhuman, both by accident and by intention, that likewise causes us to exclaim, but now in horror and unbelief, that such waste and cruelty are possible. God, then, is first of all not a being (no matter how great) but the slow (or sudden) experience that makes us aware that we are not alone—and that we are living in world of yes. Julian of Norwich's enigmatic words reach out trying to express this: all will be well. The Christian Easter attempts to say the same thing: all it says is that while we do not know how or what will be "well," we know that it will be. It simply says that a yes rather than a no rules and empowers the universe. This is all we need to know: it is the witness against our deepest fear—that despair, hatred, indifference and/or malevolence is at the heart of things. We see glimmers of the yes in the tiniest forget-me-not flower hidden under a mountain rock as well as in a piece of bread shared with a hungry person. This, not a "being" of any sort, is God.

But before we can be more specific on "intimations of the divine," we need to pull back and attempt a brief, thumbnail sketch of the paradigm of God, human being, and world that we are suggesting emerges from experiences of God's kenotic love. It is impossible to speak of God without also speaking of human beings and the world, for they form a whole, as the classic paradigm clearly shows us. In the traditional view, God is the absolute Creator and Lord of the world, creating the world from nothing, and requiring total obedience to the divine will. The created world, and especially human beings, are separate from God, living in a different place and entirely dependent on the divine will. Unfortunately, human beings sin, refusing in their pride to bow to the absolute, distant, all-powerful God, and hence they deserve punishment. However, in his mercy, God decides to take the punishment for sin upon himself, substituting his son and accepting his sacrifice on behalf of the wayward brothers and sisters. Our role is to respond to this gift of grace with gratitude and resolve to live in the future according to the commandments to love God and neighbor. This paradigm is anthropocentric, focused on human beings rather than the entire world, and it assumes that God and humans are separate beings, united by divine grace on the one hand and human gratitude on the other. While this sketch is scarcely fair to the many lives that have been lived in loving engagement with God, it does contain sufficient viability across many millennia and versions of Christianity, so it is recognizable as at least the stereotype of the Christian story.

If, however, we now attempt a similar sketch of a kenotic Christian theology, we begin not with the creation of a world separate from God, but with the history—the face of Jesus of Nazareth, his message, actions, and especially his cross. Here, Christians, those who base their lives on faith in Jesus as a limited but persuasive revelation of God, claim that the first thing to say about God is self-emptying love. Jesus' whole life was a lead-up of total giving to others, culminating in the cross, where he sacrificed his life, not for the atonement of humanity's sins, but as a witness to the totally unexpected and overwhelming gift of God's own self as the answer to our questions about who we are and how we should live. The cross of Jesus tells us that God's own life is also our life (for we were made in the "image of God" to live as God lives). And the most important characteristic of God's life is love. Here, we have the one word that we use to talk about God that is not a metaphor; that is, every other word we use to express the divine reality is something drawn from our world and used—stretched—to function somehow for God. Thus, when we call God Father or Mother or the body of the world, and so on, we are taking meanings that we understand and substituting them for the silence that inhabits God-talk. We do not know how to talk about God, so we use metaphors from ordinary life. But with this one word—*love*—we make a statement that is open, blank, unfilled: we need God to define what *love* means. And this, I believe, is where faith enters: faith is not belief that God "exists," that God is a "being" (even of the highest sort). Rather, faith is the willingness to turn to the face of Jesus of Nazareth for intimations of what love means.

And here we find a strange thing. Rather than the traditional story of an absolute, all-powerful God who relates to the world by controlling and demanding its allegiance, we see God as the one who relates to the world in a new and astounding way: as self-emptying love for the well-being of all creatures. We have hints of this kind of love in the saints, sometimes in mother love, and here and there even in the biological world where give-and-take, reciprocity, sacrifice, and even hints of altruism emerge (as we have seen), but it is in the story of Jesus that Christians find both the fulfillment and the paradigmatic expression of this countercultural love.

Who Is God?

But the kenotic-theological story does not stop with Jesus—it points to God in God's self. The doctrine of the Trinity—that seemingly abstract and often irrelevant notion that God is "three in one"—becomes central at this point. This is the case because Christianity is not Jesus-worship; it is not about him, but about God, and not just about how God relates to the world but how God is in God's self. Thus the doctrine of the Trinity—a subject that has often been used to illustrate the esoteric irrelevance of the Christian view of God: How can "one" be "three"? "Do Christians believe in three gods"?—becomes the center of a profoundly immanental understanding of divine transcendence. That is to say, rather than a conundrum to baffle people about who God is, the doctrine of the Trinity clarifies and deepens our understanding of God, if it is seen as the face of Jesus, as I have suggested. A wide range of theologians agree. Julian of Norwich, writing in the Middle Ages, maintained this connection, as one commentator observes: "Jesus himself, as she sees him bleeding on the cross, is the source of her understanding of the Trinity."[29] Now, centuries later, John Haught, an evolutionary theologian, claims: "At the center of Christian faith lies a trust that in the passion and crucifixion of Jesus we are presented with the mystery of God who pours the divine self-hood into the world in an act of unreserved self-abandonment."[30] And Jürgen Moltmann adds: "The content of the doctrine of the Trinity is the real cross of Christ himself. The form of the crucified Christ is the Trinity."[31]

This is the first and most important point to make about a kenotic theology: our understanding of who God is comes not from "above," from an external or general source, from the common misunderstanding that "everyone knows who God is," which is often the opening comment of conversations about the nature of God. For instance, when scientists and theologians gather to discuss God, an assumed generic view often prevails on the side of the scientists: God is a static, transcendent, distant, all-powerful superbeing dwelling in another world. If, however, the question of who God is starts with what Jesus did in his life, teachings, and death, we have a very different view. As Grace Jantzen says of Julian's view, "Since the revelation of God in Jesus is a manifestation of the totally self-giving suffering of love, this is also the most important fact about the Trinity."[32] Hence, it makes all the difference "where we start" to talk about God. Moreover, it also makes a difference what we understand the work of Jesus to be. If it is primarily a sacrificial atonement on the part of an all-powerful God, then the Trinity is likely to be seen as the mechanism for this transaction: thus, as in Anselm's view, the Son, the "second person of the Trinity," sacrifices himself for the sins of his brothers and sisters in order to save them from divine punishment by the "first person," with the Spirit, the "third person," conveying the benefits to the faithful. Here the focus tends to be on the "persons" of the Trinity and their connecting tasks or functions. Thus the Western understanding of the Trinity, deeply influenced by Augustine, underscores the oneness of God, with the three *persona* (traditionally called the Father, Son, and Holy Spirit) as functions, aspects, or modes of the divine oneness. The tendency is to see the Trinity as one substance with three natures, in contrast to the Eastern view, which claims that outside of the Trinity there is no God, no divine substance. The Eastern Christian view underscores the "threeness" of the divine, and in particular, the *relationality* of the three.[33]

The result of these different emphases is that the Western understanding of God verges on "individualism" in both God and humanity, while the Eastern view focuses on the process of giving and receiving. The first sees both God and humanity as "substances," separate beings, while the second sees them as "relationships," reciprocal processes of give-and-take. In other words, the Western view of the Trinity supports a paradigm of God and the world as both characterized by static, individual substances or essences, while the Eastern view assumes that life—for both God and the world—is a process in which relations are more important than entities. Love is not a property or characteristic of God, some attribute added on to God, but "love is the supreme ontological predicate" of both God and of us human beings, who are made "in the image of God."[34] In other words, we choose self-emptying love or nothing; we are not created beings who then choose love, even as God is not "God" who then decides to love. Rather, who God is and who we are defined by love, by the self-emptying action of one into the other, of God into the world and of all parts of the world into each other. Being human is simply *choosing* to be what one is: a participant in God's very own life of love. Thus, poetically, the Eastern view sees the inner life of God as an "eternal divine round dance" in which there is no inferior or superior, no first or second, but an eternal self-emptying and refilling of each by each.[35] Here we see the glimmers of mutual reciprocity evident at all levels of evolution, epitomized in the Godhead itself, now understood (for Christians who see God in the cross of Jesus of Nazareth) as the very nature of reality. The Eastern view of the Trinity is more suited to the task of conveying immanental transcendence—that is, radical self-emptying love as the heart of the divine—than is the Western view, although many, including Augustine, with his view of God as the beloved, the lover, and love itself, have attempted to emphasize kenotic love.

A second implication of starting with the incarnate, self-emptying love of Jesus, epitomized in the cross, is a different view of divine power. I have touched on this subject numerous times, as it is so central to an understanding of how we human beings should act in the world. The tendency of monotheistic religions (Judaism, Christianity, and Islam) to provide support for the current radical individualism of Western culture, a view that as we have seen underscores human domination of nature among other things, is aided by unqualified monotheism: as God dominates the world, so human beings, made in the image of God, should dominate the natural world. This view has supported centuries of human exploitation of nature, culminating in our current human-induced global warming from excess greenhouse gas emissions. It is impossible to overemphasize the significance of monotheism's contribution to this customary stance of human beings, as it is often the unspoken assumptions of "who we are in the scheme of things" that has more influence than any explicit statements of "who we *should* be in the scheme of things." Thus a radically different understanding of divine power—one in

which God epitomizes total, self-emptying openness to others, all others—
is not only an indictment of the common view of power as control, but
also a paradigm of "letting be" so profound and so inclusive that we are
speechless to suggest what it means. Buddhism's *sunyata*, the "God" beyond
God; the mystic's prayer to free us from our desire to possess God; the
statement by a Christian theologian that "the Godhead is profound and utter
claimlessness"; and Meister Eckhart's suggestion that there is no God beyond
the distinctions of the Trinity are all attempts to address this speechlessness.
In this understanding, God "gives up" all names and properties, and we are
wary of all attempts to reach to the "emptiness" of God, acknowledging the
breakdown of all human attempts to say what cannot be said—that "God" is
God. The science-fiction novelist Ursula LeGuin published a nice piece in *The
New Yorker* some years ago in which she imagined Eve deciding to "unname"
the animals, a first step toward overturning the exceptionalism of human
beings in "naming" others, from the yak to God. LeGuin notes that "most
of them [the animals] accepted namelessness with the perfect indifference
with which they had so long accepted and ignored their names." As she leaves
Adam (who is wondering where his dinner is) to join the other animals, Eve
notes how difficult it is to name (and thus possess others): "My words must
be as slow, as new, as single, as tentative as the steps I took going down the
path away from the house, between the dark branched, tall dancers motionless
against the winter shining."[36] May our words, before all else, "unname" those,
including God, whom we have so glibly named and thus sought to control.

Thus, in summary, in the kenotic theological paradigm, there is continuity
all the way from evolution to God, and vice versa: one reality that is characterized at all levels by various forms and expressions of self-emptying. Hence,
beginning with the incarnation of God in Jesus Christ, Christians believe
that we have a paradigm of God, humanity, and the world that does not
validate raw, unilateral, absolute power at any stage or level of reality; rather,
the inverse is the case—what appears as utopian, fantastic, unbelievable,
mutual, interdependent sacrifice and self-emptying is indeed what makes the
world go round. Thus one moves from this reading of the incarnation to an
understanding of the creation of the world as God's gift of pulling back and
giving space to others, that they might live (but as the "body" of God, not as
separate beings), and to an understanding of human life as itself part of the
divine life, but as its "image." We live by participating in God's very own life
(since this is the only reality there is), but not simply as parts of God; rather,
human life is learning to live into the relationality of God's own life, which
is one of self-emptying love for *others*. Such a theology is not pantheistic (the
identification of God and the world), but panentheism (the world as living—
finding its source and fulfillment—*within* God's very self, the dance of self-
emptying love that desires the flourishing of all life). It is a sacramental vision,
in which the world is a reflection of the divine in all its trillions of individual

life-forms and species; thus, as Gerard Manley Hopkins reminds us, "The world is charged with the grandeur of God," not as one shining explosion, but in all its tiniest parts, even the intricate workings of a mosquito's eye. The motto here is *Vive la différence.* We human beings are the one life-form that does not fulfill its role as being a bit of God's grandeur simply by existing; rather, we, made in the image of God, must grow into the fullness of that reflection of God by willing to do so. And, according to the kenotic paradigm, this is what "salvation" is—not release from punishment for our sins, but a call to relate to all others (from God to homeless persons and drought-ridden trees) as God would and does.

What Is Creation?

As difficult as it is to pick out parts of kenotic theology to discuss (God, Christ, creation, human beings, sin and salvation, and so on), since we cannot think of everything at once, such artificially separate discussions are necessary, as long as one keeps in mind that theology is not a laundry list of subjects, but a unified vision of those perennial questions of who God is and who we are. I have been claiming in these pages that such visions emerge from the life experiences of people who, in different times and places, and with the help of different theological paradigms, attempt to share their reflections on these issues that refuse to go away and that deeply influence our behavior. What, then, is the implication from the perspective of a kenotic theology for the way we speak of the relation of God and the world, or what is usually called "the doctrine of creation"?

Grace Jantzen notes that "we easily think of creation as the manifestation of God's supreme power, calling the beings into existence. There is truth in this, but it is truth which must be qualified by the cross."[37] The common understanding of creation is subject to the same problem as the common understanding of who God is: an assumption that creation is the product of a static, distant, all-powerful God. Hence, creation is often viewed as a product of God's mind (in the words of Genesis, "Let there be light"), followed by a string of "let there bes" listing the various parts of the world. The picture that emerges is of one individual (the Western view of God, including the trinitarian God) who, from a supernatural world, creates by intellectual fiat a finite world, also composed of separate individuals. We see how the inheritance of an Augustinian view of the Trinity has colored the Western view of creation: as Eastern theologian John Zizioulas describes this divinity: "God *is* one and *relates* as three."[38] By beginning with a generic, all-powerful God, our discussion of creation is immediately biased in the direction of individualistic power, for both God and human beings. Thus the common notion of creation is of a deistic God manipulating the world as a puppeteer pulling the strings, resulting in such simplistic and dangerous notions of an all-powerful God determining the fate of individuals in an arbitrary way. Similarly, creation is seen as a collection of "objects" to be manipulated by those created in the image of God, human beings. This is, to be sure, a caricature of the God-world relationship in Western, Christianized culture, but nonetheless it does operate as an ominous and influential backdrop behind many of our decisions in regard both to other human beings (who are often treated as objects rather than subjects) and to other life-forms, which are almost always treated as objects, never as subjects or protosubjects. Thus, as many have noted: as we imagine God to be, so also we imagine ourselves to be—in this case, as powerful controllers of the world.

If, however, we begin our discussion of creation from the perspective of Jesus as the face of God, the incarnation and the cross as the environment for the doctrine of creation, we have a very different result. It could be called radical incarnationalism, by which we mean the picture of the divine that we have sketched above: the story of the Jesus of the cross, who as the face (incarnation) of God identified so thoroughly with all creation that his life led to death on the cross (self-emptying love). Here we have a picture of the God-world relationship that is neither one of absorption of creation into God nor a distant ignoring of creation as utterly separate from God. Rather, as we have seen in our discussion of the Trinity, God's relation to creation is one of both radical intimacy and total respect for the otherness of the other. Trinitarian love is not based on the erotic paradigm (of one-to-one), but rather on a communal-covenantal pattern (of empathetic identification with the well-being of the other). It is, on the one hand, the most intimate, penetrating, communal, interdependent relationship imaginable, but, on the other hand, it does not absorb the other or remain distant from it. Rather, it makes the claim that true love (God's love), the only love that is real, is one in which each and every partner participates in the dance of give-and-take, sharing and reciprocation, sacrifice and letting be, death and rebirth, that we see in evolution and that reaches its epitome in the Trinity.

In this picture, the doctrine of creation stresses the aspect of relationality dealing with the status of the world and human beings: we are creatures with our own intrinsic value (genuine otherness) and, at the same time, creatures in the most intimate relationship possible with God, where our lives are both grounded in and fulfilled by divine reality. I have noted several times that the one word we use in an unqualified fashion of God is *love*, but it is also the word that needs God to define it. Whereas we attempt to speak metaphorically about God as father, mother, beauty, goodness, and truth, using common understandings of these terms, stretching them to their infinite application, we hesitate when we say "God is love," knowing that it is not appropriate to compare it to the loves we know. Rather, it is that extra, mysterious, surprising "beyond" that nothing in our language approaches. Therefore, I have turned (in this essay) to stories, anecdotes, parables, and even paradoxes or contradictions ("love" is losing your life to find it) to suggest what we cannot express. We point to the cross as the ultimate conundrum: How can a humiliating death be the source of the deepest, most joyous, most fulfilling life? I have suggested that Christian theology is one attempt to answer this question through the life, message, and death of Jesus of Nazareth. Beginning with this story, we then look backward to creation and forward to discipleship or the Christian life to flesh out what such love—the love epitomized in the cross, a love that we have suggested is intimated by self-emptying for others—might be. The doctrine of creation illuminates two aspects of kenotic love: its gracious giving of "space" to others and the fleshly, bodily character of creation.

On the first point: if God is all in all, if God is reality (the source of all life and its renewal), the one in whom we live and move and have our being, then creation implies a pulling back on the part of God to allow space for others, real others, to exist. It is an attempt to imagine the coming together of the most radical understanding of "transcendent immanence"; that is, a kind of intimacy that not only allows for genuine otherness but actively promotes it. This is an old and deep tradition in Christian and as well as Jewish thought, the attempt to imagine how ubiquitous, all-pervading divinity might exist as the context or environment for genuine otherness.[39] In this creation paradigm, while I am presenting a panentheistic understanding of the God-world relationship—that the world exists "within" God and is internally related to God at every moment and dimension of its existence—nonetheless, I want to express at the same time the genuine otherness of creation and all its creatures. The traditional creation view, however, stresses the transcendence of God to the world, but at the expense of radical immanence. By beginning our discussion of creation with the incarnation of God in Jesus of Nazareth, a union so total that one can say that Jesus is the face of God, I assert both intimacy and personal relationality as the hallmarks of creation.[40] Most of the traditional Christian images attempting to depict the God-world relationship have been external, intellectual, and/or artistic. That is, they have pictured God as a disembodied "mind" or "imagination" calling creation into being through a word or painting a picture—an external activity of the divine that does not involve God's very being. Creation here is not an offshoot of the radical relationality that we saw is the heart of the Trinity, God's own being. However, a doctrine of creation that begins with the incarnation, and moves to the Trinity, to the implications of Jesus as the face of God for who God is in God's self, give us an environment for everything else we say about God and the world. Everything else must, then, be characterized by kenotic, self-emptying, empathetic love. Hence, a Christian understanding of creation is an implication of the Trinity, of God as the "universal self" par excellence, bringing all others into existence to be and to become genuinely themselves as they exist in patterns of complex unity and difference with all other creatures. Again, we see this pattern stretching from the earliest forms of evolution to the Trinity understood as personal relationality, recognizing the subject-hood of all creatures as well as their openness to radical sacrifice for others.

Hence, the first implication of a doctrine of creation based on radical incarnationalism is the appreciation of genuine otherness (each creature at all levels recognized as having intrinsic value as a subject or protosubject, while at the same time serving as objects for the well-being of others). This is a form of difference-within-unity that does not absorb the many into the one or distance each from the others; rather, it points to the self-emptying dance of give-and-take within the Trinity (and evolution) that encourages thinking that both respects individuality (not individualism) and insists on radical interdependence. The second implication of a doctrine of creation based on radical incarnationalism insists that creation is about bodies, about flesh, about food, about the economics of just, sustainable sharing of the world's resources for all needy stakeholders. Creation is not a "spiritual" matter; primarily, it is about bodies. Hence, the model of the world as God's body arises almost naturally at this point. While it is only one metaphor for the God-world relationship, it is a timely one, and personally I find that the longer I attempt to live within it as a possible construct for understanding that relationship, the richer and more appropriate it becomes. Once we Western Protestants get over our conventional squeamishness for thinking of "God" and "body" in the same sentence, one can begin to appreciate the model for its limited but illuminating possibilities. I have suggested several times that joy and suffering, beauty and pain, are two of the most evident routes to experiencing the love of God. This has certainly been the witness of Woolman, Weil, and Day, each of whom in their own way found God in the beauty of the natural world and delight in human companionship, while at the same time underscoring the presence of God in all forms of oppression, starvation, illness, and

deprivation. The body model is ideal for emphasizing what the Christian tradition has often overlooked and underplayed: how wonderful it is simply to be alive on our precious planet earth and how difficult it is for many if not most individuals of most species to flourish or, as Irenaeus puts it, for "every creature to be fully alive." These two together—appreciation for the beyond-all-wonder glories of creation and at the same time agony for the beyond-all-grief, profound suffering that many creatures endure (much of it from the indifferent and/or malevolent behavior of we human beings)—make up the most necessary and appropriate responses to creation. The empathetic deepening of both our joy and our sorrow for the beauty and the suffering in the world is the kenotic response demanded of us. The growth of the universal self, the self able to empathize (stand in the place of another, imagine the experience of another creature, whether human or nonhuman), is what we are called to pursue.

Who Are We Human Beings?

We come, then, to the other crucial question of Christian theology: If God (reality) is kenotic love and creation is the pulling back of the divine to give others the chance to live and practice kenoticism in all its many forms, including the minimal ones of evolution, then who are we in the scheme of things? Again, I do not ask this question in general or "from above," but only from on the ground (looking at the experiences of our saints and our own experience) and only within the environment of radical incarnationalism or from the face of Jesus.

Archbishop of Canterbury Rowan Williams helps begin our conversation with his suggestive remark: "God gives God, having nothing else to give."[41] Hidden within this enigmatic sentence is a wealth of insight for a Christian anthropology. As we clearly see in the stories of our saints, this is precisely what they "give." It is not only what God has to give, but also all that we each have to give. That recognition is the beginning of an understanding of who we are that emerges from seeing God as kenotic love. Since we are made in the image of God, then what we say about ourselves must be based on what we say about God. As we have discovered, God is love—not a "what" but a "who," not a being or object or individual but one who relates as subject to other subjects in a totally outgoing, self-emptying way. God is more a process than a thing: the concept of the Trinity is an attempt to describe this most basic activity at the heart of things. It is probably more appropriate to say with the early theologian Irenaeus that "God" is friendship rather than that "God" is an entity or substance. While I have insisted that only God can define *love*, friendship contains a suggestive characteristic that points us in the right direction. The singular characteristic of friendship is deep and abiding concern for the well-being of another. While erotic and even maternal love are dramatic and profound kinds of love, they still contain a note of egotistic satisfaction. Simone Weil calls friendship the highest form of love, for friendship alone focuses solely on the other, wishing the best for the friend even at one's own expense. We recall that for her, "God is . . . the perfect friend," for the "infinite" nearness and distance of the Trinity epitomizes friendship.[42] In friendship, one gives oneself, for there is nothing else to give that matters, as the well-known comment from the Gospel of John states: "This is my commandment, that you love one another as I have loved you. No one has greater love than this, than to lay down one's life for one's friends" (John 15:12-13). The suggestion here is that "friendship," not erotic or maternal love but rather a more-or-less "cool" and "impersonal" relationship, is the closest human analogy to both Jesus' love for his disciples and God's love for the world (trinitarian love). The love that before all else is focused *on the other* regardless of the expense to the self appears to be the best hint we have of kenotic love.

Hence, as with our discussion of who God is, we begin our discussion of who we are with a *relationship*, the activity of self-giving that we see in our saints and that is epitomized in the life, message, and death of Jesus of Nazareth. Jesus, as the face of God, tells us that who Jesus "is" manifests itself in friendship with God—his will is totally open to God's will, wanting to do only what God wishes, no matter the cost to the self, even death on a cross. I have noted that the mysterious doctrine of the hypostatic union can be interpreted as oneness of intentionality between God and Jesus, in which Jesus empties his own will in order to be filled with the will of God. Just as Jesus became one with God by living within and for God, so also the saints practice "deification," becoming "like" God by loving others with a total lack of self-regard. The implication here is not that we become God but that we become fully human, that is, capable of empathetic love to all other creatures, becoming true friends with God and all fellow creatures.

There are several characteristics of deification as an interpretation of authentic human living that help to flesh out what is meant by the term. It originated in Eastern theology, based on the cryptic statement by Irenaeus and used extensively by Athanasius and other early theologians—"God became man in order that man might become God." It is not meant to be taken literally: it does not mean that we will all become little "gods" and lose our humanity.[43] Rather, the central insight was to stress continuity between who God is and who we are: in both instances, the intention is to underscore that God and human beings are not individuals, objects, or entities, but persons, subjects, and processes. According to this interpretation, God and human beings are not in competition but are part of the same story, a surprising tale that, contrary to our fears and expectations, claims that life is not meaningless, indifferent, or malevolent but good news, the friendship of God and the world. The real mystery and hiddenness of God is, as one theologian puts it, "the heart-stopping, breath-taking freedom of the three divine Persons to give themselves away in love to each other, and so to us and all creation—it is this which is truly incomprehensible."[44] And he adds a word about who we are in this story: "We become who we are as Christ came to be who he is, by giving self away freely in love."[45] Here we have the whole Christian story about God and human beings in a nutshell: what we learn from the story of Jesus about total self-giving love as the heart of the divine (as expressed in the Trinity) is also the heart of the human (as seen in Jesus and in the saints): empathetic, self-emptying love. Thus salvation is deification in the sense that to be fully human is to grow into what we were created to be—the image or reflection of God. We attain this slowly through the journeys of our lives, as we learn through voluntary poverty to diminish the ego, opening ourselves to the friendship of God—

divine self-emptying that we might flourish—and hence become, like God, instances of empathetic attention to all others at every level of our personal and public lives. We do not do this on our own—our wild space gives glimmers of it that, if we will accept the invitation to live outwardly, for the world and others, rather than just inwardly, for ourselves, can be the beginning of a friendship with God in which we are gradually able to invite all others into this circle of friends.

In addition to deification being a story of continuity between persons (the "I" and "Thou" of all subjects in the universe), it is also an ontological rather than just a moral story. That is, this story tells us about reality, not just about how to behave. It claims that reality is this way: from its primordial cosmic beginnings with the simplest of "subjects" to its ultimate Subject, the Trinity, deification is the attempt to express the pattern of becoming like God through the various levels of kenotic foreshadowing in the give-and-take of evolution. We human beings are part of this story, and at least on our planet, an increasingly important part since we are the only creatures capable of living consciously according to the critical law of reciprocity, which allows earthly flourishing.

Friends give themselves, having nothing else to give. This could be a mantra for the three saints that we have been following throughout this book. This is perhaps the most astonishing and persuasive characteristic of the lives of Woolman, Weil, and Day. It is also at the heart of the enigmatic kenotic statements that in losing one's life, one finds it, which has been the thread we are following as religion's most important contribution to our twin crises of climate change and the unfair distribution of resources for survival. If a critical difference between the market-capitalist view of human life and a kenotic view is that the former claims that human beings are basically insatiable individuals concerned with the satisfaction of their own narrow egotistic desires, while the latter view claims that human beings, made in the image of God, can only find fulfillment by giving up themselves for the well-being of all others, then we can clearly see that giving oneself is the heart of the matter. The doctrine of the Trinity tells us that we have nothing to give but ourselves; friendship tells us the same thing. As we seek to understand the most central thing Christians say about human beings, we have to ask, What does it mean to give *oneself*? It can only mean our bodies; it can only mean food for other bodies. At the most basic level, the saints do not preach a gospel of sharing with needy others; rather, they give their own bodies that others might live. Thus, as Edith Wyschogrod puts it: "The saintly response to the Other entails putting her/his own body and material goods at the disposal of the Other."[46] Thus, at both ends of the giver-receiver relationship, it is not words or encouragement or gifts that are exchanged, *but the body itself and the means to keep bodies flourishing*. A deeply incarnational understanding of Christianity claims that at every stage—who God is, what creation is, who we are, and how we should live—the focus is on *embodiment.* Jesus gives himself in his life and message of empathetic love to others, gives his body on the cross in solidarity with all who suffer, and thus points to God as the divine giver par excellence, whose being is composed of persons, as movements of interweaving love. Likewise, creation is the pulling in of the divine self to allow space for others to live fully embodied, physical lives, and Christian discipleship is following the pattern we find in Jesus' life and in the Trinity of limitation, restraint, self-sacrifice of one's own body that other bodies might flourish.

If we were to reach for a single word that summed up kenotic love as the heart of Christian faith, it would be *food.* This lowly, mundane, physical, nonspiritual word appears again and again in the stories of our saints and in the Christian story itself. Food is the sine qua non of existence; it sums up the entire corporeal planet, which is created by energy and is sustained by food; the evolutionary story is the tale of who gets food and who does not; and wars increasingly will be fought over food. As we consider the dual crises facing our planet—climate change and unjust resource distribution—we see that they are all about food. If we take the mother-child relationship as a quintessential example of what we mean by compassion or empathy—responding to the deepest need of another—then the mother's giving food from her body to the infant can be seen as the model of radical kenotic love. It is no accident, then, that food appears so frequently in the Christian story and that its central ritual, the Eucharist, is a common meal in which the disciples give food to one another as Christ gave his body as bread and wine for all. As we recall the four stages of conversion from an individualistic view of the self to a universal view, we see the centrality of the body and of food: the first step—the wild space of voluntary poverty for well-off middle-class people is followed by a self-emptying that allows one's attention to move from its conventional focus on the self to the needs of others, especially deprived others, whether human or nonhuman. The defining characteristic of the universal self, the inclusion of all others in one's understanding of who one is, points to the stretching of one's own body (and bodily needs) beyond the limits of one's own skin: the world becomes my body, and I must therefore consider all the world's physical needs and not just my own.

We have seen this pattern time and again in Woolman, Weil, and Day. Woolman's dream could not be more physical, more bodily: he sees a "mass" of "human beings in as great misery as they could be, and live . . . and I was mixed with them, and . . . henceforth I might not consider myself as a separate being."[47] Weil's paralytic prayer expresses the body-food connection with eerie power: "May this love be an absolutely devouring flame of love of God for God. May all this [her mind, powers of sensation, and experiences] be stripped away from me, devoured by God, transformed into Christ's substance, and given for food to afflicted men whose body and soul lack every kind of nourishment."[48] Added to these comments is Day's little way, in which every last crumb and corner of her life at the physical level, from bad food to lack of privacy, is given to others, summed up in the most mundane of comments: "Above all the smell of the tenements, coming up from basements and areaways, from dank halls, horrified me. It is a smell like no other in the world and one never becomes accustomed to it. . . . It is not the smell of life, but the smell of the grave."[49] As Day apparently mentioned many times, Dostoevsky was painfully acute when he wrote: "Love in action is a harsh and dreadful thing compared to love in dreams." More than anything else that we could imagine, embodiment of the "dream" in one's own flesh is what is called for today. It is the central focus of Christianity's incarnationalism and should be, I suggest, the central focus of an ethic for our time of climate change (which will undermine the ability of the planet to feed its inhabitants) and unjust distribution of the food that the planet can provide. The classic doctrine of Christian discipleship, that, made in the image of God, human beings should embody the kenotic love of God, means that our own bodies must be on the line. In other words, food (and the whole planetary apparatus that goes to produce food for the billions of creatures) should become the central task at all levels, personal lifestyle changes, and public policies.

Notes

[1] John Woolman, *The Journal of John Woolman and a Plea for the Poor* (New York: Corinth Books, 1961), 214.

[2] Simone Weil, *First and Last Notebooks*, trans. Richard Rees (London: Oxford University Press,1970), 244.

[3] Dorothy Day, *The Long Loneliness* (New York: Curtis Books, 1952), 317.

[4] For more thorough treatments of this model, see some of my other writings, especially *Models of God* (Minneapolis: Fortress Press, 1987); *The Body of God* (Minneapolis: Fortress Press, 1993); and *Life Abundant* (Minneapolis: Fortress Press, 2001).

[5] For a sketch of the traditional view, as well as alternatives, see Sallie McFague, "Who Is God? Creation and Providence," in *A New Climate for Theology: God, the World, and Global Warming* (Minneapolis: Fortress Press, 2008), chap. 3.

[6] Annie Dillard, *Pilgrim at Tinker Creek: A Mystical Excursion into the Natural World* (New York: Bantam, 1975), 2

[7] Gary Snyder, *The Practice of the Wild* (New York: Farrar, Straus and Giroux, 1990), 29.

[8] See Sallie McFague, "The Practice of Planetary Theology," part 1 in *Life Abundant* for further elaboration of these criteria.

[9] J. M. R. Robinson, *Jesus: According to the Earliest Witness* (Minneapolis: Fortress Press, 2007), 226.

[10] Robert Coles, "In This Pagan Land," *America*, November 11, 1972, 378.

[11] Weil, *First and Last Notebooks*, 244.

[12] David Tracy, "Simone Weil: The Impossible," in *The Christian Platonism of Simone Weil*, ed. E. Jane Doering and Eric O. Springsted (Notre Dame: University of Notre Dame Press, 2004), 233.

[13] William D. Miller, *A Harsh and Dreadful Love: Dorothy Day and the Catholic Worker Movement*, 2nd ed. (Milwaukee: Marquette University Press), 24.

[14] Dorothy Day, "Room for Christ," *Catholic Worker* 12, December, 1945, 2.

[15] *By Little and By Little: The Selected Writings of Dorothy Day*, ed. Robert Ellsberg (New York: Alfred A. Knopf, 1983), 105.

[16] Miller, *A Harsh and Dreadful Love*, 64.

[17] C. Stephen Evans, "Introduction: Understanding Jesus the Christ as Human and Divine," in *Exploring Kenotic Christology: The Self-Emptying of God*, ed. C. Stephen Evans (Oxford: Oxford University Press, 2006), 16.

[18] C. Stephen Evans, "Kenotic Theology and the Nature of God," in Evans, *Exploring Kenotic Christology*, 197.

[19] The Dalai Lama, *Ethics for a New Millennium* (New York: Riverhead, 1999), 178.

[20] Quoted in Andrew Michael Flescher, *Heroes, Saints, and Ordinary Morality* (Washington, DC: Georgetown University Press, 2003), 235.

[21] Annie Dillard, *Teaching a Stone to Talk: Expeditions and Encounters* (New York: Harper and Row, 1982), 97.

[22] Annie Dillard, *An American Childhood* (New York: Harper Perennial, 1988), 11.

[23] Dillard, *Pilgrim at Tinker Creek*, 126.

[24] Jürgen Moltmann, *The Crucified God: The Cross of Christ as the Foundation and Criticism of Christian Theology* (New York: Harper and Row, 1974), 204.

[25] See for instance the treatment of nineteenth-century Lutheran theologians in David H. Jensen, *In the Company of Others: A Dialogical Christology* (Cleveland: Pilgrim, 2001).

[26] There are many good sources for those wishing to understand this tradition more fully. Here are a few. Michael J. Christensen and Jeffery A. Wittung, eds., *Partakers of the Divine Nature: The History and Development of Deification in the Christian Tradition* (Grand Rapids: Baker Academic, 2007); Norman Russell, *The Doctrine of Deification in the Greek Patristic Tradition* (Oxford: Oxford University Press, 2004); Stephen Finlan and Vladimir Kharlamov, eds., *Theosis: Deification in Christian Theology* (Eugene, OR: Pickwick, 2006).

[27] For an outstanding example of this Christology from below, see Roger Haight, *Jesus Symbol of God* (Maryknoll, NY: Orbis, 1999), as well as his book *The Future of Christology* (New York: Continuum, 2005).

[28] Keith Ward, "Cosmos and Kenosis," in *The Work of Love: Creation as Kenosis*, ed. John Polkinghorne (Grand Rapids: Eerdmans, 2001), 164.

[29] Grace M. Jantzen, *Julian of Norwich: Mystic and Theologian* (London: SPCK, 1987), 109.

[30] John F. Haught, *God After Darwin: A Theology of Evolution* (Boulder, CO: Westview, 2000), 48.

[31] Moltmann, *Crucified God*, 247.

[32] Jantzen, *Julian of Norwich*, 110.

[33] See, for instance, the work of John D. Zizioulas and Western theologies influenced by the Eastern perspective: John D. Zizioulas, *Being as Communion: Studies in Personhood and the Church* (London: Darton, Longman and Todd, 1985), and Zizioulas, *Communion and Otherness: Further Studies in Personhood and the Church*, ed. Paul McPartlan (New York: T&T Clark, 2006); Patricia A. Fox, *God as Communion: John Zizioulas, Elizabeth Johnson, and the Retrieval of the Symbol of the Triune God* (Collegeville, MN: Liturgical Press, 2001); Haught, *God After Darwin*; Jantzen, *Julian of Norwich*; Beverley J. Lanzetta, *The Other Side of Nothingness: Toward a Theology of Radical Openness* (Albany: State University of New York Press, 2001); Karen Armstrong, *The Case for God* (New York: Alfred A. Knopf, 2009); Moltmann, *Crucified God*.

[34] See Zizioulas, *Communion and Otherness*, 46.

[35] See Elizabeth A. Johnson, *She Who Is: The Mystery of God in Feminist Theological Discourse* (New York: Crossroad, 1992), 220–21.

[36] Ursula LeGuin, "She Unnames Them," *The New Yorker*, January 21, 1985.

[37] Jantzen, *Julian of Norwich*, 134–35.

[38] Zizioulas, Communion as Otherness, 33.

[39] See, for instance, the treatment of *tsimtsum* as "the idea that God withdrew upon himself or shrank himself to make a void in which to create" (*Window of the Soul: The Kabbalah of Rabbi Isaac Luria*, selections by Chayyim Vital [San Francisco: Weiser, 2008], 22–23). Nineteenth-century Lutheran theologians took a similar view in their interpretation of Phil. 2:5-8, the classic New

Testament text on kenoticism, understanding the incarnation as a pulling back or limiting divine power in order to "fit" with human finitude (David H. Jensen, "The Incarnate, Emptying Christ," *In the Company of Others*, chap. 2.

40 For a more in-depth discussion of various models of creation, see McFague, *A New Climate for Theology*, chap. 4.

41 As quoted in Mark A. McIntosh, *Mystical Theology: The Integrity of Spirituality and Theology* (Oxford: Blackwell, 1998), 166.

42 Simone Weil, *Waiting for God*, trans. Emma Craufurd (New York: Harper and Row, 1951), 214.

43 Irenaeus: "In his immense love he became what we are that we might become what he is"; Athanasius: "He . . . became human that we might become God" (quoted by Andrew Louth, "The Place of *Theosis* in Orthodox Theology," in Christensen and Wittung, *Partakers of the Divine Nature*, 34.

44 Ibid., 194.

45 Ibid., 208.

46 Edith Wyschogrod, *Saints and Postmodernism: Revisioning Moral Philosophy* (Chicago: University of Chicago Press, 1990), xxii.

47 *Journal of John Woolman*, 214.

48 Weil, *First and Last Notebooks*, 244.

49 Day, *Long Loneliness*, 58.

8

What Next?

Living the Kenotic Life Personally, Professionally, and Publicly

What next, indeed? It is a sobering question, and not one easily answered. As I ponder it, however, a few words surface with irrepressible insistence: food, body, the world as my body, universal self, death and rebirth. Gradually, this project on kenosis and climate change is emerging not just as a program for ecological living on the planet, but for living, *period*. What I now see is an acceptance of death, my own individual death, as the test of how to live. If I can see myself in inclusive terms, the world as my body, then I might be able to accept my personal, individual death not as the end of everything but as another phase of living in and toward God. The active, historical, physical part of my existence will be over soon, but that is not the end of me. The heart of the matter is anthropology, who we think we are in the scheme of things, whether we believe we are merely single individuals who live by and for our own wits and powers, or whether we see life as a gift—from God and from all others on the earth. It is a gift of consciousness for a few years, consciousness that we have been given the gift of life—and we know it. This is nothing of our doing—it is, in every way, a *gift*, from its most physical aspects (parents checking to see if their newborn has all ten fingers and toes) to the most spiritual, creative moments of which human beings are capable. None of this is our doing. Hence, the first and last and most abiding response of human beings should be gratitude. No matter how brief or miserable one's life is, we do not deserve *any* of it. Hence, whatever smidge of life and joy we have is an unmerited gift.

With that realization as our basic stance, all the rest is a cause for thanksgiving. So, first of all, we do not include others in our definition of self in order to identify with their suffering (although that comes later), but first of all we say thank you to God and all these others for every aspect of creation that makes our existence possible and even allows us to flourish for a time. We start from zero, from deserving nothing, so *whatever* we have is a gift. That puts us all in the position of the injured man in the parable of the good Samaritan. We well-off middle-class folks are not, first of all, the good Samaritans who can hand out largesse to others. No, we are at the most basic level entirely dependent on others—on God and on all natural processes—for our very existence, not even counting our "assets" (money, power, education, influence). We all start at the same place, even God, who is not an independent, solitary, all-powerful being, but a process of reciprocal and needy love, sharing, giving, sacrificing for others.

If this is who we are and if we have internalized it—that is, actually believe it to be true and can *feel* one with the world—then what are the implications, what is *next*? First, we do not fear death as much as we did. Second, we see (and feel) the world to be our body. This means rejoicing when and where life is flourishing and suffering with the parts of the world that are not. Are we capable of really experiencing *either* of these states? Certainly we are not capable of thoroughly or always doing so, but more so than if we live within the individualistic model of the self. As an imaginative exercise, we can "stand in another's shoes" some of the time and to some extent. Through effort, training, and formation, we can practice the inclusive self. Since it *is* the way reality works, it should be easier to internalize it than the individualistic self, since one is living the truth, the other a lie.

Third, we now begin to make decisions on the basis of this new picture of the self. Our first reactions change: we no longer feel jealousy when someone else prospers, and we feel sad when they do not. The feelings that we "naturally" have for ourselves are now transferred to others, whom we include as parts of ourselves. This is quite different from responding to the other as Emmanuel Levinas does, for here the other is not totally other; rather, the other is like and unlike me in many different ways, but there is always a fragment of similarity, of "connection," of empathy that I feel with all others, including rocks, flowers, and mountains. In some primitive way, everything is a subject while also being an object. There is a continuity of empathy in which nothing is totally excluded. I feel empathy not only for the bear whose home has been destroyed by clear-cutting a forest, but also for a mountain whose top has been removed for coal production. Here there are no pure subjects or objects; we are all both to varying degrees. The narcissistic self is not the only subject with all others as objects; here, in this model, *all* are subjects in the sense of having intrinsic value, while at the same time, we are all objects in the sense that others need what we have to give in order to live and prosper.

The implications of these various insights are that we do not *own* ourselves; rather, we are "on loan," as it were, here for a time for the sake of the whole. Thus, whatever particular gifts and assets we have we should be ready to contribute to help the whole flourish. We middle-class people with education, decent incomes, connections, networks, influence and power—we have these special gifts for the benefit of the whole. Hence, voluntary poverty for us is not serving soup, but using our distinctive assets to contribute to a planet that is sustainable and where scarce resources are justly distributed. Freed from the terror of our individual deaths and formed by a new model of what it means to be a human being—the one creature who *knows* that we live only through interrelationships and interdependence—we can now act in and for the world in ways we previously could not imagine. We are saved from our worst fear (death), and we are armed with a true, realistic picture of who we are, where we fit into the scheme of things, and thus how we should act on behalf of others—for just distribution and sustainability. Each of us has received every breath we take, from our first cry to our last gasp, as a free gift, a gift that minute by minute and year by year works to give us life and consciousness. Hence, we put our considerable assets as well-off people to work for the good of the whole.

There are three levels of our lives where such practice is necessary: the personal, the professional, and the public. Briefly, at the personal level, voluntary poverty does not call us to a life of sackcloth and ashes; rather, we are called to lives of simplicity, restraint, moving way down on the index of material comfort so that others may have their fair share. This will involve such matters as the use of cars and planes and the size of our houses as well as what we eat and our mode of commuting to work. At the professional level, it means continuing to do the work we are educated in and suited for—whether it be car manufacturing, teaching elementary school children, growing vegetables, medicine, law, parenting, or others. Voluntary poverty for middle-class people does not mean giving up what one was trained for and loves to do; rather, it means doing all professional work differently, in an ecological fashion. Finally, at the public level, we should use our influence and money to elect ecologically minded politicians who will enact laws resulting in systemic changes at local, national, and international levels. It means becoming literate on ecological matters and teaching our children what is the most important education for living on planet earth: our house rules: Take only your share; clean up after yourself; and leave the house in good condition for others.

At this stage in an argument about moving from belief to action, it is usual to give a number of examples of imaginative, outstanding examples of individuals who have made such a shift. These examples are often inspiring (though exceptional), and usually leave the reader weary and discouraged about his or her ability to undertake such extraordinary and singular efforts. While I could recite many examples of such individuals who, at personal, professional, or public levels have accomplished impressive exceptions to life as usual in our culture, I think it is more beneficial to consider some attitudes, strategies, and guidelines for well-off middle-class folks to live differently—as if the world were our body. What matters is not the particular examples of amazing singular accomplishments within the narrow, individualistic model of human behavior presently dominant in our culture but, rather, the outlines of the new paradigm of the universal self to substitute for the present mode. What matters is *how* to live differently in ways that will actually help to change the paradigm that is considered normal in our culture.

The first and most important change is how we think about ourselves. As we have stressed frequently in these pages, the crucial issue is how we imagine the limits of our own selves, our own bodies. Are we singular, independent, separate entities that end with our own skins, or are we both formed and sustained by our radical interdependence with all other living creatures as well as the systems that maintain life? This single change—attempting to live into otherness as the primary focus of all aspects of our existence—is the first step. Thus, in all our reflections and actions, we need to turn *outward* toward the world to solve our dilemmas and increase our joys rather than turning *inward* toward our self. Thus I have suggested that food, understood in the most inclusive way possible—as whatever is needed for us to be created, sustained, and to flourish, from the air we breathe and calories we consume to the food for thought that fuels our imaginations, our hopes, our joys—is the most apt symbol for twenty-first-century planetary living. It is not what comes out of us, but what must come to us, be *given* to us that is our starting point. If we see our lives entirely as gift, an unmerited treasure, then we will focus our attention on what comes to us, not what goes out from us. We are the needy, the receivers, the ones who must be fed minute by minute, day by day, year by year, by the world. Hence, our primary role is to participate in giving back to the world whatever assets, talents, gifts, money, influence, and so on that we accumulate during our brief sojourn here on earth to the betterment of the whole. Hence, again, providing food for other needy creatures becomes our role, our place in the scheme of things. By "food" I here mean the necessities of existence that we by our middle-class privilege, prestige, and power can assure others have. Since we all arose together, as evident in the evolutionary history of our planet and reflected in the notions of dependent co-origination in Buddhism and the doctrine of the incarnation in Christianity, we depend on one another for everything. Thus the primary symbol for the new paradigm of the universal self is the body in need of food. This symbol should be front and center in our daily lives at the personal, professional, and public levels; it is the guiding principle by which we make both the little and the big decisions of just, sustainable planetary living.

If this is the case, then it is appropriate that we focus on "things," on material possessions that are the actual stuff whereby living, breathing creatures survive and prosper. A consumer culture, then, which is based on the accumulation of more and more things, all of which take energy to produce, becomes the principal area for critique and revision. Everything that lives—that changes, grows, develops—depends on expenditures of energy, and as our population grows within a finite, enclosed energy system (our planet), *how* we allocate energy becomes a moral issue. For instance, if we use extraordinary energy to produce meat for the privileged few who can afford it, rather than use the same expenditure of energy to produce grains to fill the stomachs of the many, we have made a decision contrary to the new paradigm that privileges bodies needing food. Whether it be potatoes or concrete, all "things," living and nonliving, require energy for production; thus, it is not a question of consumer goods *and* food, but often consumer goods *or* food. Increasingly, our planet cannot afford both at unlimited quantities, so decisions must be made of whether we will support electronic toys for the elite or basic necessities for the many. This issue of consumer desires versus necessities for existence is particularly pertinent to the well-off people of the world since our form of market capitalism is driven in large part by excessive consumer consumption. It is surely evident that our consumer culture panders to the desires of the few at the expense of the many.

Another guideline for us well-off folks as we consider our appropriate form of voluntary poverty is the issue of the "little way" versus the systemic change, or the continuity between personal behavior and public stances. Dorothy Day calls this "personalism," which points to the old, perennial problem of whether action at the individual or public level is more critical or, in other words, whether serving soup to workers or supporting their strikes for better wages is more important. She, and our other saints, refused to make a distinction between these two, demanding that the means and the end must be continuous, and for these people this meant that the intrinsic importance and dignity of every individual must be the criterion at all levels. Thus they demanded a kind of "public personalism," which assumes that we all are "needy" not only at the level of material food but also at the level of emotional food, the recognition that all beings are subjects. Thus, as Day constantly reminds us, what matters is not the grand gesture of kissing the leper (which she claims to have done twice), but the daily, laborious, mundane serving of soup—the little way. We are saved or damned by the small, daily, presumably unimportant little decisions and actions we take that often seem to make no difference. Thus personalism is not a romantic focus on needy individuals to the detriment of the big, global gestures that will "save thousands." Rather, it is a way of being in the world that demands we empty ourselves of the lie that we are the only subjects who matter, recognizing the truth that all others are subjects in some sense and demanding that we pay attention to them as such no matter what level of action we are taking—personal, professional, or public.

By implication, at the heart of the new paradigm is a different model of power than that which is current in our consumer economy. We have touched on this matter several times, as it is central to the notion that kenoticism is not a marginal, esoteric, religious notion but a widespread, though often implicit, mode of response to others. Along with the individualistic notion of human nature goes an understanding of power that is unilateral, coercive, and controlling. We see this in theology (God as a supernatural, all-powerful lord and master), in the arts (superimposing one's vision on material rather than listening to its emergence), parenting (demanding unquestioning obedience from a child rather than engaging in a discussion), interfaith conversations (the conviction that one's own religion is absolute while others are either wrong or limited), international affairs (the colonialism of invading countries superimposing their culture on native ones), scholarship (the supposition that one's position is correct while all others are inadequate), and so on. This stance is so prevalent in our culture, given the anthropological model of the singular individual, that we scarcely see it *as* a stance; rather, we see it as normal. However, when a kenotic lens is substituted, in which the human being is seen as interdependent with all others, the "normal" or "natural" stance is to assume a listening, open, receiving, appreciative, attentive, dialogical mode with all one's dealings in the world, whether they be personal, professional, or public, and whether they be in artistic, parental, religious, scholarly, or political matters. Gradually, we begin to grow into another way of standing in the world, characterized by being able to stand in another's shoes, of widespread empathy for human beings in situations very different from our own as well as for creatures very different from ourselves. We see the *continuities* across the differences, not diminishing the variety (in fact reveling in the richness of the differences), but appreciating that *all* are bodies like and unlike ourselves and all must have food. At the most basic level, we are all the same: *we need food*. Once we have internalized this most basic of all needs and gloried in the abundance of living things on this marvelous planet of ours, we cannot imagine a stance toward these others that is characterized by power over, control of, mere use of the world as if it were an object solely for our pleasure and profit. This change is probably the single most important shift that can occur as we attempt to live into, and act on, a new model of who we are in the scheme of things.

Thus, for us well-off middle-class people, it is not so much *what* we should do as *how* we do whatever we do. There are any number of specific actions we can and ought to take in order to help just distribution and sustainability on our planet, but the central issue is the *way* we do it. There is, for instance, a difference between a wealthy person who decides to give away substantial amounts of money earned through the system of market capitalism with little attention during those years of accumulation of *the conditions under which that money was earned* and the decision to work to revise the conditions themselves. In the first case, the person gives from his or her own inner bounty, having benefited from laws that privilege people like her or him at the expense of fair wages for workers. These people also decide which segments of society deserve their largesse, whether or not their gifts are appropriate or effective. But well-off middle-class people like myself have the means to actually change the system itself from an economic model that allocates scarce resources to whomever can hoard the most to an economic model that privileges the sustainability and just distribution of necessities as priorities. Most of us are willing to be charitable, especially when it is a matter of our excess, but few of us see our role as using our influence and money to change the fundamentals of an economic system. Yet, it is the latter that is most needed as our form of voluntary poverty. We must give up our power to control who receives from us, while opening our assets to the basic need of various creaturely bodies. This mundane, other-directed, kenotic form of giving deprives us of our exceptionalism, our privilege, our superiority.

Thus what we see emerging from these reflections is a modest, relative, qualified—indeed, humble—mode of operation in which we are moved by a vision for a better world, but not in an absolute way. Utopias are important: imagining another way is critical to actually moving toward that new vision, but again, it is not up to us, the few privileged ones who can set the stage for what should happen and then control others so that our vision will dominate. We have seen many instances of totalitarian thinking—people who are certain that their vision of the way things should be is the only right way, and if not their way, no way! This mind-set is entirely alien to kenosis. Just as capitalism has set out its goal of the abundant life in terms of the accumulation of unlimited things, so this new way must imagine its abundant life in concrete, attractive ways, seeing it as a world of relative adequacy for most living things rather than excess for a few at the price of misery for the many. Does this mean mediocrity? Yes, it does, if the criterion is how much one can hoard. But if the goal is a decent life of material necessities as well as time for developing one's uniqueness, then success is measured in terms of fulfillment of each and every form of life. The flourishing of difference in the network of radical interrelationship and interdependence is the given "rules of the game" for life on our planet: each and every leaf on every tree is different from all others and has particular needs for its development. So each and every human individual is different from all the others and has the need for certain basic components for his or her flourishing. Difference within radical unity or unity only by unimaginable diversity: to the extent that most human beings and most forms of life have the opportunity for such fulfillment, the model is successful. That is to say, it is commensurate with what we presently know of reality, of how the world works, and its goal is the well-being of the whole through the flourishing of the parts. No model is perfect; the most that human beings are capable of is approximations, paradigms of relative adequacy, which are better than alternatives. It should be obvious after the experience of the last several years resulting in financial disaster for most people and increasing deterioration of our planet's health that the current model of market capitalism has been tried and failed. It is failing in a spectacular fashion, in a way that should be a wake-up call to the one species of the planet that can consciously decide to "live differently" that it is time to do so and at basic levels. Cosmetic changes to the market model are no longer enough; the fundamentals of this paradigm have been questioned and found wanting. It is scarcely a leap into the unknown to suggest that an economic/ecological model for living on the earth that begins with different priorities—just distribution and sustainability—deserves a chance. If not now, then when? If not us, then who?

The kenotic model of reciprocity, of paying attention to the other, of sharing, of give-and-take, of sacrifice and openness, of the rhythm of life and death, is claiming that it is closer to reality than its alternative, and it has the support of most major religions over the centuries. It claims that unilateral power, the privilege of the one over the many, the exceptionalism of the human subject, the turn inward for insight, the objectification of the world—that all of this is a lie. It is not the way the world is put together and therefore cannot be a model for abundant human living or for any kind of earthly flourishing. The kenotic model is not an esoteric bit of mysterious religious knowledge; rather, it is the gospel, the good news of how to live well on planet earth for all of its inhabitants. We well-off people of the middle class have, I believe, along with the religions of the world, the special task of spreading this good news as deeply and as widely as possible. It is no longer sufficient to undertake charitable acts within the present system to provide band-aids for its most egregious faults—schools and hospitals for those who fall between the cracks of our present broken model. The model itself must be changed—and we have the power, the money, the influence, the networks, the know-how to undertake such a revolution of thought and action.

It is false and unfortunate that the link between these two—thought and action—is so often overlooked or not taken seriously. Action is not only marching with banners protesting various kinds of oppression. Action is also, for those of us who deal in words, concepts, and images that form peoples' most basic assumptions about the world, the suggestion of new models changing those assumptions. We live within the models we create, and when they control our actions in ways that are diminishing and destructive, we have the responsibility to suggest alternative models. This is, I believe, action of the highest order and the greatest importance; to refuse this task is to refuse the role of human beings on the planet. We are fast destroying the planet by our actions taken within a false model, and we owe it to our earth and to each other to imagine and to embody a different vision, a different model.

And finally when we ask, What next? we are asking what the next concrete steps are if one does indeed accept this role. There is no one answer, no magic bullet that will save us, no program for salvation from our worst enemy (ourselves when focused *on ourselves*). I will close with a few humbling comments about myself, of how I answer this question each morning when I crawl out of bed and face another day, more or less certain that we are headed for a very bad if not apocalyptic future. Do I feel confident that we will turn things around, that we will in fact begin to live within a different model at all levels of our existence? No, I do not. So, I think small, like Dorothy Day; I think of the little way, the tiny fragment that I can bite off and chew on during the particular day that lies ahead of me. I am trained to think and write, specifically as a Christian theologian. I have spent most of my life trying to figure out the particular contribution that the Christian model (or one interpretation of it) has to make to the betterment of life on our planet for all its creatures. It is a small piece, but my responsibility is to do it as well as I can and to keep working at it day after day. At two years old, I was determined to learn to tie my own shoes. I worked at this task for over a month until I finally succeeded—I didn't tie my shoes very well, but I did tie them. Things can't get much smaller than that. I am still trying to learn to tie my shoes better, and even if I don't succeed, I will have made an effort. That is, perhaps, all we can do—but we do need to try to tie those shoes.

Index

Hallie, Philip, 136–37
Haught, John, 161, 192
Havel, Václav, 25
Hawken, Paul, 31–32
Hawking, Stephen, 155
Heller, Erich, *xii*, 112
Herbert, George, 54
Hick, John, 19, 34, 136
Highfield, Roger, 123–24
Hoffman, Martin L., 125
Hopkins, Gerard Manley, 195
hospitality, 69, 84, 104, 119
house rules for planet earth, 114–15
human beings, 21, 25, 131–33, 199–203
hypostatic union, 188–89, 200

incarnationalism, Christian and radical: belief to action, 133; doctrine of creation and, 197–98; Dorothy Day, 119, 180; John Woolman, 177; kenotic theology and, 171–73; meaning of, 186; Simone Weil, 50–55, 90, 101–2, 118, 178–79
inclusiveness, 129–31
individualistic model, 141–43
inner/outer lives, 17–18
interdependency: described, 20–24, 26, 84; focus on, 97–98, 126–28; model of, *xii–xiii. See also* democracy of life; world view of, 175–76
Irenaeus, Saint, 9, 28, 188, 198, 199

Jablonsnki, Carol J., 66
James, William, 136
Jantzen, Grace M., 192, 195
Jeeves, Malcolm, 144
Jeffers, Robinson, 18–19, 19, 184
Jesus, understanding of God and, 157–59, 173–77, 181–82, 185, 188–89, 196
John Paul II, Pope, 161
Johnson, Elizabeth A., 82
justice, love and charity, 93–94, 133

Kant, Immanuel, 24
kenosis. *See also* self-emptying: broad-based notion of, 144–45; Christian understanding of, 153–56; conditions for acceptance of, 160; described, *xii*, 2–3, 6, 35–36, 74, 85, 171–72; impersonal approaches and, 46, 60–61, 128, 131;